C000098997

CRIMSON
WATERS

CRIMSON WATERS

True Tales of Adventure, Looting, Kidnapping, Torture, and Piracy on the High Seas

DON MANN
AND KRAIG BECKER

Skyhorse Publishing

Skyhorse Publishing books may be purchased in bulk at special discounts for sales promotion, corporate gifts, fund-raising, or educational purposes. Special editions can also be created to specifications. For details, contact the Special Sales Department, Skyhorse Publishing, 307 West 36th Street, 11th Floor, New York, NY 10018 or info@skyhorsepublishing.com.

Skyhorse® and Skyhorse Publishing® are registered trademarks of Skyhorse Publishing, Inc.®, a Delaware corporation.

Visit our website at www.skyhorsepublishing.com.

10 9 8 7 6 5 4 3 2 1

Library of Congress Cataloging-in-Publication Data is available on file.

Cover design by Mona Lin
Cover photo credit: Getty Images

Print ISBN: 978-1-5107-5487-4
Ebook ISBN: 978-1-5107-6041-7

Printed in China

Table of Contents

Foreword

Who was "Frogman?" I asked myself, reading the business card this tall athletic gentleman just handed to me. Having spent much of my life exploring the world for sunken shipwrecks, and having discovered Captain Kidd's Adventure Galley and the world's only pirate treasure, my curiosity ran wild.

Later that evening at the Vail Round Table, where I've been honored to share my lifetime adventures with men who'd walked on the Moon, war heroes who survived months in solitary confinement at the Hanoi Hilton, and many other legendary men and women, I would come to know this extraordinary fellow explorer, world-class triathlete, and Navy SEAL combat veteran.

After exchanging adventure stories of Panama in the early '90s, when Don was involved in classified Navy SEAL missions and I was searching for the Viper Pit and Captain Morgan's *Satisfaction*, it was as if two long-lost shipmates had returned to port to swap yarns. We talked of the ruthless bad guys we'd encountered, and the bewitching Kuna sorceress who led me through the jungle to the mythical Viper Pit. With Don as my jungle sidekick, we hope to return someday . . . but that's another book.

The next week after returning to Cape Cod, I began reading *Crimson Waters*, and again found myself enthralled with Don's lucid storytelling.

Over the decades countless books have been written about pirates, none of which were written from the perspective of an intrepid Navy SEAL pirate hunter who survived captivity. He has brought us this intuitive historical resource of skullduggery, mayhem, and murder, to the dread of countries that enslaved entire populations to mine precious metals, and companies that sold millions of Africans at auction.

Escaped slaves were experimenting in democracy with multiethnic crews aboard pirate vessels.

Beginning with pirates of the ancient world, three thousand years before Blackbeard had whiskers, we'll meet mysterious Greek pierato and dreaded Tuscan Tyrrhenians who wreaked havoc up and down the Mediterranean, through the Golden Age of Piracy when renegade seadogs plied crimson waters for silver and gold, to modern day Somali pirates confronted by Don's courageous brethren of SEAL Team Six.

Thus, with utmost sincerity, I am honored to present this foreword to *Crimson Waters*.

Introduction

The pirate captain stepped out onto the deck of the ship just as a wave crashed against its hull, sending sea foam soaring high into the air. The water hung over the bow of the vessel for just an instant, before it came crashing down on top of several crew members who scrambled to stay on their feet. A massive storm was quickly closing in, bringing high winds, heavy rain, and rolling seas along with it. The only question the captain had was whether or not the storm would arrive before the English frigate that was already bearing down on their position.

The Royal Navy had been dogging him and his crew for three days, giving chase around several islands in their attempt to engage the pirate ship in battle. The captain knew that if they caught him, he'd be hanged for sure. Even outnumbered and outgunned, he wasn't about to let that happen.

Stepping to the stern of the ship, the crusty old buccaneer pulled a brass navigational telescope from inside his long, weathered jacket. Extending it to its full length, he raised it to his uncovered eye and peered back across the undulating sea behind them. On the horizon were the sails of the frigate, swelled to capacity as they caught the growing wind. Atop the main mast sat the Union Jack blowing wildly in the breeze, taunting him even from a distance.

"They're still there," he said quietly. "Still closing."

Turning back towards his men, the captain barked an order, imploring them to raise the main sail. Until now, he had relied on maneuverability and guile to help him stay one step ahead of his pursuers, but with

A pirate captain.

the storm quickly approaching, time was quickly running out. Now, speed would have to be their ally, allowing them to escape both the British pirate hunters hot on their trail and the growing ferocity of Mother Nature.

Grabbing the wheel of the ship from his first mate, the old pirate steered the vessel out towards the open ocean. If they were lucky, they would lose their enemy in the wind, rain, and surf. If not, they would almost assuredly be sent to the bottom of the ocean.

If popular culture is to be believed, these kinds of cat-and-mouse scenes played out on the high seas on a regular basis during the so called "Golden Age of Piracy." This name was given to the era that ran from roughly 1650 to about 1730, when thousands of pirates were active not just in the Caribbean, but in the Indian Ocean, off the coast of West Africa, and along the eastern coast of North America too. Some of those pirates stayed in relatively small areas, using their geographic knowledge of the region to their advantage. Others sailed the globe in search of easy targets, plundering ships the world over in a never-ending quest for fortune and glory.

When most people think of pirates, they often envision larger-than-life characters from the Golden Age of Piracy. After all, books such as Robert Louis Stevenson's classic *Treasure Island* and movies like the *Pirates of the Caribbean* series have clearly defined exactly how we envision what a pirate looks and sounds like. Stevenson himself helped create the perfect pirate archetype, with the introduction of Long John Silver, the main villain in his genre-defining book. Even though *Treasure Island* was first published in 1883, the image of a tall, imposing man, complete with a thick black beard, a wooden leg, and a parrot on his shoulder, remains in our collective unconscious even to this day.

While it is true that Golden Age pirates were often larger-than-life figures, the history of piracy predates that era by thousands of years. Almost since the first humans ventured out onto our planet's seas and oceans, others have sought to prey upon them on the water, claiming their cargo, crew, and ships for their own. In fact, history shows that pirates were active in a number of locations around the world dating back as far as 2500 BCE. And as we all know by now, the end of the Golden Age didn't put a stop to piracy either. Even now, in the twenty-first century, there are still parts of the world where seafaring bandits are an active threat to commercial shipping and passenger ships alike.

Within this book, we'll explore the history of piracy around the globe, from its origins in the ancient world, right up to the modern day pirates who still stalk the coastlines of continents and islands. Along the way, we'll meet some of the most colorful characters to ever take to the seas; sharing strange, entertaining, and enthralling tales of their exploits. We'll separate myth and legend from reality, and explore what life was like for a buccaneer. As you'll see, the life of a pirate rarely involved secret hideouts, treasure maps, or a ship's hold filled with plunder. More often than not, it was a difficult and challenging way of life that was fraught with danger. Many sailors who were pressed into service aboard a pirate ship were just as likely to end up hanging from the mast as they were to returning to a normal life.

Still, there is something undeniably alluring about the life of a pirate and the freedom of the open seas. So raise the Jolly Roger, buckle on your sword, and chart a course for adventure. This is going to be quite a journey.

CHAPTER 1

The Pirates of the Ancient World

Historians believe that the first maritime trading routes began operating about four thousand years ago. This likely means that the first acts of piracy followed almost immediately thereafter. Opportunistic individuals have existed since the dawn of time, and the most ancient of mariners probably could not resist the temptation to seize ships filled with all manner of goods.

While the practice of using the sea as a medium for trade developed at roughly the same time in parts of Asia and the Middle East, the civilizations that lined the Mediterranean were amongst the first to truly reap the benefits from ships durable enough to row over long distances and remain stable in rougher conditions. The Phoenicians, for example, were an early power in the region thanks to their seafaring capabilities and willingness to facilitate trade with their neighbors. Similarly, Cyprus gained wealth and notoriety for shipping copper to places like Egypt and Mesopotamia, where the metal was in both short supply and high demand. Even in an age were international trade was still in its infancy, this provided a degree of leverage and superiority over other nations, quickly establishing Cyprus's sense of superiority and dominance in the region.

The creation of these trading routes initiated between the Phoenicians, Greeks, and Egyptians, amongst others, along with more durable and sophisticated boats, marked a turning point in human history. The Phoenicians also built the first cargo vessels, which meant for the first time, goods and services could be shipped over longer distances in a relatively short timeframe. This created opportunities for emerging civilizations and distant fiefdoms that had previously been unaware of each other's existence to establish contact and begin exchanging a wide variety of items, including cloth, spices, wood, and other natural resources.

Perhaps more importantly, it also facilitated the spread of art, literature, and ideas. In this way, these kingdoms and city-states were able to maintain their own unique identities, while gaining knowledge and enlightenment from their neighbors at the same time. These trading routes also gave them the ability to adopt certain customs and philosophies, while sampling exotic delicacies and extravagant luxuries that could only be found in distant lands. In this way, Greek philosophy reached the distant shores of Egypt, while Phoenician cartography and navigation skills taught others to explore farther from home too.

The Egyptians, Minoans of Crete, and Phoenicians, who were especially adept at sailing, were able to parlay those skills into wealth and influence. They not only sold their own goods to neighboring states, they also bought products from some of those kingdoms and transported them to other parts of the Mediterranean where they were solid for a substantial profit. By adding more ships to their fleet, their commerce network continued to grow, allowing them to reach farther abroad and facilitate larger cargos. Naturally, that display of wealth and power didn't go unnoticed for very long.

Egypt versus the Sea People

When, exactly, the first pirate attack took place has been lost to the mists of time and the shadows of history. But the earliest record of such raids can be found in Egypt, dating back to around 1350 BCE. At that time, clay tablets were the preferred method for recording important information and to commemorate historical events that had taken place. One such tablet from that era depicts an image of unidentified attackers making an assault on a ship, clearly displaying a band of brigands attempting to violently capture the vessel and its cargo.

What actual events inspired this carving remains unclear, but we do know that a battle took place and that a ship served as the battleground. It most likely wasn't the first time that Egyptian sailors had experienced such an attack and it's possible it was a fairly common occurrence even at that time. This particular clay tablet not only has the distinction of showing a naval battle taking place, but also having survived across the millennia, allowing modern day historians to discover it.

In 1208 BCE during the reign of Pharaoh Merenptah, a strange and mysterious people arrived on the geopolitical stage of the Mediterranean. Exactly who they were and where they came from remains a mystery, but they routinely launched attacks on both land and sea, striking fear in the hearts of their adversaries. At times, they seemed to have an almost supernatural ability to appear as if from out of nowhere, conducting fast and efficient raids, only to disappear again just as quickly as they had arrived. Where they went, no one knew, but they usually hauled off vast amounts of goods, gold, and captives with them when they went.

Today, modern historians and archeologists have taken to calling this mysterious group the "Sea People," despite the fact that we know almost nothing about where they came from. We do know that they arrived at a time of political upheaval in the Mediterranean, with numerous kingdoms and factions—including the Egyptians and Libyans—at war. What isn't clear is if the Sea People were the cause of that upheaval or only took advantage of it for their own gain. Regardless, they were one of the first recorded groups that actively understood the tactics and strategies necessary for attacking while at sea, often leaving chaos and destruction in their wake.

Evidence of their existence can be found on the walls of the Mortuary Temple of Ramses III at Medinet Habu, which was built in 1190 BCE. Inside that structure, which still stands near modern day Luxor in Egypt, visitors will find depictions of naval battles between Egyptian forces and those of the Sea People. These images are believed to be the earliest ever recorded of such battles, with the enemy ships featuring prows shaped like the head of a bird and using elaborate sails, rather than oars, as a form of propulsion.

Even today, the motivations of the Sea People remain as big of a mystery as their true identity. They would often side with the enemies of Egypt, indicating that by standing up to the wealthiest and most powerful kingdom of the day, they may have had altruistic intentions. But at other times they seemed to act very much in their own self-interest instead, grabbing loot and plunder wherever it could be found. Historical researchers have searched for clues as to their origins and what they were hoping to achieve on a grander scale, with the most likely explanation simply being that they wanted to acquire wealth and material goods. While it is possible they may have had ambitions of becoming a power on the Mediterranean, it seems just as likely that they simply were motivated by greed and ambition on a smaller scale.

During their years of raiding along the Mediterranean coast, the Sea People made devastating strikes against Syria, Palestine, Anatolia, and the Hittites. But even when they had those civilizations on the ropes, they never managed or bothered to deliver the killing blow to any of their enemies. Instead, they preferred to conduct raids that destroyed governmental seats of power, palaces, and temples, while leaving the residential districts that were occupied by the lower-class citizens alone. It seems they had no interest in conquering, but were instead just looking for plunder. Their tactics and approaches would be emulated by other pirates that followed in their wake for hundreds of years to come.

The Sea People's reign of terror and destruction came to an end around 1175 BCE, when the "Battle of the Delta" took place close to where the Nile River flows into the Mediterranean Sea. According to ancient accounts of the battle, the seagoing invaders attacked Egypt but were repelled on land by forces led by Ramses III. As they fled back to their ships, Egyptian archers sent volleys of arrows raining down on them, slaughtering the Sea People by the dozens. This humiliating defeat not only decimated their ranks, it had a devastating effect on their ships too. With their fleet in tatters and the invasion turned back, the Sea

People sailed away in defeat, rarely making an appearance in the years that followed.

The decisive battle exacted a significant toll on Egypt as well, and it would be many years before the country fully recovered. Ramses III won a hard-fought victory against a terrible foe, but it came at the cost of the lives of thousands of Egyptian soldiers. Of his enemy, the pharaoh would record in his personal accounts only, "Their hearts and their souls are finished unto all eternity." After the Battle of the Delta, the Sea People slowly faded from the world stage, becoming just another mysterious footnote in history.

While the Sea People were almost certainly not the first pirate force to take to the sea, their success against the major powers of the day drew more attention than the less organized and focused brigands of the past. Using their swift ships to make quick, yet decisive, attacks on their enemies allowed them to disrupt trade, amass wealth, and shake the very political foundations of the Mediterranean. Ultimately, they may have lost the war, but the blueprint that was established in terms of sea tactics emboldened other pirates that followed. As a result of their defeat as a group, more than a few of the Sea People likely became independent pirates, pursuing their own self-interests instead.

Greek *Pieratos*

The Egyptians weren't alone in their fight against pirates. In fact, the very term "pirate" can actually be traced back to the ancient Greeks. They used the word *pierato* not to describe seafaring outlaws, but mercenaries who would sell their services to the highest bidder. In this case, the one paying the bill was likely to be a political faction or a city-state, who hired these *pieratos* to provide protection from rival factions. The leaders of these *pieratos* were even given the title of *archpierato,* which roughly translates to "pirate captain."

During an age when Greece dominated the Eastern Mediterranean, particularly around the Aegean and Adriatic Seas, piracy was actually encouraged. City-states allowed their citizens to become privateers, which meant they could outfit their own ships with weapons and use them to attack enemies of the state under an official charter from the government itself. This essentially amounted to state-sponsored piracy, with sailors given free rein to attack enemy ships, seize their goods, and even sell these stolen items off for a profit.

The privateer model was emulated by dozens of city-states and nations throughout the centuries. Not only did it offer a country the opportunity to quickly bolster its naval forces, it also gave pirates an opportunity to earn a pardon by sailing in defense of a royal sovereign or for a specific cause. Privateering also served to create a gray area when it came to defining exactly what piracy was, lending a measure of legitimacy and credibility to certain acts of the profession.

At times, these privateers would band together, finding strength in numbers or some other benefit from joining forces. Sometimes this would result in whole pirate fleets that had the strength to not only take on enemy armadas, but raid and sack entire towns as well. Those fleets often found safe harbor on islands that were sympathetic to their cause. Places like Melos and Aegina evolved into thriving markets where pirate crews could sell off their plunder, including men and women that had been captured during their raids.

Piracy was such an accepted way of life for the Greeks that even the heroes of Homer's *The Odyssey* had no qualms about raiding and plundering enemy ships and towns. While Homer himself never refers to Odysseus and his men as pirates per se, he does note that they sack a city in Thrace on their way home from Troy following the conclusion of the Trojan War. During that raid, the Greeks not only kill the men of the village, but they also capture the women and steal all of the valuable goods, including the cattle. They then divide up the plunder amongst them as the spoils of war.

Other Greek storytellers also told tales about the most notorious pirates of the day, including the dreaded Tyrrhenians. These fearsome seagoing people were also referred to as the "Etruscans" and made their home in what is now Tuscany. Situated on the Adriatic, they earned themselves a reputation as shrewd traders and merchants, often sailing to Greece and Carthage to conduct business. They also happened to play a

Odysseus and the Sirens.

central role in the bustling slave trade, routinely raiding the coastline of the Mediterranean in search of potential victims that they could sell in a slave market and press into a life of servitude.

In the poem *Homeric Hymn to Dionysus*, Tyrrhenian pirates come across Dionysus, the Greek god of wine, as he wanders along the seashore. He is so handsome that they think he must be the son of a wealthy king or some other aristocrat. Believing that they can ransom him for a large sum of money, the sailors set upon Dionysus, overpowering him with their superior numbers. But when they drag him back to their boat and attempt to bind his hands and feet, they discover that the rope will not stay in place. One of the men, recognizing that great powers were at work, tries to warn the captain and his fellow crew members that they should let their captive go, lest something awful befall them.

This story being a classic example Greek tragedy, the captain fails to listen to his companion and is instead intent on carrying out his original plan. However, once Dionysus is brought onboard the ship he reveals his true nature. As the story goes, wine starts to flow throughout the vessel and a large vine—complete with grapes and flowers—grows out of the hold and around the mast and sail. The god then shape-shifts into a massive lion while also summoning a giant bear to fight by his side. The creatures instantly kill the commander of the pirates, while the rest of the crew dive overboard. As they hit the water, they are transformed into dolphins, swimming out to sea, cursed to live the rest of their lives in that aquatic form.

The causal mention of the pirates in that story is an indication of how well known they were when the poem was written. It is also an indication of how fearsome the Tyrrhenians were, as they were able to subdue a god, even if for just a short time.

Even though ships began to grow in size and became more capable of venturing farther from shore during this era, sea battles involving oceangoing vessels remained relatively uncommon. While naval encounters did occur from time to time, it was far more likely for pirates to attack seaside villages, which often proved to be much easier and more lucrative targets. Towns situated along the coast usually had more valuables on hand that could be looted than those carried in a single ship. These towns' populations were also targeted by raiders. A bustling slave trade across the Mediterranean Sea turned human beings into an important commodity that could easily be bought or sold.

However, not all captives were destined for the slave market. Kidnapping young aristocrats and ransoming them back to their rich families—as demonstrated in the *Homeric Hymn to Dionysus*—also proved profitable. Pirate captains learned early on that wealthy friends and relatives would be willing to pay exorbitant amounts of money for the safe return of their loved ones. This quickly became a new revenue stream for industrious brigands and continued on as a popular tactic amongst generations of pirates.

Eventually, piracy fell out of favor with the Greeks; it went from a profession that their mythological heroes took part in, to a profession that was largely looked upon with scorn and derision. Occasionally, pirates were employed by generals and kings to serve as reserve forces or to help create a diversion from the sea, but for the most part they were viewed as outcasts that earned a living on the fringes of society. Just as banditry was viewed as a dishonorable act on land, piracy was seen in much the same way on the ocean.

During the Greek Classical Period, which began after the defeat of the Persians in the Battle of Salamis in 480 BCE, Athens rose as the dominant power in the region. Greece's most preeminent city-state used its navy to maintain peace across the Aegean and Adriatic, suppressing pirate activity wherever it was found. Those efforts were largely successful, opening a new era of trade and prosperity in the Mediterranean, and bringing security and stability along with it.

Athens was able to maintain its position of power and keep pirate activity fairly low until its defeat in the Peloponnesian War in 404 BCE. After that, piracy returned with a vengeance, disrupting trade routes and creating chaos along the shores of the Mediterranean. It would take almost another century before the Athenians could reassert control in the Adriatic, reestablishing a measure of security for its trading ships. But its dominance over the seas never returned to its former glory, which meant piracy remained a constant threat, even if it was somewhat contained.

Diomedes and Alexander

The names of very few of the pirates that were active during this era have survived the passage of time. While many were no doubt notorious and rightly feared in their day, most of their deeds weren't permanently recorded for future historians to study. While we do know that piracy was rampant, and a major concern of the Greeks, we generally don't have any idea of the identities of any of the major pirate captains. However, the name of one such outlaw has survived the centuries, more so because of the man that he is linked with, rather than the deeds that he committed.

According to legend, Diomedes was a pirate of some renown who made a name for himself by raiding and plundering numerous Greek towns and villages. He managed to avoid capture, infuriating the authorities who had been charged with bringing him to justice. Smart, bold, and swift on the water, the pirate had earned himself a reputation for being fearless, confident, and clever. He built upon this reputation as he continued to elude capture and amass a small fortune in plundered booty.

However, Diomedes' luck eventually ran out and he was taken into custody by Greek forces. Before long, he was dragged in front of Alexander the Great, who was emperor of all of Greece—and much of the rest of the known world—at the time. According to legend, Alexander turned his intense gaze upon his captive, ready to pass judgment. The pirate had been a thorn in his side for years and he was eager to be rid of him. But before he passed sentence, he asked Diomedes, "What gives you the right to sail the sea, taking that which is not yours and leaving destruction in your wake?"

Diomedes reportedly returned Alexander's gaze without flinching. Boldly and without hesitation he answered that question with one of his own. "Let me ask you this," he said. "What gives you the right to travel the world, taking things that do not belong to you either?"

Caught off guard, Alexander was momentarily stunned by the pirate's words. But before he could respond, Diomedes pressed on. "You have occupied the land of Egypt, made yourself king of Persia, and have invaded India with a force of arms," he said. "You have used your armies and your navy to conquer the world and have proclaimed yourself emperor. Yet I have used my boat in a similar fashion and you have labeled me a pirate and criminal."

A hush fell over Alexander's court. Rarely had those in attendance seen their great king spoken to in such a manner. They watched intently, waiting to see what fate would befall the pirate who feared not the emperor nor certain death.

"If you were to ask me, who is the greater criminal, I could not say," Diomedes continued. "But know this; if I had the tools that you have at your disposal, I would be emperor too."

Alexander paused for a moment, pondering the words of the pirate. He heard insolence and defiance in the voice of Diomedes, but he saw wisdom there as well. He could not deny that the two men were kindred spirits in a way, both looking out for their own self-interests.

The legend says that Alexander respected Diomedes for speaking truthfully and directly, something that didn't happen often in the presence of the emperor. With begrudging respect, Alexander ordered his men to set the pirate free, allowing him to return to his life on the high seas. The eventual fate of the outlaw is unknown, but his name lives on as the pirate who stood unblinking and unimpressed before the most powerful man in the world, not only sticking to his convictions, but calling into question those of the emperor as well.

Alexander the Great would famously rule for just thirteen years, dying under mysterious circumstances at the age of thirty-two. Before his death, he amassed a vast empire that stretched from Macedonia to India in the east, and across the sea to Egypt in the south. During that brief time, he had dominion not only over the Mediterranean, but the Red Sea, the Persian Gulf, and the Arabian Sea as well. And while piracy was still rampant, the Greek navy did its best to maintain trading routes and protect against coastal invasions.

The Isle of Rhodes

As Greek influence in the Mediterranean Sea began to wane, others took up the mantle of power. For a time, the responsibility of battling pirates fell on the isle of Rhodes, which was once a part of Alexander's vast empire. Following his death, the island gained independence in large part because of its wealth and complex sea trading network. As one of the main suppliers of grain for many parts of the Mediterranean, Rhodes soon found itself the target of pirates looking for a quick and easy score. Eventually, piracy became such an issue for the merchants of Rhodes that the government decided to take matters into its own hands. In order to combat the growing threat to its newfound power, Rhodes built a war fleet to help patrol trade routes to and from the five largest and most prosperous ports on the island. That fleet eschewed the design and tactics of previous navies, doing away with larger vessels that required hundreds of rowers in favor of boats that were smaller, lighter, and faster. The result was a flotilla of ships that attacked in swarming squadrons and at surprising speed. This change alone was enough to disrupt the balance of

Pirates fight for control of a ship.

power out on the water, putting the seafaring marauders on the defensive and transforming the hunters into the hunted.

This new approach to naval warfare proved to be an effective one. By 200 BCE, piracy in the Mediterranean had been reduced to almost nothing. By going on the offensive, Rhodes managed to secure its trading routes and grow into an economic powerhouse along the way. It had even managed to turn the well-known pirate haven of Hieraphytna into an ally. The town, which was located on the island of Crete, had previously served as a base of operations for some of the most notorious pirate groups of the age, but thanks to the efforts of the Rhodian navy, piracy was no longer a profitable venture. Hieraphytna saw the writing on the wall and turned to legitimate trade instead, seeking partnerships with its one-time rival.

Unfortunately for traditional traders, Rhodes' dominance over the seas did not last. In the ensuing decades, a series of wars throughout the Mediterranean would undermine its power, eroding its economic might and leaving its navy a shell of its former self. This cleared the way for Rome to rise to prominence, eventually becoming the most dominant force that the Mediterranean geopolitical sphere had ever seen.

The decline of Rhodes was due in part to Phillip of Macedon, who had long envied the island's wealth and the iron grip that it held over the seas. In order to break Rhodes' hold, Phillip enlisted the aid of pirates from Sparta and Crete, promising them that they would find plenty of plunder aboard the Rhodian ships. After being systematically hunted for decades, pirates eager for payback soon began attacking their former antagonists with wild abandon.

Beginning in 205 BCE and running through 167 BCE, ongoing conflicts completely eroded away the influence that Rhodes exerted over the Mediterranean. By then, their rivalry with Rome was on the rise as well, which saw the Roman Senate enact economic measures that had a direct impact on the island nation's diminishing wealth. With less money in its coffers, Rhodes could no longer afford to cover the expense of its pirate patrols, which created new opportunities for seagoing outlaws to wreak havoc across the Adriatic and Aegean Seas once again.

But Rhodes wasn't the only traditional Mediterranean power to find its star fading just as the Roman Republic's influence was on the rise. In 146 BCE, Carthage was utterly annihilated by Roman forces, bringing a violent and dramatic end to one of the region's oldest civilizations. Meanwhile, in the east, the Seleucid Empire was in sharp decline too and the Ptolemaic Dynasty in Egypt had become a shadow of its former self. As a result, there was a power vacuum on the sea that the Romans weren't yet in a position to fill, which created new opportunities for mayhem on the open ocean.

With Rhodes, Carthage, and other traditional powers filling diminished roles on the world stage, and Rome seemingly unconcerned with piracy in general, it was a good time to be a marauder on the Mediterranean. The island of Delos created a major slave market, which served to fuel the demand for captives. When this market was paired with a decline in anti-piracy patrols, it opened the flood gates for seafaring raiders to return in great numbers. It should come as no surprise then, that out of this era came one of the most powerful and notorious band of outlaws in history—the Cilician pirates.

Cilicia and Illyria

Without a major naval power to enforce law out on the seas or protect the towns and villages that lined the coast, many of the smaller, less powerful communities were forced to broker deals with pirates instead. Typically, those deals consisted of towns providing a safe haven for the pirates in exchange for amnesty from attack and protection from other marauders. Thanks to these arrangements, hundreds of small pirate refuges sprang up all along the Mediterranean coast.

One of these places was in a stretch of the coastline known as Cilicia. Part of the Seleucid Empire, and located along the shores of modern day Turkey, Cilicia featured numerous rocky cliffs that were well suited to serve as natural harbors. The rugged terrain along these shores made it difficult for attacking fleets to locate pirate strongholds. Additionally, those outposts were relatively easy to defend, making it a potentially costly proposition to pursue marauders when they fled back to their bases of operation. Thus Cilicia was the perfect hiding place for large bands of pirates, who could easily sail out onto the sea, attack merchant vessels and raid towns, then return to the safety of their hidden coves relatively unmolested.

Unable to deal with the pirates directly, the weakened Seleucid Empire could only watch as its southern coast turned into a lawless land ruled by oceangoing outlaws. Only Rome was in a position to do anything to prevent piracy in the region, but because the marauders provided the Republic with a steady supply of cheap slaves, there was no real incentive to address the problem. This would become an ongoing theme for the Romans, whose unquenchable thirst for slaves only continued to grow over time.

By 140 BCE, sea travel had degenerated into a decidedly risky affair. The predominant naval force in the Mediterranean was, without a doubt, the Cilicia pirates. This band of brigands had become so well known and feared that the term was used to describe all of the raiders who were operating in the Eastern Mediterranean at the time, whether they sailed out of Cilicia or not.

As the dominance of the Cilicians grew, massive pirate fleets sprang up and began working with one another. These armadas would coordinate attacks, share information, and provide support for their brethren, allowing them to range farther afield on the Mediterranean. Some of the outlaws actually grew so bold as to conduct raids inland, operating miles from the sea. Others even attacked coastal cities in Italy, most notably Ostia, which served as the port of Rome. Towns were sacked, fortresses assaulted, and temples pillaged. It was as if the pirates had impunity to go wherever they wished and take whatever they wanted—not even the might of Rome gave them reason to take pause.

If the Greek philosopher and writer Plutarch is to be believed, the Cilicia pirates were a formidable force indeed. In his writings, he estimates that the pirate armada at its height consisted of more than a thousand ships and that the marauders were responsible for capturing over four hundred cities. The ransoming of entire towns was not uncommon, and as piracy spread across all of the Mediterranean it completely choked off traditional commerce and trade. Merchants were forced to take over-land routes rather than travel by sea, which required far more time and added expense. The prices of goods also rose dramatically, directly impacting rich and poor alike.

With such a large section of the world completely under their sway, the Cilicia pirates began to set up satellite bases in other parts of the Mediterranean. This gave them even greater freedom to strike at will and to operate farther from the safety of their rocky hidden ports. With their ships sailing to every corner of the region, the sea had become a desperate, hostile place. Anyone who dared sail on it risked losing their cargo, being killed, or being sold off into slavery.

Pirates with prisoner.

Not yet a naval power itself, Rome was content to allow the pirates to rule the seas rather than confront them directly. At times, the massive pirate presence in the Mediterranean served as a proxy for the Republic's interests, supplying a steady stream of slaves to be used as labor through-out the Italian Peninsula while keeping many of Rome's rivals preoccupied too. The alliance was a tenuous one at best however, as the waterborne outlaws had no qualms about capturing Roman ships or pillaging Roman towns. Still, the Senate usually turned a blind eye to those activities, as the raiders often proved to be extremely useful in promoting Rome's military and economic agenda in the Adriatic and Aegean Seas.

However, the Romans did not tolerate all piracy. In fact, the Republic went to war against the kingdom of Illyria to put an end to its state-sponsored pirate activities. During the second century BCE, the Illyrians saw piracy as just another form of politics and warfare that could be used to further its own ends. For the upstart nation, sending its citizens to sea on raiding missions was just as useful as sitting down at the negotiating table. Because of this, many Illyrians became privateers, arming their ships to attack merchant and enemy vessels alike. From time to time, that included raiding Roman ships, which often had cargo holds full of precious loot.

The seat of power for Illyria was located in what is now modern day Croatia, although the kingdom spread out into parts of Bosnia–Herzegovina, Montenegro, and Albania. As some of the more traditional Mediterranean powers waned in influence, Illyria grew in stature, in part due to its swift and powerful navy. Eventually, its aggressive tactics brought Illyria into contact with Rome, particularly as its privateers increasingly attacked and raided Roman vessels.

Looking to put an end to the conflict before it spiraled too far out of control, two Roman ambassadors traveled to Illyria in 230 BCE to negotiate a peace settlement. At the time, the kingdom was ruled by Queen Teuta, who was a strong proponent of the use of piracy as a diplomatic and political tool. Teuta defended the right of her nation to use its navy as it saw fit and refused to sign an agreement ending the practice. The pirates that sailed under her command were given full permission to raid enemy coastlines and expand the borders of Illyria as they saw fit. She was not about to abandon that approach at the request of her Roman rivals. This earned her the nickname of "pirate queen," even though she never sailed out to battle herself.

Their diplomatic mission a failure, the two Roman ambassadors set out for home. But before they could reach their destination, the ship that was carrying them was unfortunately—and ironically—beset by pirates. The attack left one of the dignitaries dead and served to infuriate the Roman Senate, which had attempted to extend an olive branch to Queen Teuta.

It is unclear as to whether or not Teuta ordered the attack on the Roman ship or if the raid was simply an untimely coincidence. Either way, with one of its envoys dead, the Roman Republic soon declared war on Illyria, and by default the privateers that flew Queen Teuta's banner. According to historical records, more than two hundred ships were mustered for an invasion, carrying several Roman legions to the rival kingdom. Those ships made short work of the pirates they encountered while en route and quickly subdued any land forces that stood in their way. Seeing she had no chance of defeating the Romans on the battlefield, Teuta sued for peace and by 228 BCE Illyria and its coastline were completely under Roman control.

In the years that followed, Rome curtailed pirate activity and revoked the privateer status of the Illyrian ships. Piracy in the area dropped off dramatically, although it did not disappear altogether. Much like in Cilicia, the Illyrian coast had many rocky inlets and natural harbors that were difficult to map out and attack. Therefore, marauding ships continued to be a problem even long after the Romans took power.

Decades later, the Romans found that they faced a similar challenge with the Cilicia pirates, although this time there was no central ruler that they could negotiate with, nor was there a single seat of power that they could attack. In spite of the Seleucid Empire, the pirates controlled the coastline.

Eventually the incessant raids and pillaging across the Mediterranean grew untenable. Roman interests in the entire region grew steadily and while the pirates were once seen as a valuable asset, they were quickly turning into a serious liability. By 102 BCE, the Senate decided that it was finally time to take action, so they dispatched Marcus Antonius—the Orator to Cilicia—with a powerful fleet and a well-trained army at his disposal. His mission was to crush the pirates irrevocably.

It did not take long for the seafaring raiders to realize that they were completely outclassed by the Roman forces. Antonius steamrolled over all who opposed him on land and sea, sending the pirates fleeing as he approached. He quickly cleared all of the outlaws from Cilicia and returned to Rome as a conquering hero. The Senate even threw the general a triumph to celebrate his victory. Serving as both a victory lap and a parade, the triumph was the highest honor a Roman general could receive.

As it turns out, the pirates were not defeated as many regrouped on the island of Crete. There, they continued their lawless ways, biding their time and waiting for Rome to lose interest as it had in the past. Eventually, the Senate was distracted by other conflicts and matters of state, allowing the outlaws to sail back to Cilicia and take refuge amongst the cliffs once again. It didn't take long for them begin raiding vessels throughout the Mediterranean, regaining their status as a constant thorn in the side of the Republic.

From 79–74 BCE, the Romans waged another active campaign against the pirates of Cilicia. But this time the Roman approach was less focused and determined, and while piracy was greatly reduced by those efforts, the Republic was never able to completely wipe out the threat. It was at this same time that a young Roman by the name of Julius Caesar encountered pirates on several occasions, which taught him some valuable lessons that he carried with him later in life.

Julius Caesar and Gnaeus Pompey Magnus

In 75 BCE, at the age of twenty-five, Caesar set out by ship from Rome to Rhodes where he planned to study public speaking in order to sharpen his oratory skills. As a young lawyer, he knew that improving his vocal abilities could further his political ambitions and potentially allow him to rise up the ranks of the Senate. He even hoped to one day be named Consul, claiming the rank of the highest elected official in the Republic.

While en route to the island, the ship he was traveling aboard was beset by pirates, and the young nobleman was taken prisoner. According to Plutarch, Caesar did not behave like any captive that the pirates had ever taken before. As was typical, the brigands held the young man for ransom, demanding a sum of twenty talents of silver (roughly 1,455 pounds) for his release. When Julius heard this, he reportedly scoffed at the demand, rebuking his captors for not asking for more. After all, he was a prominent member of Roman society and from an upstanding family no less. Caesar himself dispatched members of his own entourage to instead raise fifty talents of silver, the equivalent to about 3,400 pounds, effectively outbidding his own captors.

While he waited for the revised ransom to arrive, Caesar made himself at home amongst the pirates. It wasn't long before he was giving them orders and making demands of his own. He would tell them to be quiet when he was trying to sleep and force them to listen to the speeches and poems that he composed while in captivity. He even joined the pirates in their training and recreational games, although—ever the Roman nobleman—he continually looked down upon them. According to the existing stories, young Caesar would often disdainfully address the men as if he were their commander rather than their prisoner.

From time to time, one of his captors would do something to annoy or enrage Caesar. Plutarch says that it was not uncommon for Caesar to lash out at the pirates, calling them uncultured and illiterate savages. He would even threaten to crucify all of them, which invariably led to a round of chuckles from his captors.

After thirty-eight days in captivity, the ransom was delivered and Caesar was set free. His first order of business was to travel to the nearby city of Mietus, where he immediately set to work raising a naval force. His aim was to procure a few ships and well-trained Roman men so that he could return and deliver on his promise of exacting revenge upon the pirates. Despite the fact that he was just a private citizen, and held no public office or military titles, he succeeded in those efforts, taking charge of a strong fighting force.

It was not long before Caesar sailed back to the island where he had been held prisoner. Once there, he discovered his captors were still in the same camp, having grown complacent in their confidence. Ordering his recently acquired forces into action, he managed to not only capture all of the pirates, but reclaim the fifty talents of silver that had been paid out as his ransom. He even confiscated all of the outlaws' possessions in order to increase his own wealth.

With the pirates subdued, Caesar delivered them to a prison at Pargamon, where he petitioned the proconsul of the region to have them all executed. The proconsul refused, preferring to line his own pockets by selling the pirates into slavery instead. Caesar was not one who was known for going back on his word, thus he immediately returned to the prison and had his kidnappers brought before him. After they had all been gathered, he gave the order to crucify them. Just as he had promised them while he was in captivity.

By 67 BCE, the Romans decided that the pirate threat had once again risen to such a high level that it called for mass action. The Republic turned to one of its greatest generals, granting unprecedented power to Gnaeus Pompey Magnus, or Pompey the Great as he had come to be known. At a young age, Pompey displayed a talent for war, continually leading Roman legions to victory both at home and abroad. He also served as the consul of Rome on three separate occasions, making him an outstanding candidate for leading the attack against pirates on the Mediterranean.

The Roman Senate boldly granted Pompey full power in the Mediterranean Sea, which allowed him to deal with the growing pirate threat as he saw fit. His sovereignty wouldn't end at the coastline however, but would instead extend up to fifty miles inland, allowing his forces to pursue the outlaws wherever they fled. Furthermore, Pompey was awarded this unusual level of power for three years, giving him all of the time that he needed to stamp out the enemies of the Republic.

According to Plutarch, Pompey was given five hundred warships with full crews, 120,000 soldiers, and five thousand mounted cavalry, along with six thousand talents as a budget to conduct his war. He was also assigned twenty-five assistants, who were given senatorial rank, to allow them to efficiently cut through the bureaucratic red. Rome had finally grown serious about eliminating piracy from its expansive territorial waters.

Pompey's first move was to divide the Mediterranean Sea into thirteen districts, each of which was assigned its own fleet of warships and a commander to oversee their operation. With those forces in place, the great general himself took a fleet to the far western edge of the Mediterranean and started to sail eastward. As the marauders fled Pompey, they invariably found themselves running headlong into a waiting fleet.

It took Pompey just forty days to cross each of the thirteen districts, effectively stamping out piracy in each region as he went. Records show that along the way he captured four hundred pirate ships and destroyed another thousand. Reportedly, ten thousand pirates were killed, while twenty thousand more surrendered. It was a decisive victory for the Romans.

With the pirate fleet swept from the sea, Pompey ordered the commanders in each of the districts to seek out and destroy any remaining strongholds. It wasn't enough to just eliminate the ships and capture the men, he wanted all of their hiding places and safe havens cleared out too. If the pirates did not have a place to return to, they would have a harder time surviving and reorganizing for more attacks in the future.

Surprisingly, Pompey showed mercy on many of the pirates who surrendered to him. Rather than execute them or sell them into slavery, he chose instead to pardon them and relocate the former outlaws throughout the Republic. Many became framers, merchants, and craftsmen, earning an honest living and contributing to the greater prosperity of Rome.

Pompey's campaign against the pirates was a rousing success and the Mediterranean became a safe and profitable place to conduct trade once again. His actions not only secured a steady supply of grain to keep Rome fed, but also ensured that travel to and from the far corners of the Republic would be safe and reliable. Trade routes with distant kingdoms were reestablished and Rome—along with many of its neighbors—prospered greatly.

The military might and wealth of Rome brought an end to the largest and most feared pirate organization that the ancient world had ever seen. With the Cilicia pirates gone, the coasts of the Mediterranean saw an era of unprecedented security and stability.

That era was interrupted briefly during the Roman civil war, during which the one-time allies, Pompey and Julius Caesar, fought one another for control of the Republic. Caesar emerged victorious, but was famously assassinated on the Senate floor, which threw Rome into disarray while several powerful men vied for control. This struggle divided Rome's attention and allowed piracy to return in the Mediterranean, although not to the lofty levels that it once had achieved.

Eventually, Caesar's heir Octavian seized control and took the name Augustus Caesar. He became the first emperor of Rome and restored order not only to the country, but to the Mediterranean Sea as well. Augustus established a permanent Roman fleet specifically built to suppress piracy in the Aegean and Adriatic Seas, establishing an era of seafaring stability that lasted for the next three hundred or more years.

By the time Augustus ascended to the throne, piracy had been elevated to such a terrible crime under Roman law that the sentence was swift and brutal. Anyone who was convicted of being a pirate was either crucified, beheaded, or fed to wild animals. Furthermore, that sentence would be carried out in a public place, such as a town square, and preferably in front of a large crowd. This was meant to serve as a deterrent to others who may have considered joining the ranks of the Mediterranean pirates in the future.

However, Rome had always been a place of contradictions, and as the Republic made way for the empire, the need for slaves only continued to rise. While pirates had been all but eradicated from the Mediterranean, there were still some who were allowed to operate so long as they provided a steady stream of labor for use throughout Italy and other Roman provinces.

During the height of the Roman Empire, even the Cilicilian pirates were allowed to return in modest numbers. This time however, they were working for the interests of the Romans and were allowed to conduct their raids both at sea and along Mediterranean coastlines. And while they never again came anywhere close to their previous levels of power, Cilicia had once again become a haven for seafaring outlaws.

Still, the might of Rome kept the trading routes open and made the Mediterranean a much safer place in general. "Pax Romana"—the peace imposed by Rome—was extremely beneficial for the region, as it not only prevented wars between nations, but also maintained open and safe seas as well. For a time, it appeared that piracy had been stamped out entirely, although history proved that to be wrong. Very, very wrong.

By the late 400s CE, the Roman Empire was on the verge of collapse. When the Visigoth and Vandal armies sacked the Eternal City, its power and influence had waned greatly. In the east, the Byzantine Empire was growing from the ashes, but it would never hold the same level of control and influence over the region as the Romans had at the height of their power. With the pirate-hunting fleet on the Mediterranean gone, piracy soon returned in force. This time, the pirates would remain relatively unchecked for the next 1,300 years, not facing any serious opposition until the arrival of the British navy in the seventeenth century.

The Tale of Blackbeard

There is no question that the most famous pirate to ever sail the seven seas was the buccaneer who became widely known as Blackbeard. In the early eighteenth century, when he prowled the Caribbean Sea and the east coast of the American Colonies, he was amongst the most feared and cunning pirate captains the New World had ever seen. His towering legend far outlived his career as an oceangoing outlaw however, and today he is widely seen as the model for modern depictions of pirates.

For such a prominent figure in pirate history, very little is actually known about the early years of Blackbeard's life. It is believed that he was born sometime around 1680 in the English city of Bristol, which was an important international trading port at the time. This would have provided him with opportunities to not only hone his skills as a sailor, but to also find work aboard ships even at a young age.

Who Blackbeard's parents may have been also remains a mystery as even his real name is not known. Early in his career, he reportedly went by the name of Edward Teach or even Edward Thatch, although like many pirates of the era he used pseudonyms to mask his real identity. However, some believe that young Edward may have come from a wealthy background, as he knew how to read and write, something that was not common amongst the majority of citizens living in Bristol at the time.

Further details of Teach's life remain obscured, including how exactly he made his way to the Americas. There is some speculation that as a teenager he served aboard a merchant ship running supplies—or even slaves—to the New World. His home port of Bristol was a key player in the slave trade during the era and it is possible that he served aboard such a vessel. Most historians estimate that he arrived in the Caribbean around the turn of the eighteenth century, with some evidence that he may have lived and sailed out of Jamaica for a time.

We start to gain more insight into Blackbeard's life and personality around the outbreak of Queen Ann's War, which raged from the start of the eighteenth century for more than a decade as the French squared off against the English for control of North America. Both sides were backed by Native American tribes and used privateers to fight a proxy war against one another in the Atlantic Ocean. One such privateer was Edward Teach, who distinguished himself as part of just such a crew, helping to defend English interests in the New World.

Queen Ann's War served as an extension of the War of Spanish Succession, which was playing out amongst the European powers in the early 1700s. That conflict began when Charles II of Spain passed away without any children, naming his grandnephew Phillip of France as his heir. In effect, this would have made Phillip the ruler of both France and Spain, unifying both nations under a single flag. The other monarchs of Europe were not about to let that happen, so England, the Netherlands, Portugal, and several other countries declared war to stop the coronation. This led to the Treaty of Utrecht, in which Phillip renounced his claims to the French throne and ascended to become the King of Spain, ending a struggle that lasted for fifteen years and waged across two continents.

It was during that war that Teach began to forge his reputation as a bold and ruthless individual. He is said to have fought with courage and distinction, often acting in a decisive manner to help turn the tide of battle. He also honed his fighting skills and nautical tactics throughout the conflict, which would come to serve him well later in life.

After the War of Spanish Succession ended, Teach traveled back to the Caribbean where he took up residence on the island of New Providence in the Bahamas. Prior to the war the island had been mostly uninhabited, but a former privateer by the name of Henry Jennings created a colony that would soon become a safe haven for buccaneers. Due to its location, New Providence was the perfect place to launch raids against ships sailing in the Florida Strait, as well as larger merchant vessels sailing to and from Europe.

The fact that Teach relocated from Jamaica to New Providence indicates that he was already planning to make the leap from a life as a legitimate sailor and privateer to one of piracy. After the signing of the Treaty of Utrecht in 1715, most of the letters of marque that granted ships permission to prey on enemy vessels without fear of legal reprisal were revoked. Thus, there were a lot of sailors out of work and looking for a way to earn a living. Jennings gave them a new opportunity by creating a pirate-friendly environment in which large numbers of brigands joined forces with one another, creating a secure place to live and conduct raids. In sum, Jennings's outpost had become a colony for professional buccaneers.

One of the pirates who sailed out of New Providence was a man by the name of Benjamin Hornigold. Much like Teach, the Englishman had come to the Caribbean years earlier, and embarked on a pirate career in 1713, not long after the end of Queen Ann's War. Hornigold and his men preyed upon French, Spanish, and Dutch ships, although he made it a point to leave British vessels alone. Over the following four years he grew to become one of the most successful and feared marauders in the Americas. He also had a hand alongside Jennings in creating the pirate colony at New Providence.

By 1716, Teach had joined Hornigold's crew aboard a ship called the *Marianne*. It wasn't long before the captain named Teach his second in command. But later that year the crew mutinied, overthrowing Hornigold as their leader and putting him, and his officers, aboard a small sloop that they had captured during a previous raid. The mutineers then sailed off with the *Marianne*, along with her cargo hold full of plunder.

Undeterred, Hornigold, with Teach by his side, soon set to work finding a way to improve their current status. They soon captured a much larger ship, which the captain christened the *Ranger*. He then went to work outfitting it with as many as thirty guns, making it one of the most well-armed vessels in the entire Caribbean.

With the *Ranger* under his command, Hornigold turned control of the sloop over to Teach, who quickly settled into his role as captain. The duo soon made their presence known by capturing three merchant ships in rapid succession. Their early success included taking a Spanish galleon that was hauling 120 barrels of flour to Havana, a small sloop carrying rum from Bermuda, and a Portuguese ship loaded with white wine that had just arrived from the Madeira region back home.

It was around this time that Teach's reputation for being a fearsome pirate and sharp tactician began to emerge. While his friend and mentor Hornigold was already well known for his exploits prior to the two men joining forces, Teach had been a relatively anonymous up until that point. Their stunning level of success was enough to draw the attention of local authorities and to make opposing captains weary. One such man was Captain Mathew Munthe, who was a pirate hunter out of North Carolina. In his journals from that era he prominently mentions a "Captain Thatch" who commanded a sloop of six guns and a crew of more than seventy.

Teach and Hornigold's raids continued throughout all of 1717, and in September of that year they added yet another vessel to their small, but growing, fleet. An aristocrat turned pirate named Stede Bonnet encountered the two outlaws at sea at a time when he was not only healing from a wound suffered in battle, but his own men were growing restless and discontented with his leadership. Bonnet's crew expressed their wishes to join forces with the *Ranger* and its sister ship, which the captain willingly granted. Teach quickly took the helm of Bonnet's vessel, which had been dubbed the *Revenge*, putting another seventy men under his command. A month later, the fleet expanded to four boats when they captured yet another sloop.

By November of 1717, the relationship between Teach and Horngiold deteriorated, with the two men parting ways. It is unclear exactly why the pirates had a falling out, but they left the partnership with two ships each. Teach kept the *Revenge* and one of the sloops, while Hornigold sailed away with *Ranger* and the other captured vessel.

A month later, the English Crown offered a general amnesty to all

Edward Teach's moniker was indicative of his physical appearance.

pirates operating in the Caribbean. If they turned themselves in, and displayed a measure of remorse for their actions, the King would pardon them of all crimes. Eager to put his life of crime behind him, Hornigold did just that, accepting the pardon. Later, he would change careers and become a feared pirate hunter, although he and Teach would never cross paths again.

Not long after Teach set off on his own, the real legend of Blackbeard began to take shape. Using his two sloops, Teach attacked a large French merchant ship, capturing it using well-placed cannon shots that forced its captain to surrender even before the boarding parties were mustered. That ship—*La Concorde*—was outfitted to carry a sizable contingent of slaves, with dozens chained up in the hold below.

After taking possession of *La Concorde*, Teach and his crew sailed to a remote beach on the isle of Bequia, in the Grenadines of the West Indies. Once there, the pirate released the crew of the French ship, along with all of the slaves that were aboard the vessel. A few of those prisoners elected to join Teach's crew rather than stay on the island, assisting in the efforts to retrofit the ship to more effectively accommodate their needs. When that job was done, Teach rechristened the ship as *Queen Anne's Revenge*, making it his flagship.

A massive ship of two hundred tons, the *Queen Anne's Revenge* was everything a buccaneer could ask for. Durable, well built, and capable of hauling large numbers of men and plenty of cargo, it was exactly what an enterprising pirate needed. Teach further outfitted the ship with forty cannons, which gave it enough firepower to contend with most of the ships in the Royal Navy. Even though the vessel was a bit large and ponderous, she was still nimble enough to capture quite a few prizes in her brief career on the Caribbean Sea.

In the days that followed, Teach, now with three ships under his command, launched a series of raids against passing merchant traffic. Those raids typically ended with the enemy ship disabled by gunfire, then boarded by a group of marauders. The cargo hold would usually be stripped bare and sometimes the ship would even be set ablaze, left to burn out on the open water. On other occasions, Teach would allow the opposing captain and his men to sail away, which is how we gained the first real description of what the buccaneer looked like, not to mention how he gained his famous moniker.

In December of 1717, just a month after acquiring the *Queen Ann's Revenge*, Teach's pirate fleet attacked a merchant sloop named *Margaret* off the coast of Anguilla. Over the better part of a day, the buccaneers tore apart the ship, taking anything of value that they could find. But as the day wore on, and *Margaret* had fewer treasures to share, the captain of the ship—a man named Henry Bostock—was allowed to take his crew and resume command of the vessel. When he sailed back to his home harbor on Saint Kitts, he immediately reported the raid to the authorities, painting a colorful description of the man who had robbed him at sea.

Bostock described the pirate captain as a tall, lean man, "with a very black beard which he wore very long." It didn't take long for that striking image to take hold and the now-infamous nickname of "Blackbeard" to supplant the name of Edward Teach. So much so that most people have heard of the pirate Blackbeard, but few can actually tell you his real name.

As the number of encounters with the mysterious pirate grew, more reports of his physical appearance took shape as well. Some of his opponents described him as fearsome and fearless in battle, with a wild look in his eyes, and a terrible wrath in his voice. Author Charles Johnson, who wrote a famous book titled *A General History of the Robberies and Murders of the most notorious Pyrates* in 1724, said Teach was "such a figure that imagination cannot form an idea of a fury from hell to look more frightful."

Teach, it seems, fully embraced his Blackbeard persona as he knew the value of employing a more psychological approach to defeating his enemies. Over time, he took to wearing his beard tied into tails using the fuses of guns and cannons to hold the hair in place. His tall, broad-shouldered body was often adorned with fine dark clothes, including a wide-brimmed hat and boots that reached up to his knees. In battle, he'd wield three pistols and, according to Johnson, he'd fight with slow-burning matches ablaze and tucked behind his ears to further enhance his frightening appearance.

In the early weeks of 1718, Teach and his pirate flotilla continued to grow in size. He captured as many as five ships in the Bay of Honduras, another vessel in Grand Cayman, and a small Spanish ship near Havana. While en route between those locations, he and his crew, which had likely grown to well beyond three hundred men at that point, also raided and plundered several more merchant ships, putting one or two to the torch along the way.

It had only been about a year and a half since Blackbeard had joined the crew of Hornigold and less than a year since they had been reduced to sailing in just a single tiny sloop. During the ensuing months, Teach grew into a powerful pirate captain who was feared and respected across the entire Caribbean. He was an outlaw who didn't seem to fear pirate hunters, the Royal Navy, or any other ship that he encountered out on the water. Over that time, he had also sailed the length and breadth of the region, while occasionally venturing into the Atlantic Ocean, seemingly unchallenged by any maritime authority.

As the success of his raids increased, Blackbeard promoted himself to the rank of commodore and in May of 1718 he set sail for the English colonies in North America. His target was the harbor at Charles Town in South Carolina, where he set up a blockade and proceeded to board and plunder any ship that was unlucky enough to wander past. Over the span of about six days, the pirate armada captured a total of nine vessels, stealing valuable cargo along the way. But when Teach decided to leave the area, he released all of the ships and their crews, allowing them to continue their voyages.

While in Charles Town, word reached Teach that a famous pirate hunter by the name of Woodes Rogers had been dispatched from England and was on his way to the Caribbean. Rogers' orders were to eliminate piracy from the region, and he came armed with a fleet of powerful ships to help him accomplish that task. Privateers and pirates had fallen out of favor, both with the monarchies of Europe and the public in general. It was only a matter of time before Rogers and his crew would come looking for the infamous Blackbeard, who had grown into one of the most successful pirates of the age in a very short time.

Sensing that he would likely be near the top of Rogers' list of targets, Teach took his fleet north to a place called Topsail Inlet. There, off the coast of North Carolina, he hoped to perform a few routine repairs and maintenance on several of the ships in preparation for a potential showdown with the pirate hunter. But several of the vessels—including the *Queen Ann's Revenge*—ran aground on a shallow sandbar, leaving them not only locked in place on the beach, but damaged beyond repair. This was a serious blow to the pirate captain, whose options were starting to run low.

Knowing that there was still time for him to accept the royal pardon, Teach considered reaching out to Charles Eden, the governor of the North Carolina colony, to strike a deal. But unsure if he could trust the man, Blackbeard sent one of his trusted lieutenants instead. That man received his pardon within a few days and returned to Topsail Inlet to share the news with his captain. Upon arriving back at the beach however, he discovered that Teach had abandoned a portion of the crew, took the two remaining ships, and had set sail, leaving a large portion of his loyal followers behind in the process.

Some historians believe that Teach had planned to run the *Queen Ann's Revenge*, and the other ships, aground all along. Sensing that his large fleet and crew were becoming a liability, Blackbeard decided it was best to reduce his profile in an effort to move faster and travel more inconspicuously. His flagship had become a very well-known ship, easily spotted and recognized out on the water. By ditching the vessel, he and his remaining men would be harder to track should Rogers come looking for them.

However, within days, it seems that Teach may have had a change of heart and begun looking for a way to escape his life as a pirate. He requested, and received, a pardon from Eden, and for a time he settled down in North Carolina. There are some indications that he may even have gotten married and was preparing to put his marauding ways behind him for good. Ill-suited for that kind of lifestyle, Blackbeard returned to raiding ships in the Atlantic by the fall of 1718, capturing several French vessels and a Spanish sloop in fairly short order.

In an effort to avoid a showdown with the authorities, Teach did his best to hide his activities from Eden and other local administrators. But after he joined forces with another well-known pirate by the name of Charles Vane, it did not take long to draw the attention and ire of high-ranking English officials. This included Alexander Spotswood, the governor of Pennsylvania, who had little tolerance for piracy. In order to put an end to the pirate's reign of terror, Spotswood commissioned a lieutenant of the Royal Navy, Robert Maynard, with the task of finding the two men and putting an end to their marauding.

Maynard located both pirates at Ocracoke Island. There, Teach, Vane, and their crews had set up a small base of operations, frequently entertaining other pirate captains passing through the area. The out-of-the-way location had proven itself perfect for avoiding the ships that were hunting them, while still affording the buccaneers privacy and comfort.

After scouting their location and assessing the best plan of attack, Maynard and his men sailed off with two sloops to launch a morning assault. Their hopes of catching the pirate camp off guard were soon dashed however, as Teach's new ship—the *Adventure*—opened fire on the approaching vessels as soon as they were within range. Within minutes, a pitched battle broke out, with the attackers looking to pin their quarry into a confined space, while the pirates worked quickly to maneuver their ships into a defensive position.

At some point, the *Adventure* was able to turn in place and fire its powerful array of cannons directly onto Maynard's sloops. The cannon fire caused a devastating amount of damage, killed numerous men, and quickly eliminated one of the ships from the battle. For a time, the outcome of the battle did not look good for the pirate hunters.

At some point however, the *Adventure* sustained damage to its sails and the crew briefly lost control of the vessel. It careened headlong into a sandbar, running aground, suddenly becoming a stationary target. Within moments, Maynard steered his one remaining sloop into the side of Teach's ship.

Throughout the battle, Maynard had kept the bulk of his forces hidden below deck in order to conceal their numbers and to protect them from cannon and musket fire. When the pirate hunter's ship approached, Teach thought that he and his men far outnumbered their attackers. As the two vessels slammed into each other, the pirate captain confidently ordered his men to prepare for close-quarters combat, leading them forward to meet the enemy.

Blackbeard's confidence was momentarily shaken when he strode onto Maynard's ship, only to have dozens of men burst out from the cargo hold below. But Teach was a grizzled veteran of many battles by that time, so he held his ground and rallied his troops around him. A ferocious battle broke out on the deck of the sloop, with the sound of gunfire and the clashing of weapons ringing out through the air.

The two captains met at the center of the battle; Teach wielding a cutlass and Maynard a sword. The duo stood toe to toe, neither giving quarter, as they faced off in a battle to decide the fate of both crews. At one point, Blackbeard managed to break the sword of his opponent, sending it sprawling across the deck. Sensing the end was near, he moved in to press his advantage.

Fearing that his final moments were upon him, Maynard raised his firearm to take one last desperate shot. But before either he or Teach could land the killing blow, another member of Maynard's crew slashed out at the pirate, cutting him deeply across the throat. Blackbeard stumbled backwards in shock and pain, only to be quickly overwhelmed by more attackers. Within moments Maynard's crew cut him down where he stood, ending the life of one of most feared and notorious pirates the world has ever seen.

Later, when his body was examined, it was said that Blackbeard had suffered at least five gunshot wounds and more than twenty cuts. After confirming Teach's identity, his head was severed from his body and hung from the mast of Maynard's ship, a gruesome prize for all to see. The pirate hunter would need that head in order to collect the expected reward for the death of the pirate. The rest of Teach's remains were tossed overboard.

The capture of Blackbeard by Robert Maynard.

In the wake of his death, the crew of the *Adventure* soon surrendered and were rounded up by Maynard's men. Most eventually received pardons for their crimes and were allowed to go free. As was typical, some headed home and adopted a more normal life, while others continued sailing. None ever met up with a pirate of Teach's stature again, including those who would return to a life of piracy.

Contrary to popular belief, the infamous pirate Blackbeard did not have a long and prosperous career. Just two years had passed from the time that he joined Hornigold's crew to his death at the hands of Maynard. But Teach certainly made the most of those two years; raiding ships, amassing a small fleet, and gaining the loyalty and trust of hundreds of men. Over that time, he also managed to become one of the most feared brigands in the Caribbean and along the American coast, with his exploits helping to spread his legend far and wide.

Perhaps Edward Teach's greatest accomplishment is how his reputation has stood the test of time. Few other pirates from any era are as well known as Blackbeard, even if the actual details of his story aren't particularly common knowledge. In the more than two hundred years since his death, Blackbeard has become the model for modern depictions of what a pirate should look and sound like. His image, real or perceived, has been the influence for countless pop culture references including books, television shows, movies, and video games.

Without a doubt, there were pirates who were more successful, diabolical, and cunning than Teach. There were many who had longer careers too, sailing the globe in pursuit of wealth and plunder rather than operating in a relatively small theater like the Caribbean. But most of them have long since been forgotten, with only a few historians and pirate enthusiasts remembering their names. Somehow, the tale of Blackbeard hasn't just survived, but thrived since his death, turning him

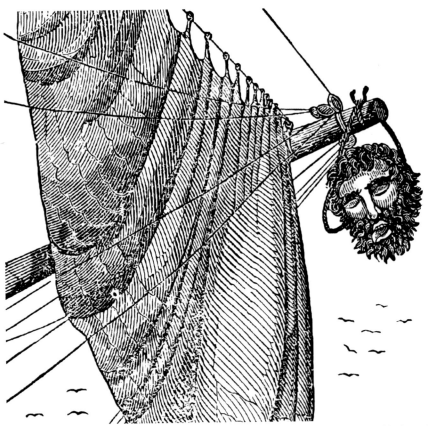

The hanging of Blackbeard's head.

into the quintessential seafaring rogue by which all others are measured.

The shadow of Blackbeard continues to be cast even many years after his death. In 1996, the remains of the *Queen Ann's Revenge* were found in what is now known as Beaufort Inlet off the coast of North Carolina. The ship was later entered into the National Registry of Historic Places, further cementing the pirate's place as an indelible part of American history. Since its discovery, archaeologists have continued to find a number of items scattered around the site, including many of the vessel's cannons.

If tales are to be believed, the story of Edward Teach doesn't end even there. On occasion, on the darkest of North Carolina nights, strange lights can be seen out on the sea. This unexplained phenomenon is often referred to as "Teach's Light," and as the legend goes it is the ghost of Blackbeard himself still haunting the coastline, searching for his missing head.

These superstitious stories help to maintain the romantic notions for a bygone era when pirates still sailed the oceans.

CHAPTER 2

The Pirates of the North

After Rome

The Fall of Rome put an end to *Pax Romana*, the peace that was imposed first by the Republic and later by the empire. Without the mighty Roman legions to maintain order, local tribes and fiefdoms soon found themselves in conflict with one another, battling over scarce resources and territory. It was a brutal time in Europe in particular, where an age of knowledge and enlightenment was snuffed out and would not return for more than a thousand years.

Chaos and conflict erupted across the waters of the Mediterranean as well. Without a Roman fleet to maintain control of the shipping lanes, merchant ships soon found themselves at the mercy of pirates once again. After four hundred years of almost no pirate activity, the Adriatic and Aegean Seas became lawless environments where seafaring marauders preyed on passing ships and coastal villages with little to no resistance.

It is difficult to overstate just how devastating the fall of Rome was for the Western world. The demise of the empire created a power vacuum that had a profound economic, military, and political impact on the region. In the wake of the collapse, hundreds of thousands of people were left scrambling to find a way to survive. For many, the only real alternative was to turn to banditry and piracy, as they sought ways to profit at the expense of others.

In the Roman Empire, anyone who was convicted of piracy was quickly crucified or beheaded. Sentencing was usually swift and the punishment was meted out just as quickly. This alone was usually enough to deter most people from rushing off to join a pirate crew. But once that deterrent was no longer a factor, and economic conditions turned desperate, piracy became an increasingly more viable way to survive in a hostile world.

Throughout ancient history the motivation for becoming a pirate generally had nothing to do with seeking out adventure on the high seas or amassing a fortune in plundered treasure. For most, it was simply a way to eke out a living when few other options were available. If a young man—there were exceedingly few female pirates at the time—found himself without any prospects, no discernible skills, and a dim future, he might choose a life of piracy simply because he did not have a lot of other options. He was willing to accept the danger that came with this profession with the hope that it would someday allow him to carve out a better life.

In some cases, the members of a pirate crew quite literally may not have had any other choice. Sometimes, able-bodied men serving on captured boats or who were captured during raids on coastal villages were pressed into service aboard a pirate ship, becoming outlaws against their will. For them, the options came down to either joining the crew or being cut down where they stood. More than a few decided to enter a life of crime, which at least gave them the hope of one day being free.

Most of the pirate ships that operated in the Mediterranean at this time went in search of targets of opportunity. They would usually stumble across merchant vessels traveling on established trading routes or search for vulnerable towns and villages along familiar coasts. Rarely did they make coordinated assaults on strategic targets or plan their raids to maximize their rewards. Since they operated in a region of the world that had been thoroughly mapped by that point in history, they had fewer chances to attack communities that hadn't already been assaulted by marauders from the sea.

Rome's demise cleared the way for smaller, regional powers across

Europe to rise in prominence. Some were able to stake out a kingdom of their own on ancestral lands that they had occupied even before the Republic was founded. Others took territory from their neighbors, establishing new nations by force. The Saxons, for example, began establishing themselves in Britain in the decades that followed Rome's fall, while the Franks moved into what would become modern day France. And far to the north, in a part of the world that would eventually be labeled as Scandinavia, a group of fierce and proud warriors called Norsemen began to emerge onto the world stage, charting a course that would leave their mark on history.

The History of the Vikings

The Norsemen were a Germanic tribe that inhabited parts of what would eventually become Denmark, Norway, and Sweden. Their exact origins are unknown, but it is believed that they had migrated to the region hundreds of years earlier in order to escape conflicts with other Central European tribes. It is possible that they may also have been displaced by the expansion of the Roman Empire, which routinely pushed indigenous people off their land in an effort to maintain steady growth.

Regardless of where exactly they came from, the Norse were descended from tough and hardy stock. The part of the world that they chose to call home was remote, rugged, and harsh. Summers were warm, but short, and the winters were long, cold, and dark. Survival was rarely easy and individuals needed to be strong and self-sufficient in order to carve out a place for themselves. It was no place for the weak or indecisive.

Still, the Norsemen managed to survive along the coasts of the North Sea. There they became fishermen and farmers, and occasionally traded with other Norse tribes or their German cousins to the south. For centuries they subsisted in this way, with their immediate neighbors knowing of their existence, but rarely paying them much mind. The kingdoms that the Romans once categorized as "barbarians" saw the Norsemen as being even more uncivilized and unsophisticated, and often dismissed them as nothing more than pagan infidels.

However, over time, living in the harsh north began to impact the

Norsemen. As the centuries passed, they became stronger and harder, learning to not just survive in the cold north, but to thrive there. They believed that the rugged land that they called home was no place for lesser men, snuffing out the life of outsiders in a quick and brutal fashion. Thanks to their environment, the Norse became fiercely independent, aggressive, and powerful. That land would also give rise to a subset of the Norse that would come to be feared and respected by all who encountered them, with a reputation that remains formidable to this day—the Vikings.

It is important to point out that while the Vikings were Norsemen, not all of the Norse were Vikings. That's because the term "Viking" is used to describe the groups of warriors who routinely went on exploratory missions and raids to pillage nearby towns and villages. In fact, the vast majority of Norsemen were content to stay at home and continue their lives as fishermen and farmers, rather than venture out into the unknown world. As hard as it may be to believe, the Vikings were just a very small segment of the Scandinavian population, most of whom rarely ventured more than a few miles from home.

Where the name "Viking" actually comes from has long been a matter of debate. Some say the word meant to go raiding or plundering in the Norse language, while others say it describes the place these seafaring warriors originally came from. Viken is a location found inside the Oslo Fjord where some of the Norse may have launched their earliest attack ships. There are indications that in the Scandinavian tongue the word *viking* meant pirate as well, although plenty of historians believe that the name was simply a generic label referring to "people who came from the sea." Over time, as the northmen ventured farther away from home, and conducted more and more devastating raids, the term Viking became synonymous with oceangoing marauders and warriors, which is an image that the word continues to conjure to this day.

The first recorded Viking raid took place in 793 CE, and by most accounts it came as a major surprise to Europeans. While it seems likely that other raids took place prior to that date, attacks by the Norsemen were apparently so unusual and unexpected that it was a shocking revelation to those who took the brunt of the assault. That initial raid essentially marked the dawn of the Viking Age, which lasted for more than 270 years and left an enduring mark on European history.

It is unclear why exactly the Norsemen decided to begin raiding their neighbor's villages or plundering passing boats at this time. Some historians believe that a population surge resulted in a lack of resources in the north, pressing the Scandinavians to go looking for the things they needed elsewhere. Others point to the increasing sophistication of ships, which gave them the ability to travel much faster and farther abroad. By the seventh and eighth centuries CE, the use of oars as a primary source of propulsion had given way to sails instead, creating greater opportunities for the Vikings to explore and plunder farther from home. Either way, the Norsemen announced their presence in a swift and startling fashion, serving notice that there was a fearsome new force to be reckoned with on the North Sea.

Viking ships traveling along a coast.

The target for the first known Viking attack was a priory on the island of Lindisfarne, just off the northeast coast of England near what is now Northumbrian. For the Norsemen, it is likely that the monastery that was located on the island simply promised them little resistance and plenty of plunder that was easy to transport back home. Whether or not there was much strategic thought put into the location beyond that remains unclear.

The Lindisfarne priory happened to be extremely wealthy, largely due to the fact that it was an important pilgrimage site for many Christians in the British Isles. Founded by St. Cuthbert nearly a century and a half earlier, the location was said to be the site of numerous miracles presided over by Cuthbert himself. It is possible that even the Norsemen were surprised by how much plunder they found at the monastery, which no doubt encouraged them to raid similar locations in the future.

From the Anglo-Saxon point of view, the raid wasn't just an attack on a remote abbey located on an island in the North Sea. Instead, it was viewed as an assault on Christendom itself, with heathen forces squaring off against God's Earthly servants. The fact that the Norsemen sacked a place that was seen as sacred ground made the attack all the more shocking and horrible. Such a sacrilegious act sent fear and despair across Britain and farther abroad into the very heart of Europe itself.

That attack took place on June 8, 793 CE, with few actual details surviving the test of time. According to some accounts, the Vikings appeared on the scene as if from nowhere and laid waste to the church, carrying off goods of great value in the process. Amongst the treasures that were taken was a fine metal case that was constructed to house the famed Lindisfarne Gospels, a priceless work of art that survived the raid in part because it was deemed of little value by the marauders. The ornate box that housed it was shiny enough to draw their attention however, along with whatever else of value they could haul back to their ships.

Lindisfarne would serve as a blueprint for future Viking raids. Approaching from the sea on Norse longboats, the marauders would come ashore as close to their target as possible. This allowed them to use speed and surprise to their advantage, creating as much chaos as possible along the way. With their enemies in disarray, the skilled Viking warriors could loot, burn, and pillage almost unchallenged, routinely hauling off gold, silver, and other treasures, not to mention captives.

The success of their first major attack sent the Vikings home with plenty of loot, but it also served a second purpose. The brutality and audaciousness of the assault stunned not just the Anglo-Saxons, but others who learned about the raid on the European continent too. The infidels from the hinterlands were a terrifying new force that appeared to hold human life in low regard, at least when there was silver and gold to be acquired.

As bold and cunning as the Vikings were, their reputation was enhanced even further by the tales of the inhabitants of Lindisfarne. In the weeks preceding the attack, many claimed to have seen frightening sheets of lightning, massive whirlwinds, and even fire-breathing dragons streaking across the sky. To make matters worse, a great famine had struck earlier that year, leading many to believe that God was angry with the Brits or had forsaken them altogether. These signs and portents pointed to some kind of looming disaster. The Norsemen were that disaster personified.

At the time, churches and monasteries were generally viewed as off limits when it came to armed attacks, which generally meant they were left unguarded. The armies on the European continent went to great lengths to make sure that no blood was spilled on holy ground and that priests and monks were not assaulted in any way. The mere fact that the Vikings didn't seem to share this same outlook was enough to shock and terrify kings and peasants alike. If these strange, fierce men from the north didn't fear the retribution of God, what exactly were they afraid of?

The Vikings had their own pantheon of powerful gods, led by the All-Father Odin. The deities that they worshipped were usually depicted as powerful warriors who reveled in glorious combat. They hurled thunderbolts, battled giants, and were just as bold and vengeful as the Norsemen themselves. These gods starkly contrasted with the one God of the Christian faith, who preached peace, understanding, and forgiveness.

Christian monasteries were thus easy targets for the Vikings, who had zero hesitations about attacking the scared places of a God in whom they didn't believe. To make matters worse for the Britains, many of their churches and abbeys were located close to the sea, which only made them more tempting targets for the seafaring men from Scandinavia.

A ship full of Viking warriors could arrive as if out of nowhere, conduct a swift and merciless raid, and escape back to their boats just as quickly as they had appeared. This efficiency contributed to the notion that Norsemen had an almost supernatural quality about them, which when paired with their legendary ferocity and propensity for violence, quickly turned the Vikings into the bogeymen that stepped out of the darkest nightmares.

In the years that followed the attack on Lindisfarne, the Vikings continued to raid other islands that were home to remote priories. They targeted the monasteries on Sky and Iona, plundering the latter three times over the span of a single decade. On each occasion, they burned buildings and destroyed property, killed locals, and spirited away untold treasures. It was as if the Church, the Anglo-Saxons, and God himself were helpless before the Viking onslaught.

As the success of their raids mounted, the Norsemen only grew in confidence. By the turn of the ninth century, their ships had begun to venture farther afield, striking at more targets in distant lands. What began as lightning-fast attacks against small and remote outposts in the islands of the North Sea soon spread to raids against England, Scotland, Ireland, and the north of France. There are even some indications that they sailed all the way to Italy, exploring the waters of the Mediterranean and potentially coming into contact with the more traditional pirate and merchant vessels of that region.

The farther away from home that they sailed, the more the Vikings began to realize that the resistance they faced was light and mostly inconsequential. This only served to embolden them further, leading to increased raids and luring even more Norsemen to sea. While finding plunder was always of the utmost concern, the Vikings also valued conquest, glory, exploration, and the pure exhilaration of adventure.

Viking Ships

Having settled in the coastal regions of Scandinavia many centuries earlier, the Norsemen had been competent seamen long before they began launching raids against the British Isles. There is evidence to suggest that the first, simple boats made by the Norse can be traced back as far as 2300 BCE, or perhaps even earlier. Those vessels were not seaworthy enough to venture far from shore and they used oars as a form of propulsion, which was the norm at the time.

However, the Norse would learn to craft more sophisticated ships, first by borrowing from the designs of others and later by perfecting their own techniques. For instance, the sail was likely introduced to the Vikings thanks to Germanic and Celtic traders, who had adopted it from the Romans. This simple, but innovative upgrade supplanted the use of oars for long-distance travel, even as the Norse longboats were becoming faster, more stable, and easier to control. The invention and addition of the keel added to their maneuverability and precision steering to the point that by the time of the raid on Lindisfarne, Viking ships were likely amongst the very best on the sea.

A traditional Viking ship featured a low-lying hull and could have measured as much as ninety feet in length and roughly sixteen feet in width. These vessels could hold as many as fifty or sixty men, delivering a sizable fighting force into enemy territory. Usually made from oak, the ships were extremely durable and designed to be swift out on the water. This proved particularly useful in the early days of the Viking Age, when hit-and-run tactics were the norm. Because the hull sat so low, the ships didn't require a dock or any kind of harbor, but could instead be beached directly on the sand. This was also extremely useful for quick strikes against targets located along the coast, giving the Norsemen the ability to land, disembark, and wreak havoc just about anywhere.

Part of what made fighting the Norsemen so frustrating for their adversaries was that they would often attack a lightly defended town or monastery, overcoming the opposition with relative ease. They could then sack the village, make off with the plunder, and be long gone before a larger military force could arrive on the scene to engage them. The swiftness of the longboats was crucial to this type of raid, helping to confound and frustrate the Viking's enemies, who never seemed to know exactly when and where they were going to strike next.

The unique design of the Viking longboats, which featured a narrow and shallow hull, gave the Norse warriors another strategic advantage that their enemies did not expect. While the ships were clearly fast and maneuverable out on the ocean, they happened to be able to move surprisingly well in shallow water too. This didn't come in handy just when making a beach assault, as it gave the Norse pirates the ability to travel upstream on rivers as well. By dropping their sails and picking up the oars, the Viking raiders were able to reach targets farther inland by using Europe's rivers to their advantage.

In the early years of the ninth century, the Vikings mostly stuck to their tried and true battle plan, rarely deviating from the tactics that had proven so effective in the past. After all, they had found a great deal of success with their hit-and-run attacks on coastal towns and villages. Just like the ancient pirates that had come before them, the Norsemen had discovered that those locations were generally very difficult to defend, often put up little or no resistance, and offered plenty of valuable items to plunder.

River Raids

It didn't take long before the Vikings realized there were targets along some of the major rivers in Europe that their ships would allow them to strike at as well. By 815 CE, the Norsemen had already launched raids along the Thames River in England, as well as the Volga River in Russia, and both the Seine and Loire Rivers in Frankish-controlled regions. Thanks to the unique design of their ships, traveling upstream was not a deterrent for the Vikings, who would often go to great lengths to attack a distant, yet wealthy, target. Conversely, for the enemies of the Norse, it felt as if there was no place that was safely out of the reach of the marauding bands.

During this era, Emperor Charlemagne ruled much of central and Western Europe. His kingdom was harassed by the Vikings on an almost continual basis, which gave him the foresight to build both coastal and river defenses that could help stymie those assaults. Charlemagne's defense system proved to be somewhat successful, reducing the number of successful attacks for a time. However, after the emperor's death in 814 CE, his kingdom began to splinter and those defenses fell into disrepair. This gave the marauders from the sea the window of opportunity that they needed to begin venturing farther up river to attack some of the larger settlements that were found there.

Much like their early attacks along the sea coast, these river raids often came as a complete surprise to the targeted settlements. For years, English, German, and Frankish citizens had heard tales of the giant, fearless warriors from the north who swept down on their foes without warning or mercy. But most thought that because they lived farther inland they would be spared from such attacks. Some even believed that the stories of the Vikings were actually tall tales that had been overly exaggerated to frighten the young. So when the Norse invaders began to strike at cities and fortresses that were increasingly farther from the sea, it brought a new level of fear and panic to an increasing number of Europeans.

One of the more famous of these river raids occurred in 845 CE when a large force of Vikings rowed up the Seine River and attacked Paris. Even then, the city was ancient, tracing its roots back to sometime in the third century BCE. As time passed, Paris grew into a trading center, drawing merchants from across Europe. This, of course, made it a prime target for an invading force looking to haul off a large amount of loot. But thanks to its inland location, it had generally gone unscathed from such attacks for centuries.

The Viking fleet that attacked Paris is said to have been made up of more than 120 ships carrying as many as five thousand men. It was led by a legendary Norse chieftain by the name of Ragnar, who had conducted many successful raids against the Europeans in the past. He was known to be ruthless, determined, and utterly fearless, which only served

Viking longboats attacking Paris.

to inspire his men to follow him into battle. Those same characteristics also drove him to take great risks and set out on bold expeditions.

The local Frankish king during that era was Charles the Bald. He vowed to prevent the Vikings from taking Paris and sacking the wealthy Abbey of Saint-Denis that was located nearby. Charles raised a large army and split his forces in two, with half on either side of the Seine. He believed that this tactic would allow his troops to attack the invaders from two directions at once as they rowed up the river towards their target. However, by dividing his men, he weakened his tactical position.

Ragnar and his Viking force engaged and defeated one of Charles the Bald's armies, taking more than one hundred men prisoner in the process. In order to dishearten his foes, and honor the Norse god Odin, he ordered all of captives to be hanged and put on display along an island on the Seine. This tactic seemed to achieve its purpose, as the remaining Frankish army provided little resistance. On March 29, 845 CE, the Norsemen captured and looted Paris, sending many of its inhabitants fleeing in terror. The day also happened to be Easter Sunday, a fact that was not lost on the superstitious Parisians.

The occupying force stayed in the city for a time, as the Frankish army couldn't muster enough strength to dislodge them from their position. Eventually the Vikings did leave, but not until they were paid to do so. In order to convince Ragnar and his men to depart Paris, Charles gave them a ransom of more than 5,670 pounds of silver and gold, adding substantially to the plunder they had already collected when they initially sacked the city.

The Siege of Paris, as the battle eventually came be known, marked a turning point not only for the Vikings themselves, but for their European adversaries as well. From then on, it was not uncommon for the wealthier kingdoms to simply pay the Norsemen to leave them alone rather than try to face them on the battlefield. The logic behind these payments was that win or lose, the Vikings were going to inflict massive damage to towns and villages, probably making off with a good deal of treasure in the process. By paying them a ransom, the Vikings would leave the towns—and people—alone, resulting in far less bloodshed and destruction.

For their part, the Norse were happy to collect the ransom and move on to another target. There were always other regions that would not—or could not—pay them off, so they set their sights on pillaging those locations instead. In this way, they not only filled their coffers with more treasure, but they still marched into battle. Every true Viking craved glory in battle as much as they did silver and gold. How else were they to earn a place in Valhalla—the mythological hall of heroes ruled by Odin—if they didn't vanquish their foes on the battlefield and prove their worth as warriors?

While Charles the Bald paid one of the first ever recorded ransoms to the Vikings, it took a bit longer for the practice to reach the shores of Britain. According to historians, a ransom of 7,275 pounds of silver was given to the Norsemen following the Battle of Maldon, which was a particularly harsh defeat for the Anglo-Saxons in 991 CE. Rather than continue a protracted war with the Norsemen, the monarchy decided it was best to pay them off and send them on their way instead. This marked the first official occasion that such a tactic was employed by the Brits, although it seems likely that it was a common practice even before being noted in the history books.

After the Battle of Maldon, it became increasingly common for the Anglo-Saxons and Franks to pay off the Vikings. For example, Æthelred the Unready, who was the King of England in 1007 CE, is said to have paid the Norsemen nearly three hundred thousand pounds of silver in exchange for two years of peace. Five years later, they were given an additional four hundred thousand pounds of silver after a Danish army sacked Canterbury as well.

In order to pay these exorbitant sums, monarchs across Europe began instituting a special tax that was specifically earmarked to cover the expense of bribing the Norsemen into leaving them alone. This tax eventually came to be referred to as the *Danegeld*, which quite literally translates to "Dane tax" in reference to the large numbers of Danish marauders that continued to raid the coasts. Later, after the Viking Age came to an end, the Danegeld remained as a way of paying Danish mercenaries off.

Eventually, even vast quantities of silver and gold were not always enough to quench the thirst of the Vikings, who were increasingly sailing against their enemy not just for plunder, but for conquest. Over time, there was a subtle, but important, shift in Norse tactics as they switched from the traditional hit-and-run approach that had been so successful in the past to a focus on capturing and holding land. Often the disputed territory was retaken by a force of arms from the European defenders, but on occasion it was ceded to the Vikings by a monarch as an additional way to prevent ongoing warfare. In this way, giving the Vikings territory became a new type of ransom that soon proved just as effective as precious metals.

More often than not, the lands that were given to the Norsemen were located along the coastlines and at the mouths of important rivers. These regions somewhat resembled their homelands back in Scandinavia, allowing them to settle in much more quickly and comfortably. But there were ulterior motives for European powers giving the Vikings those territories, as they happened to be particularly well suited for defending them against foreign invaders, including other Norsemen. By gaining ownership of the land, these former seagoing raiders now had a vested interest in protecting it, which again marked an important and subtle shift in their culture.

As more and more Vikings settled into these conquered territories, fewer and fewer of them returned to the sea as marauders. It was becoming increasingly less profitable for them to continue their raids against the coastlines as improved defensive fortifications and more sophisticated weapons made that lifestyle more difficult and dangerous. The combination of these factors was enough to convince the once fearsome warriors from the north to all but abandon their pirate heritage in favor of a more settled existence.

The End of the Viking Age

Historians generally mark the start of the Viking Age with the attack on the priory in Lindisfarne in 793 and ending with the Battle of Hastings in 1066, when William the Conqueror took the throne of England and became the first Norman sovereign of that nation. By that time, even the Scandinavian leaders were rich, powerful, and influential; a far cry from the chieftains that had ruled when the Vikings first appeared on the world stage. Their kingdoms had also started to gain legitimacy from the Vatican, particularly as an increasing number of Norsemen forsook their own pagan religion to adopt Christianity.

Over the span of a few hundred years, the Vikings had gone from a ruthless band of raiders that had carved out a wide path of destruction wherever they went, to a people who had settled into lives as farmers, merchants, and craftsmen. The enemies that once fled in terror at their approach had found a way to tame them with offers of silver, gold, and land of their own. The Norsemen assimilated into local regions across the European continent, where their unique heritage soon diminished.

Unsurprisingly, as the Vikings tapered off their raids, piracy along the coasts of Europe diminished as well. With the Norsemen giving up their seafaring ways, it soon became much safer for merchants and the communities that were located along the coast to take to the open waters once again. This allowed some of the newly formed, emerging nations across the continent to begin trading with one another, creating diplomatic and economic ties that would set the stage for a new era of prosperity to come.

Of course, this lull in pirate activity wouldn't last for very long and a new breed of marauders would soon take to the sea. But for a time, those efforts were much less focused and organized than they had been under the Vikings, who were a force of nature when they first appeared out of the icy north. Those that immediately followed the Norsemen were simply opportunists looking to take advantage of new economic conditions, rather than a determined, organized group hell bent on conquest and glory.

For decades, there has been an ongoing debate amongst historians as to whether or not the Vikings were ever truly pirates at all. On the one hand, they clearly exhibited some of the common characteristics that have come to define what a pirate is—sailing the open waters, attacking ships and coastal villages, seeking plunder, and leaving chaos and destruction in their wake. If the most basic definition of piracy includes committing illegal acts while at sea, the Vikings are most definitely guilty as charged.

On the other hand, the Vikings also had some unique traits, which make them to stand out from the ancient pirates that had plagued the Mediterranean and other coastal regions for centuries before them. For instance, they all shared a Scandinavian heritage, a common history, and a unique pantheon of gods. That alone is enough to make them unique amongst other pirates, but the fact that they had common goals and were more apt to work with one another to enhance their success further distances them from traditional oceangoing marauders.

In the early days of the Viking Age it was clear that the Norsemen were acting much like the pirates of antiquity. Their raids were meant to harass coastal settlements and to capture as much treasure as they could carry back home aboard their ships. But over time, their attention turned to land conquest, which is something that most of the ancient pirates that operated in the Mediterranean had little interest in. For the Vikings, taking the land of their enemies was just as good as capturing their precious treasure. Conversely, more traditional pirates would generally view the acquisition of land as a liability, tying them down to a particular region and giving their enemies a place to strike at them more directly.

As a fighting force, the Vikings were much more organized, well trained, and willing to engage in conflict than other pirates. Seeking glory in battle was part of their Norse heritage and an important aspect of their society. This allowed them to operate in a more efficient and coordinated manner when it came to combat and warfare, something that most other seafaring raiders lacked. And while the Norsemen trained in the use of weapons and shields, traditional pirates rarely had any formal training at all, which often left them lacking when it came to engaging in hand-to-hand combat.

The pirates of the ancient world generally took to the sea because it provided them with opportunities for economic gain. The Vikings saw those same opportunities, but they were generally better sailors because they were an oceangoing people before they ever started raiding the European coastlines. They also possessed a more sophisticated understanding of navigation and shipbuilding, which allowed them to range farther from home and stay out to sea for longer periods of time. These skills also made them a more formidable force on the water when they engaged in ship-to-ship combat, where they employed more advanced tactics too.

Unlike previous bands of pirates, the Norsemen were natural explorers. While most Vikings stayed close to Europe, some traveled far and wide in search of new lands. They discovered places like Iceland, Greenland, and even North America, where they established a far-flung colony in what is now Newfoundland in Canada. It is difficult to imagine why any ancient pirates would have sailed so far and for so long, not knowing if their voyage would be a profitable one. But the Scandinavians were not afraid to set out into uncharted waters if it meant the potential for discovering a new world or potentially carving out a place for themselves amongst the honored heroes of Valhalla.

Despite these unique characteristics, the Norse dominance of the seas during the Viking Age is unquestionably a byproduct of their pirate ways. While ship-to-ship combat remained a relatively rare occurrence, their constant pillaging and raiding of the coastlines allowed them to largely go unchallenged for more than 270 years, making the Vikings the most successful pirates that the world had seen as of yet.

Over the course of those three centuries, the Vikings managed to transform from a group of loosely affiliated tribes occupying the northernmost regions of Europe, to wealthy, land-owning monarchs found across the continent. Piracy played a significant role in making that happen, although when it was no longer a viable and profitable way of life, they abandoned it for other opportunities instead. While the Viking conquers of old were eventually assimilated into the greater European community, their legacy and legend lives on even to this day.

These fearsome warriors who came from the sea are still a part of popular culture to this day, thanks in large part to their unique history and heritage. That too makes them unique amongst the early pirates, most of whom came and went without leaving any kind of lasting impression on history or the world around us. That certainly wasn't the case for the Vikings, however, who for a time were the scourge of the seas and the most feared force on the planet.

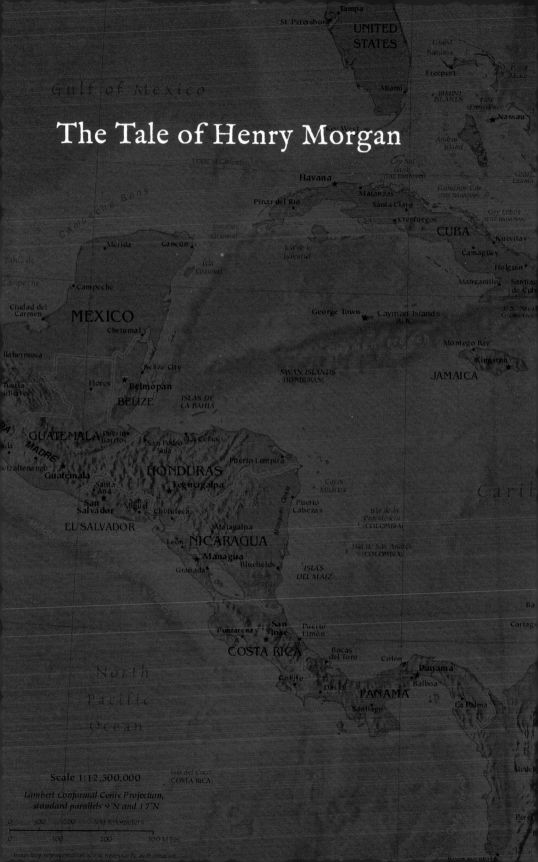

The Tale of Henry Morgan

If ever there was a man who was the living embodiment of the idea that one nation's hero is another's scoundrel, it is Sir Henry Morgan. For the British, he was without a doubt a great patriot who was respected for his honor and integrity. But England's enemies—Spain in particular—saw him as a despicable and untrustworthy outlaw. To them, Morgan was no better than any other pirate who sailed the seven seas, lawlessly plundering ships without regard to life or property. The reality was that he was respected and admired by allies and enemies alike, making him the kind of man you'd prefer have on your side rather than sailing against you.

As with many of the famous seaman who rose to fame and fortune during the seventeenth century, not a lot is known about Morgan's childhood. It is thought that he was born in the country of Wales sometime around 1635. Most historians believe that his parents were simple farmers who eked out a meager living. Young Henry may have been inspired to seek a life adventure and fortune thanks to uncles who had served in the military. Listening to tales of their exploits, the boy dreamt of sailing off to see the world at a young age before he later set out to pursue those ambitions.

How exactly he came to be in the Caribbean is also somewhat nebulous, although it seems likely that he arrived there around 1655 as part of an English invasion force. That year, English general and statesman Oliver Cromwell charged General Robert Venables with wresting control of Jamaica away from the Spanish. The island held particular strategic value, providing opportunities to attack and defend shipping lanes throughout the West Indies.

That operation was a success, with Morgan serving in a junior officer role, learning tactics that would serve him well on both land and sea throughout his career. Jamaica was claimed for England and the island's main colony soon had the familiar colors of the Union Jack flying overhead. In the years that followed, the island became home to a steady stream of pirates and privateers, with as many as 1,500 calling Jamaica home.

After the English captured Jamaica, Morgan stayed in the Caribbean, either by choice or circumstances. Finding the weather and climate to his liking, he explored the region. During his travels he was abducted and sold into indentured servitude as strong backs were needed to work the sugar plantations that were sprouting up throughout the West Indies in the mid-1600s. How exactly he found himself in such a predicament, and how he managed to free himself, remain a mystery.

By the 1660s, the facts of Henry Morgan's life become much easier to follow. During the early years of that decade he served under a privateer named Sir Christopher Myngs, further honing his skills as both a gifted sailor and a brilliant tactician. Myngs and his men routinely conducted raids up and down the Caribbean and along the Yucatan Peninsula, mostly attacking Spanish targets. Morgan played an important part in those raids, serving with distinction.

It didn't take long for Henry Morgan to rise through the ranks in this environment and by 1662 he had taken command of his first ship. During that time of his life, he sailed in support of Myngs's expeditions as the captain of one of the ships in the privateer's flotilla. That fleet eventually grew to include at least fourteen vessels and as many as 1,400 men. This gave them the ability to attack hardened fortifications such as Santiago de Cuba and Campeche on the Yucatan, complexly plundering those cities of their riches.

When England and the Netherlands went to war with one another in 1664, English governors in the Caribbean began handing out letters of marque. These official documents allowed privateers to hunt down the enemies of the Crown, which in this case meant attacking and looting Dutch ships with permission from the king. While there were a number of privateers who were quick to apply for such a letter, Morgan and his closest allies chose not to join the fight against the Dutch. Instead, they continued to focus on Spanish colonies throughout the Caribbean and along the coastline of modern day Mexico. Those raids served to infuriate the Spanish, who were just beginning to realize how daring and resourceful of a man Morgan could be.

Thanks to his incessant harassment of enemy vessels and villages along the Spanish Main, Morgan was by all accounts a wealthy man after just a few years of marauding. So much so, that by 1667 he had purchased his first planation on the island of Jamaica. He also oversaw the construction of the defenses at the cities of Fort Charles and Port Royal, indicating just how much of a trusted advisor he was becoming amongst the English leadership, both in the Caribbean and back home.

Just a year later, Morgan was promoted to the rank of admiral and was given command of ten ships and more than five hundred men. He was also issued a new letter of marque giving him permission to attack Spanish ships wherever and whenever his fleet encountered them. He and his men were allowed to keep any plunder that they captured during those raids. However, Morgan's charter did not allow him to attack Spanish interests on land and came with a warning that such actions would result in the forfeiture of any loot that he captured.

Ignoring this warning, Morgan's first plan was to attack Havana, one of Spain's seats of power in the Caribbean at the time. But the city was very well defended, even for his fleet and small force of men. Quickly switching plans, he instead attacked the town of Puerto Principe, easily overwhelming the forces there. Much to the disappointment of Morgan and his men, there was little treasure to be found, leaving them to sail back to Port Royal with almost nothing to show for their actions.

While en route to Port Royal, Morgan devised a plan that—if successful—would wipe the taste of disappointment from his mouth. He planned to sack the city of Puerto Bello, which was one of the wealthiest outposts on the entire Spanish Main. The town, which is located in modern day Panama, sat along lucrative trade routes, with ships

Henry Morgan sacking Puerto del Principle.

bringing a seemingly never-ending supply of goods to its port. The only problem was that Puerto Bello was also protected by not one, but three citadels, making it a very difficult target to raid.

After a brief stopover in Port Royal to resupply and pick up reinforcements, Morgan and his fleet set sail for Panama. But as they neared Puerto Bello he decided to drop anchor and wait for nightfall. After the sun had set, Morgan chose a select group of men, clambered into canoes, and silently paddled through the night. They arrived at the outskirts of the city just before dawn, launching their assault as the skies to the east began to brighten.

Catching the fortress completely off guard, Morgan and his men were able to take the three citadels, and capture the city, in surprisingly short order. They then occupied Puerto Bello for a full month, repelling at least one attempt by the Spanish to reclaim it. Eventually, the privateer negotiated a ransom with the Panamanian governor, who agreed to pay one hundred thousand pesos for the Englishmen to depart. When they did, they took nearly £100,000 worth of goods and supplies with them, the equivalent of over $2 million today.

Returning to Port Royal, Morgan and his men divided up the plunder, with each and every member of the crew receiving a share that came out to about £120. That was a handsome sum of money for the day, coming to about five times what they would make in a typical year at sea. Morgan took home about 5 percent of the total revenue. His benefactors and sponsors were also richly rewarded for supporting him, although his actions were not without controversy.

Because he was not chartered to attack the Spanish on land, the tactics that Morgan used were seen as potentially unlawful. But considering the success of the raids, the amount of wealth it brought in, and the humiliation it delivered to the Spanish, the English Crown decided to turn a blind eye to the actions. Back home, his success against Britain's enemies made him a hero, while managing to infuriate the Spanish at the same time.

Following his success at Puerto Bello, Morgan grew even bolder. His next plan was to attack Cartagena, Colombia, the richest town in the New World. With that objective in mind, the English captain gathered his fleet and set sail across the Caribbean, rendezvousing with a Royal Navy vessel named the *HMS Oxford* along the way. The *Oxford* was a gift for Morgan from the king and was meant to convey prestige and power. Upon acquiring it, he immediately took command and made it his new flagship. Unfortunately for Morgan, not long after the *Oxford* arrived, tragedy struck.

Just after the New Year in 1669, Morgan called a meeting of his officers to discuss their battle plans in the captain's quarters of his new flagship. While that meeting was still in session, a powder keg in the ship's magazine exploded, tearing the ship apart in the process. The explosion caused the death of more than two hundred men, including half of the officers who were sitting around the conference table. The other half of the officers—Morgan included—were sent flying into the water, miraculously suffering only minor injuries from the blast.

The loss of his flagship meant that attacking Cartagena was off the table, so Morgan went looking for other viable targets instead. Thanks to some illuminating information from a French member of the crew, the privateer decided to set his sights on the cities of Maracaibo and Gibraltar in Venezuela instead. To reach those cities, he had to sail through a narrow channel that separated the Caribbean from Lake Maracaibo, defeating a small, undermanned fortress along the way. Once that task was completed, the fleet took the two Spanish settlements with relative ease, plundering both towns of their valuables. Rumors suggest that in order to discover where that loot was hidden, Morgan may have tortured some of the locals.

After spending more than month in Venezuela, the English captain decided it was time set sail back to Jamaica. But before his fleet could exit Lake Maracaibo and return to the Caribbean, the privateer received word that the Spanish had set up an ambush to destroy his fleet. An armada of ships armed with more than one hundred cannons was stationed at the narrow choke point where the two bodies of water met. In order to make good on his escape, Morgan would have to find a way to either evade or confront the Spanish fleet and avoid the rearmed fortress that defended the route.

The Spanish commander signaled the English ships, expressing his wish to negotiate a peaceful resolution to the standoff. He told Morgan that if they surrendered all of their plunder, he and his men would be allowed to safely sail into the Caribbean. But if they kept any of the treasure they had taken, the Spanish would bombard them with cannon fire, reducing their ships to rubble.

Thinking this was too weighty of a decision to be made on his own,

Morgan called for a vote amongst his men. The crew, showing their loyalty and belief in their captain, elected to fight, despite their tactical and numerical disadvantages. Morgan and his officers planned to allow a ship to be captured as a decoy, sending it out with a skeleton crew to ram the *Magdalan*, the flagship of the waiting Spanish fleet. That plan worked to perfection, and the decoy ship was set ablaze as it approached, severely damaging the enemy vessel and quickly taking it out of the fight. Another Spanish ship called the *Soledad* also caught fire, while a third was sunk by the English cannons, quickly reducing the Spanish Armada to a harmless collection of driftwood.

Despite their success against the Spanish ships, the English privateers still had to make their way past the fortress that guarded the entrance into the Caribbean. Once again, Morgan showed his ingenuity and cunning, waiting for the tide to rise and carry his fleet through the channel without the need of their sails. The Spanish defenders inside the fortress had prepared for a ground assault, expecting the privateers to attack as they had a month earlier on their way into the lake. But Morgan had outwitted them all, with his fleet—still packed with treasure—floating by completely unnoticed.

Upon return to Port Royal, Morgan was shocked to find that he was once again being reprimanded for his actions. While at sea, King Charles II of England had been swayed into taking a softer stance on the Spanish, and was looking for potential ways to negotiate for peace. Morgan's raids on Spanish settlements put those discussions in jeopardy, resulting in the revocation of the privateer's letter of marque. No longer given free rein to attack the enemies of the Crown, the Welshman took his newly acquired gold and purchased a second plantation, once again further enhancing his wealth and status.

It didn't take long for the cessation of hostilities between England and Spain to evaporate. By 1670, Spanish privateers were once again preying on English ships, which prompted the governor of Jamaica to issue yet another letter of marque to Morgan. As usual, his orders were to do what he did best—sew chaos and uncertainty amongst the Spanish. This time when he set out, the Welsh admiral had over thirty ships under his command. That fleet was not just an indication of how much respect and trust King Charles II had in Morgan, it also happened to be the largest ever assembled by a privateer in the Caribbean.

With such a large force at his disposal, the privateer set his sights on a number of Spanish targets, including the town of Chagres on the Isthmus of Panama. This city was strategically important, as it was the port from which most of the goods being shipped back to Spain were loaded onto cargo vessels. The city was so significant that it was defended by the well-fortified Fort of San Lorenzo, which was an excellent deterrent to any invading force. Morgan and experienced crew made short work of those defenses however, taking the city and the fort within a few days.

The privateer's real goal was to attack Spain's main outpost in Panama, which was located in Old Panama City. However, that settlement was located on Panama's Pacific coast, which required Morgan and his men to travel on foot and by canoe through dense jungle to reach their latest objective. It took them two weeks to complete the journey and when they arrived, they found the Spanish forces already waiting for them. But Morgan's tactical genius won the day once again, with the English forces taking the city with relative ease. When the smoke had cleared, the Spanish had lost more than four hundred men, while English casualties numbered just fifteen.

In an effort to keep Old Panama City from falling into the hands of the enemy, the Spanish governor set the city on fire. Using strategically placed barrels of gunpowder, the entire place went up in an inferno that burned for the better part of two days. When it was over, only two stone buildings remained, and much of the wealth that had been accumulated there had turned to ash. Some of the more priceless items had been collected by the Spanish ahead of Morgan's attack and were sent away aboard ships. Despite having plenty of advanced warning, there were still countless other treasures that were consumed in the flames.

Morgan's army stayed in Panama for three weeks, sifting through the rubble and collecting as much plunder as they could recover. Despite the governor putting the torch to the city, enough loot was located to make

Cap.ᵗ Hen, Morgan before Panama which he took from the Spaniards.

Henry Morgan before attacking Panama.

the operation a rousing success, sending Morgan's fleet back home to Jamaica with full cargo holds. When they arrived back on the Caribbean Island, they were once again greeted as conquering heroes who had embarrassed the Spanish with their bold attacks.

The celebration was short lived since not long after Morgan returned home, word reached the Caribbean that England and Spain had signed a peace treaty. That agreement had been ratified prior to his attack on Panama, although news of the accords hadn't arrived until well after Old Panama City had been destroyed. Morgan's actions created a predicament for the two countries, who had hoped to establish a lasting peace between one another in the New World.

One of the provisions of the treaty was that all letters of marque would be revoked immediately upon its signing. The treaty also called for the removal of Thomas Modyford as governor of Jamaica due to the part he played in issuing those letters and ordering attacks against the Spanish. It did not matter that Modyford was doing so under orders from the Crown, he was now seen as a liability when it came to maintaining peace between the two European powers. For his loyalty, the former governor was arrested and sent home to England in irons.

When word of Morgan's audacious attack and looting of Panama reached Europe, it instantly opened old wounds. The Spanish were incensed by the news, which was made all the worse because the operation was conducted by Henry Morgan. The Welshman had been a thorn in their side for years, continually raiding ships and towns no matter what Spain did to try and stop him.

Hoping to appease the Spanish Crown, King Charles II sent word to Jamaica to have Morgan arrested. Just like Modyford before him, the privateer was put aboard a ship and sent to London in 1672. With the delicate peace hanging in the balance, the English knew they had to at least look like they were doing something to curb the activities of one of their most experienced and successful privateers.

While the English government officially declared Morgan an outlaw and sentenced him to imprisonment in the Tower of London, there is no evidence that he ever actually spent any time there. His exploits in the

Caribbean had made him a hero back home, where it made little sense to lock him up for following his orders. In fact, most historians believe that his time in London was mostly spent at leisure, entertaining noblemen and scholars with his harrowing tales of battle against the Spanish. While there, the privateer was also able to present compelling evidence that he had no knowledge of the signing of the peace treaty prior to his attack on Panama. Because of this, no charges were ever officially filed against him.

Two years later, the political winds shifted in Morgan's favor once again and he was allowed to leave London and return to the Caribbean. Before he went, he provided the King with a detailed plan on how to bolster the defenses of Jamaica. In appreciation, and in honor of his years of service to the throne, Charles II knighted Morgan, conferring on him the title of "Sir."

In early 1675, Morgan set sail for Jamaica, with Modyford in tow. Unlike the Welshman, the former governor had been imprisoned in the Tower of London, where he had been held without charges for months. Upon release, he had been promoted to Chief Justice of Jamaica and was returned to the island to assume the duties of that position.

After his stay in London, Morgan also accepted a new role upon his return to Jamaica. He was charged with hunting down and eliminating any pirates that operated in the waters surrounding the island, of which there were more than a few. After the war with Spain had ended, all of the letters of marque had been revoked, causing many of the former privateers to take up piracy to make ends meet. But pirates had fallen out of fashion with the English Crown, aristocracy, and the general public alike. In order to return law and order to the seas, a concentrated effort was being made to clean up the Caribbean, with Morgan overseeing that operation.

Due to his close ties with many of the former privateers who had turned to piracy, Morgan often turned a blind eye to pirate activity in Jamaican waters. Sometimes, he would even invest in the ships of those buccaneers, making a bit of extra profit from their endeavors. Unsurprisingly, the Welshman saw privateers as useful tools for diplomacy, war, the acquisition of goods, and in maintaining the all-important trade lanes. Despite the fact that the use of privateers had been banned by the peace treaty between England and Spain, the old sea captain continued to employ them in a variety of fashions.

In the years that followed, Captain Henry Morgan played an active role in Jamaica's leadership, serving as both governor and lieutenant-governor for a time. In recognition of his experience as a military commander, he also filled the role of lieutenant-general in charge of the island's defense. Those duties did not slow his entrepreneurial spirit in any way, as he also purchased a third plantation, becoming one of the largest exporters of Jamaican sugar.

Morgan remained active in the politics and decision making of the colony throughout the rest of his life, using his reputation and substantial influence to guide Jamaica through some of its most challenging growing pains. At times, he found himself at odds with the leadership of the island, and yet he continued to be a guiding force. Even in his final years, he served as an unofficial advisor to the governor, who appreciated the former privateer's experience and wisdom.

Morgan passed away in August of 1688 at the age of fifty-three. Due to his service to the Crown and the island of Jamaica, his body lay in state, allowing the public to pay its respects. The Jamaican governor even declared a state of amnesty for a time, giving the countless privateers and pirates who knew and respected the Welshman the opportunity to visit without fear of arrest. Following a suitable time of mourning, he was buried in the Port Royal cemetery, with the ships in the harbor issuing a twenty-two-gun salute in honor of their fallen comrade.

At the time of his death, Henry Morgan was probably the most well-known privateer in the entire world. His exploits had become the stuff of legend, even in his own time. For the English, he was a national hero, defending the high seas for king and country. The Spanish, on the other hand, saw him as less of a privateer and more of an outlaw. To them, his activities were strictly illegal, despite the fact that he always conducted his raids while under an official letter of marque. This point of view is

IVAN MORGAN

Illustration of Henry Morgan.

completely understandable, particularly when considering the scope of the damage that Morgan inflicted on Spanish ships and settlements over the years.

The tales of Henry Morgan typically underscore the challenges privateers faced with their governing bodies. Even while sailing under legitimate orders, they still ran the risk of being branded pirates and sent to prison or hung for their crimes. It was a dangerous tightrope act for many buccaneers, who crossed back and forth between being legitimate businessmen and outlaws on a regular basis. Despite that, Morgan always found a way to stay honorable and true to the Crown and his English ideals. In the end, this allowed him to not only become one of the most respected men of his age, but it also made him a very wealthy man along the way.

Five years after he was laid to rest in the Port Royal cemetery, a massive earthquake struck Jamaica. The natural disaster inflicted serious damage on the city, destroying many of the existing buildings. During the quake, a thirty-three-acre section of the cemetery broke off from the island and sank into Kensington Harbor, taking Morgan's body along with it. Due to the damage and chaos that followed, his remains were never recovered, and were forever lost to the sea. Considering his love for the ocean, it seems a suitable burial ground.

CHAPTER 3

The Pirates of the Barbary Coast

The turbulent waters of the Mediterranean Sea located off the northern shores of Africa once teemed with some of the most violent and feared pirates the world has ever known. Dubbed the "Barbary Coast" by sixteenth-century Europeans—a reference to an ethnic group known as the Berbers—this part of the world was ruled by pirate kings and slave lords for centuries. Those individuals built outlaw empires that struck fear into the hearts of the more traditional world powers, as they attacked without warning or mercy. For three hundred years, stretching from 1530 CE to 1830 CE, the so-called Barbary Pirates were a direct threat to trade and travel, conducting daring raids and capturing hundreds of thousands of people in the process. But their history begins well before that time, with origins that can be traced all the way back to the Age of Antiquity.

The power vacuum created after the fall of Rome did not just have long and lasting consequences for Europe, but for other Roman-controlled provinces as well. At the height of its power, the empire stretched the length of the Mediterranean Coast, encompassing parts of the Middle East and Northern Africa. When the last Roman legions were ordered to abandon those regions, chaos and conflict soon followed. But unlike their European counterparts, it wouldn't take long for the people living in those regions to rally behind a unifying force. In fact, a powerful new actor soon took its place on the world's stage and gave rise to a new breed of pirate that was unlike any other that had sailed the high seas before. Over the centuries these pirates wreaked havoc on some of the greatest imperial powers of the age.

The Umayyad Caliphate and the Byzantine Empire

After Rome defeated Carthage in the third Punic War in 146 BCE, it established the province of Africa to maintain control of the region, levy taxes, establish trade, and defend the frontier from barbarian invasions. Over the course of the next two hundred years, that province would grow to encompass what is now Morocco, Algiers, Tunisia, Libya, Egypt, and Syria. Those places stayed firmly locked under Roman rule even after the empire crumbled in the late fifth century, quickly being absorbed by the Byzantine Empire during its rise to prominence.

Two more centuries would pass before Northern Africa would finally shake off the yoke of Roman control once and for all as the Umayyad Caliphate, a Muslim dynasty that vied for power with the Byzantines, swept through the Middle East and westward across Africa's Mediterranean Coast. The Caliphate spread Islam throughout that part of the world during the eighth century, fundamentally changing the political, cultural, and religious landscape forever. Eventually, Umayyad forces crossed the sea into Europe itself, establishing strongholds in the Iberian Peninsula, where its Caliphate's influence can still be felt to this day.

Over this time period, the waters of the Mediterranean went from well controlled and regulated, to lawless and wild once again. The absence of a Roman fleet specifically designed to hunt pirates allowed marauders to reappear in every corner of the sea, making trade and travel by ship extremely difficult. The seagoing outlaws also resumed raiding coastal towns and villages, although for the most part these activities were largely unorganized and lacked any driving force other than the drive for material gain.

The Umayyad Caliphate was not against using these pirates to further its own ends. The Arab kingdom had frequently clashed with the Byzantine Empire, which had established itself as a world power by holding onto—and reconquering—much of the territory that once belonged to Rome. The two fledgling empires routinely found themselves at odds with one another. Armed conflicts frequently broke out over territorial disputes and the use of trade routes, not to mention religious and ideological differences too.

The situation turned dire for the Byzantines in 674 CE when their Muslim rivals laid siege to Constantinople itself. The city had been the capital of the Eastern Roman Empire since Emperor Constantine had transferred power there in 324 CE. From there, the direct lineage of the Romans continued, weathering some massive changes to the geopolitical landscape in the centuries that followed. One of the biggest of those changes was the rise of the Caliphate, which grew into an expansionist power, setting its sights directly on destroying Byzantium and claiming the territory for its own.

The siege of Constantinople consisted of both land and sea forces attacking, with an army marching on the city to cut off supply lines and prevent Byzantine leaders and military units from making their escape. Meanwhile, a naval blockade was put into place in the city's harbor with the aim of using the Muslim fleet to accomplish the same task at sea. Both strategies proved extremely effective in shutting the city off from the outside world for months at a time, creating an unbearable living experience for those trapped inside its walls.

The bulk of the Caliphate's armada was made up of ships that had been built specifically to take on the Byzantines. That said, a large number of those vessels belonged to pirates who had been hired by the Muslims to help control the waters in the Sea of Marmara. This strategically important waterway links the Black Sea to the Aegean, with Constantinople situated right where those two bodies of water meet. This location remains incredibly important even to this day and is home to the modern city of Istanbul in Turkey.

Over the course of the next four years, the Arab army and navy continually harassed the Byzantines, with well-paid pirates helping to patrol the seas just off the coast of Constantinople. While the Caliphate's main fleet was able to concentrate directly on maintaining the siege and limiting Constantinople's ability to fight back, the pirates were given free rein to raid, burn, and destroy enemy vessels and villages. The chaotic, unpredictable nature of the pirate activity served to keep the Byzantine forces off balance and continually guessing as to where their adversaries would strike next.

It would take four years for the Byzantines to destroy the Caliphate's navy, scatter their pirate allies, and break the siege. Without the blockade in place, reinforcements and supplies began flowing back into the capital city, providing the resources needed to eventually defeat the Muslim armies as well.

The defeat of the Caliphate prevented it from destroying the Byzantine Empire or capturing much more of its territory in the years that immediately followed. But the loss did little to slow the Umayyad expansion across Northern Africa, where it met with far less resistance. By 711 CE, Muslim forces had marched all the way to the Atlantic Ocean, assimilating the entirety of the southern Mediterranean Coast in the process.

Not long after claiming North Africa, the Caliphate also made a bold move into Europe when invading Muslim armies defeated the Visigoths and conquered what would one day become Spain. This made the Islamic Empire one of the largest the world has ever seen, incorporating vast amounts of land and a sizable population at the same time. This victory also made it one of the preeminent actors on the world stage and the first empire based on the Islamic faith.

The Return of Piracy to the Mediterranean Sea

As the Muslim forces swept across Africa and into Europe, their pirate allies became increasingly more emboldened out on the Mediterranean Sea. With no unified force working against them, the waterborne raiders were free to attack any target they came across and often faced little or no resistance. Looting ships and towns provided plenty of material incentive for these attacks, but the largest driving force for pirate activity was a familiar one—the slave trade.

Just as the Roman Empire before it had relied heavily on slave labor, so too did the Umayyad Caliphate. In fact, slaves had been used throughout the Middle East for centuries, although the rise of Islam brought a significant challenge to that practice. The religion forbids Muslims to use other Muslims as slaves, which meant that their labor force had to come from another source other than from within the Caliphate's domain. Fortunately for this endeavor, there were plenty of Christian communities along the Mediterranean coast for the pirates to raid, carrying human cargo to Muslim slave markets to be sold into bondage. Even in ancient times, the law of supply and demand dictated economics, and the slave trade was no different.

It was about this time that ownership of slaves actually fell out of favor within the Byzantine Empire. The general feeling was that owning other human beings was morally wrong, and an anti-slavery movement took form in Constantinople and spread throughout Byzantium. Still, slavery wasn't outlawed altogether in the empire and many noble houses and business owners continued the practice despite the change in public opinion. Those individuals were able to continue purchasing slaves at the Islamic markets or directly from the Muslim pirates and slave traders themselves, ensuring that they still had the labor they needed in order to maintain their lifestyles.

Despite slavery being frowned upon by the two largest empires of the age, the market for slaves was booming across Europe, the Middle East, and Northern Africa. Just as it had during the Egyptian, Greek, and Roman eras, this played a significant role in driving piracy's popularity during the early Middle Ages. Capturing loot and treasure was fine of course, but it was even easier to attack a ship or town, subdue the enemy, and then carry them off to a market to be sold to the highest bidder. Despite the fact that Rome was no longer the most powerful empire in the world, the demand for slave labor did not slow down, it just changed locations.

By the eighth and ninth centuries, piracy in the Mediterranean Sea had grown to such high levels that some familiar locations had once again fallen under pirate control. Most notably amongst those was the island of Crete, which at the time was occupied by Muslim forces. As the Emirate of Crete, it served as a safe haven for marauders, who brought plenty of slaves to be sold and traded there. This turned the island into an economic powerhouse on a level that it hadn't seen for hundreds of years, revitalizing its place in the region.

Unsurprisingly, Cilicia once again became a popular pirate hideout during this time as well. The towering cliffs and rocky terrain that had allowed it to become a pirate haven 1,800 years earlier had not changed much since Pompey Magnus and the Roman navy had smashed the ancient pirate fleet. But during the time of the Byzantine Empire and the Umayyad Caliphate, a large number of outlaws once again took refuge along the coast of what is now Turkey. From there, they were able to launch attacks against large sections of the Mediterranean, only to flee back to the safety of those hidden coves and harbors when an enemy flotilla approached.

When the Umayyad Caliphate invaded the Iberian Peninsula in 711 CE, piracy also rose sharply in the Western Mediterranean. Previously, the Muslim ships mainly stayed to the east or occasionally prowled along the shores of Northern Africa. But as the power of the Caliphate grew, it continued to use pirates to support its efforts throughout the region. This meant that aquatic trade and travel were largely disrupted once again as pirates found a willing patron in the form of the Islamic Empire, whose Muslim forces sewed chaos on land, while their allies did the same out on the water.

Not long after capturing Iberia, the Caliphate began a slow, but steady decline. Facing resistance on multiple fronts, the Umayyad soon saw its empire start to crumble from both the west and the east. Renewed conflicts with the Byzantines, coupled with humiliating losses in India, left the Islamic kingdom in disarray. Eventually, the Caliphate disintegrated altogether, making way for another to rise in its place.

The Berbers' Rise to Power

One of the most significant challenges to Umayyad rule came in Northern Africa, where an indigenous people known as the Berbers launched a revolution to retake control of their homelands. The Great Berber Revolt took place from 740–743 CE, which liberated large sections of the region. It also gave rise to the first independent Islamic states,

Barbary corsairs.

with Muslim nations existing outside of the Caliphate's control. These nations included Morocco, which remained free and independent until it became a French and Spanish protectorate in the twentieth century.

Under the rule of the Caliphate, the Berbers often served as front-line troops and played an instrumental role in the invasion and capture of the Iberian Peninsula. More importantly, they had also taken to the seas in defense of the empire, wreaking havoc on enemy ships and coastal regions. With their newfound independence, those tactics did not need to change much, as the lucrative slave trade provided plenty of incentive for continuing such activities. This time however, they were not sailing for the greater good of a foreign leader, but were instead seeking to fortify their own presence on the Mediterranean.

Over the next several hundred years, the Berber pirates came to rule the seas off the coast of Africa, becoming a feared power in their own right. During that time, piracy became an indelible part of their culture and grew into an accepted economic, military, and political policy. While they had fought a long and difficult revolution to win independence from the Muslim Caliphate, the Berbers still maintained an important economic relationship with the Middle East, providing a steady supply of non-Muslim slaves that could be put to work by their Islamic cousins.

Just how efficient and effective were the Berbers when it came to acquiring slaves? So much so that by 1198 CE, an organization called the Order of the Most Holy Trinity and of the Captives—the Trinitarian Order for short—was formed with the express purpose of freeing Christians who had been taken captive by Muslims. Some of those efforts were applied to negotiating for the release of prisoners of war taken during the crusades, but much of the organization's time and energy was directed at paying the ransom of those who had been captured in pirate raids conducted by the Berbers. Members of the Order would even go so far as to offer themselves up as captives in order to take the place of others who were already being held as prisoners.

Over the course of the next three hundred years, the Trinitarians played an instrumental role in freeing thousands of people from Muslim captivity. Their goal had always been about peacefully negotiating for the release of innocent civilians who just happened to get caught up in the larger affairs of kings and emperors. Over time, the organization both diminished in size and spread out to other countries. It even exists today, with the ongoing goal of working towards freeing kidnapped or wrongfully imprisoned Christians from captors across the globe.

Despite the best efforts of the Trinitarians, the Berbers continued to display an impressive level of efficiency when it came to conducting

A French ship attacked by Barbary Pirates.

coastal raids and attacking rival ships. It is estimated that in the first few centuries of the Berber reign of terror, thousands of enemy vessels were taken at sea, while more than two hundred thousand people living on the Iberian Peninsula were captured and sold into slavery. These constant attacks along European shores even forced the inhabitants of Spain and Italy to give up their coastal towns and villages altogether, electing to retreat inland instead. For centuries, those areas were left almost completely uninhabited out of fear of the Berber pirates. It wasn't until the nineteenth century—when order was restored to the Mediterranean—that settlements began to reappear along the seashore.

This state of affairs went largely unchanged and unchallenged for decades on end. The Berbers continually harassed European merchants and towns where they could, even though their ships were growing increasingly inferior to those of their enemies. Even as the vessels built by the Europeans made the transition to sails as a means of propulsion, the Muslim pirates clung to their use of oared galleys, using the smaller—and often more maneuverable—boats to harass and confound their enemies.

The Berber pirates were a tremendous source of frustration for the Europeans, who despite their faster, better-built, and more heavily armed ships, found themselves continually losing out to the more agile and elusive Berber galleys. Those smaller vessels were often very lightly armed, but usually carried a large crew that made it easier to overwhelm the merchant ships that they preyed upon. The pirate boats did not rely on the wind, which limited their speed on the open water, but provided a huge advantage when maneuvering in tight quarters or when ocean breezes were nonexistent.

Some European privateers tasked with hunting down and eliminating the pirates found their job to be much easier if they used similar galleys in their pursuit. By employing a strong and determined crew at the oars, they were much more likely to be able to catch the Berber marauders and engage them in combat directly. A few of these hunters even went so far as to build hybrid sailing galleys that allowed them to use both the wind and oars, and while these particular ships were extremely effective, they were never used in large numbers in the Western Mediterranean.

English and Dutch shups in Algiers.

Other Pirates of the Mediterranean Sea

While the Berbers were the most dangerous and successful pirates of their age, it is important to point out that they were not the only ones who were operating in the Mediterranean. Throughout the ninth and tenth centuries, a Slavic tribe known as the Narentines created havoc in the Adriatic Sea. For decades, they practiced state-sponsored piracy and managed to rule the waters there. Their favorite tactic was to harass Venetian merchants who were some of the most prolific traders of the era. The Narentines were so successful in their attacks that they even managed to reach Venice itself and raid some of its outlying suburbs of the city from time to time.

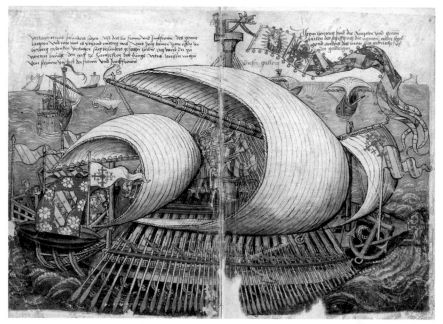

A Venetian galley.

European pirates were common in the Aegean and Adriatic seas too, increasingly attacking ships that they encountered on both bodies of water. Thanks to the development of more maneuverable ships in the twelfth century, it became easier to mount waterborne assaults, something that had been difficult to accomplish in the past. This gave marauders the ability to strike at more targets of opportunity, particularly as easily raided coastal settlements became rarer and rarer.

In 1192, an incident involving pirates operating out of the Italian Peninsula created an international incident between the Byzantine Empire and the city-state of Genoa. Genoese pirates, working with allies from the city of Pisa, attacked and pillaged a fleet of Venetian ships that they encountered on the Mediterranean. During that attack, the outlaws made off with a considerable amount of loot, including some extremely valuable treasures. As it turns out, a sizable portion of the plunder that was taken was actually gifts from the sultan of Egypt to the Byzantine emperor. The Venetians were merely facilitating the delivery when they had an untimely encounter with the pirates.

Incensed by this attack, Issac II Anglos, the ruler of Byzantium, sent envoys to Genoa demanding that the pirates responsible be punished and that compensation be paid for the loss of property. As leverage, the emperor ordered the confiscation of goods and cash of Genoese merchants living and working in Constantinople, promising that it would be returned once the Byzantine's demands had been met. Eventually the two kingdoms came to an agreement over reimbursement for the losses, with Genoa also promising to bring the pirates to justice. There are no indications that the Genoese ever made good on that promise, as piracy was not necessarily seen as a nefarious act amongst the city's elite. On the contrary, pirate activity was seen as playing an important role in maintaining the city's fortunes.

While some of these other pirate factions found a measure of success in the Eastern Mediterranean, Muslim pirates sailed largely unchallenged throughout the entire region. The Berbers of North Africa were highly successful in attacking the Iberian Coast, while Moorish raiders sailed in the east, sewing chaos and discord wherever they went. Over time, the clashes that occurred began to take on religious overtones, with the Islamic pirates raiding the Christian infidels in the name of Allah. This battle was being played out on land in the form of the Crusades.

Nowhere was this religious conflict more evident than in the clashes that took place between Muslim pirates and the Order of Saint John. This Christian organization was originally headquartered in Jerusalem and was charged with caring for sick or injured pilgrims who made the arduous journey to the Holy Land. But when the city fell to Islamic armies during the First Crusade, the members of the Order were forced to evacuate to the island of Rhodes before eventually resettling on Malta off the coast of Sicily.

Over time, the Order of Saint John morphed into a military unit that consisted of more than seven hundred knights and eight thousand troops. Although they only had a handful of ships at their disposal, the Order often sailed the Mediterranean to engage enemy vessels. They even conducted four campaigns against the Berber pirates themselves, fighting them on the high seas. Despite their best efforts, the North Africans continued to hold the upper hand on their European counterparts, while the Order of Saint John became little more than a minor speed bump to their ambitions.

The Ottoman Empire and the Growth of Piracy

The fourteenth century ushered in a major shift of power within Europe, the Middle East, and Northern Africa. It was then that the Ottoman Empire began its rise to power, annexing large chunks of land across those various regions. Over time, the empire came to hold great influence and power over the Mediterranean basin, while serving as a major trade and political crossroads for East and West alike. It grew into a major player on the world's stage, and remained so for more than six centuries, and well into the twentieth century.

European and Ottoman galleys in a battle.

In 1453 CE, the Ottoman Empire won a major victory by capturing the city of Constantinople. This effectively brought an end to the Byzantine Empire, with its territory being absorbed in the process. With their most powerful rival removed from the playing field, the Ottoman Turks were able to move into completely new territories, including North Africa. While they were never able to fully conquer the Berber nations, their shared Islamic heritage eased the way for the Ottoman Empire to convert those nations into satellite states. This connection gave rise to Ottoman-backed pirates who became some of the most feared marauders of all time.

The other significant change that occurred around this time was that an increasing number of European pirates began making their way to the Barbary Coast. Some came to escape prosecution back home, while others were lured there by a chance to trade with Arab merchants and slavers. They brought with them their European sensibilities when it came to designing ships and it was not long before the Berbers took notice. The North Africans soon adopted the use of sails, while also improving the hulls, masts, and keels that were employed on their own vessels. The result was faster, more agile, and more rugged ships that would carry them farther. These advances allowed them to strike targets along the European coast and in the North Sea, eventually reaching as far away as Iceland.

The Age of the Barbary Pirates

Despite the fact that the Berbers had been conducting raids in the Western Mediterranean for hundreds of years, most historians mark the start of the age of the Barbary pirates as the early sixteenth century. It was then that these North African states began to take a more measured and organized approach to their pirate activities. By then, it was the Ottoman Empire that needed a steady supply of slaves to keep it in operation, which the Berbers were more than happy to provide.

Prior to the 1500s, the Berber pirates often worked independently from one another or occasionally in small groups. But once the sixteenth century arrived, whole fleets sailed out into the Mediterranean Sea, the

Atlantic Ocean, and the North Sea as unified forces. By now, the cities of Tripoli, Tunis, Algiers, Rabat, and Salé had grown into large, thriving ports that were largely supported by the constant pirate ships that came and went from their docks.

These new fleets were made up of faster and more nimble ships called "corsairs." This moniker was eventually applied to the pirates themselves, who were often referred to as the Barbary or Ottoman corsairs by both historians and their European foes. The ships, and the pirates who piloted them, would be a constant source of frustration for their adversaries for the next three hundred years. Over that time, it is estimated that more than one million Europeans were captured by the Muslim pirates and sold in the slave markets of North Africa and the Ottoman Empire. That was a considerable number of people for a continent that was only then beginning to shrug off the shackles of the Middle Ages.

Cossacks fighting Turkish Coarsairs. Credit: Grigory Gagarin.

As the lawlessness of the Mediterranean continued, and the pirate states of North Africa grew more influential, they began to attract the attention of large numbers of European outlaws. During the sixteenth and seventeenth centuries, it was not uncommon for European pirates and outcasts to make their way to the Barbary Coast seeking fame and fortune of their own. More often than not, these men were wanted for piracy back home, where acts of raiding and plundering ships were seen as unlawful. That wasn't the case in places like Tunis or Algiers, thus exiles from England, France, the Netherlands, Portugal, and Spain routinely flocked there.

Jack Ward and Zymen Danseker

Two of the most dangerous and ruthless of these criminals were Jack Ward and Zymen Danseker. Both arrived on the Barbary Coast within a few years of one another after having their privateer status revoked by their monarch patrons back home. Ward stole a ship and sailed from England, while Danseker—who grew up in the Netherlands—did the same while living in France. These would not be the only parallels of their careers, although they would meet with very different fates in the end.

Experienced and able seamen, Ward and Danseker quickly rose through the ranks of the Barbary corsairs. Within a year of their arrivals, each of them commanded a fleet of ships operating out of Algiers and Tunis. From time to time, they even combined their ships to create a formidable force out on the water, attacking merchant vessels and enemy warships with equal enthusiasm.

Ward had a knack for capturing the ships of his adversaries and adapting them to his own needs. Often, these vessels were small, fast, and agile, which matched the Englishman's own tactics on the water. But in 1607 he and his men took control of a massive ship called the *Reniera e Soderina*, which he eventually turned into his personal flagship. Part of the retrofit process included adding more gun ports and installing sixty cannons, which was enough firepower to sink just about any foe that he would encounter.

Capturing the *Reniera e Soderina* proved beneficial in other ways too. When the ship was taken by Ward and his men it was said to have been carrying treasure that was worth at least two million pounds. This did not exactly sit well in Venice, which had served as the home port for the merchant vessel. When the city lodged an official protest over the action with King James I, one of the ambassadors described Ward as "beyond a doubt the greatest scoundrel that ever sailed from England."

At some point in his career, Ward found himself lamenting the fact that he had abandoned his home country. Wanting to return home, he requested a pardon for his actions from the king himself, but his request was denied. By that time, he was known far and wide, including across the Atlantic in the Caribbean and all the way up the coast to England. His deeds had caused political headaches for the Crown and forgiveness was simply out of the question.

With nowhere else to go, he returned to Tunis and converted to Islam, changing his name to Yusuf Reis. He continued to conduct raids across the Mediterranean for several more years before retiring in 1612 having amassed a small fortune. Not one to venture too far from the action however, he reportedly filled his time by teaching a new generation of corsairs how to sail, navigate, and operate their guns. According to historical records he lived to the age of seventy, passing away in 1622.

Zymen Danseker had a similarly successful career in the Mediterranean, raiding merchant vessels and attacking slave ships from one end of the sea to the other. He became so successful that the French and Spanish tried on numerous occasions to hunt him down and capture or kill him. On one such occasion, a French fleet working in conjunction with at least eight Spanish galleys cornered the Dutchman. However, a powerful storm brewed on the ocean, allowing Danseker and his crew to outrun their pursuers and make good on their escape once again.

Amongst the Barbary pirates, Danseker was seen as a skilled sailor and an expert navigator. Putting those skills to the test, he became the first captain to lead a fleet of corsairs through the Strait of Gibraltar and out into the Atlantic Ocean. At the time, that was the farthest that any of the Muslim sailors had ever traveled before, opening the doors for raiding parties to spread to the distant coastlines of Western Europe and beyond.

Much like Ward, Danseker eventually came to miss his family and his home. Prior to sailing for the Barbary Coast, he lived in Marseilles,

France, along with his wife and children, and although he was highly successful as a pirate, he desperately wanted to see them once again. In 1609, through intermediaries, he reached out to King Henry IV to request a pardon. Later, with that pardon in hand, he was allowed to return home, where he—along with his four heavily armed ships—were greeted with a hero's welcome. Not only was he presented with Turkish slaves as a gift, he also received a small fortune in confiscated Spanish gold.

Due to his association with the Barbary corsairs, Danseker later found himself pressed back into service by the French. A year after his return to Marseilles, he led a small fleet against the Islamic pirates, once again managing to avoid capture by the enemy when things went wrong. Then, in 1615, Louis XIII asked the Dutchman to help negotiate the release of several French ships that had been captured by pirates. When he traveled to Tunis to meet with the Turks, he was lured ashore under a false promise of safety and security. Once he arrived in the city, he was captured and reportedly beheaded.

The stories of Ward and Danseker show the fluidity of pirate allegiance along the Barbary Coast. Both men served in European navies as privateers in the early parts of their careers, only to grow disillusioned when their charters were revoked. Seeking fame and fortune, they sailed to North Africa, where each carved out a name for himself by ruthlessly attacking any ships that crossed their paths. When they grew weary of that life, the two men both sought a pardon so that they could return home. For Ward, that pardon never came and he lived out the rest of his days in exile. Meanwhile, Danseker tried to return to a normal life, but found he had a hard time escaping his past.

Sayyida al Hurra

There is no question that the vast majority of the Barbary and Ottoman corsairs were undoubtedly men, but a few women managed to work their way into their ranks too. The most famous of these women was Sayyida al Hurra, who become a pirate queen and was recognized as the undisputed leader of the pirates in the Western Mediterranean for more than three decades.

Sayyida was born into an affluent family in the kingdom of Granada on the Iberian Peninsula in 1585. At the time, Granada had been controlled by the Muslim Moors, since the Umayyad Caliphate had invaded and captured the region more than eight hundred years earlier. But in 1492, at the age of seven, Sayyida and her family were forced to leave their home and flee to Morocco as the Catholic king and queen of Spain launched a campaign to reconquer all of Iberia.

While Morocco wasn't home, Sayyida lacked for nothing. Her wealthy family saw that she received a proper education, learning to not only read and write, but speak several different languages. Even at a young age, they knew she was destined to be the wife of a powerful man, having pledged her hand in marriage to Ali al-Mandri while she was just child. The two wed when Sayyida was just sixteen years old and al-Mandri was the governor of the city of Tétouan, an important outpost in North Africa at the time.

Despite her young age, Sayyida proved an indispensable resource to her husband and soon found herself taking on an advisory role. Smart, well educated, and wise, she ran the city while her husband traveled on diplomatic business. The people living in Tétouan became accustomed to seeing her in that position, which she officially ascended to when al-Mandri passed away.

In the years that followed, Sayyida became a respected and powerful leader whose role grew into more of that of a monarch rather than a governor. During that time, she married a sultan, granting her even more influence and admiration. As the Queen of Tétouan, she deftly used the city's large and powerful pirate fleet to her advantage, filling the town's coffers, while simultaneously waging war on her enemies.

Of those enemies, Spain was the most prominent. Sayyida would never forget that it was the Spanish that forced her, and her family, to leave their home in Granada. She took every opportunity that she could to deliver some form of payback. To that end, she supported pirate activity throughout the Mediterranean and encouraged raids on Spanish and Portuguese ships in particular. She even struck an alliance with the infamous pirate Oruç Reis—also known as Barbarossa of Algiers—who controlled the Eastern Mediterranean.

The pirate queen proved to be a quick study in using piracy as a political tool. Not only did the fleets under her command disrupt Spanish and Portuguese trading routes, they also managed to capture a good deal of plunder and hostages along the way. But her crowning achievement as a leader of pirates came in 1540, when forces under her command assaulted and plundered Gibraltar, a strategically important location. At the time, the fortress at Gibraltar was ruled by Charles V, the Holy Roman emperor. He had been at odds with the Ottomans for years, and the sacking of Gibraltar was a massive embarrassment for him.

Sayyida rose to such power that even her European rivals recognized her as holding the unofficial title of Queen of the Western Mediterranean. As such, emissaries from Spain and Portugal often negotiated directly with her for the release of prisoners that were taken during her pirate raids and those of other marauders. Usually, they found her to be a shrewd and challenging negotiator who rarely gave quarter save when it served her interests to do so.

Sayyida would rule for more than thirty years before being forced out of power by her own son-in-law. She then stepped away from the limelight and lived another twenty years in seclusion. When she passed, she became the last Muslim woman to independently bear the title of al Hurra, which roughly translates to "queen."

The Barbarossa Brothers

Without a doubt, the most notorious of the Barbary corsairs were Oruç Reis and Hisir Barbarossa—better known as the Barbarossa brothers. The two men were born on the Greek isle of Lesbos, but sailed for the Ottoman Empire, helping the Turks to secure control of the Eastern Mediterranean and Northern Africa. The two brothers played an instrumental role in the liberation of Algiers, and Oruç's victory at Preveza, Greece, served to open Tripoli for renewed trade and commerce. During that battle, the pirate used a fleet of 122 oared galleys to defeat a force of more than three hundred enemy sailing ships.

The Dutch in Tripoli.

Spanish vessels were amongst the brother's favorite targets, in part because their ships often carried plenty of precious cargo. But the Ottomans had a long-standing rivalry with the Spanish as well, which served as extra incentive for the brothers to attack their boats wherever they encountered them. At the time, the Spanish and the Ottoman empires were the two greatest powers on the planet and their interests in the Mediterranean and elsewhere often clashed. The Barbarossa brothers routinely played a role in helping their Muslim patrons defeat their European adversaries.

Under their collective watch, the Barbarossa brothers strengthened the Ottoman Empire in the Mediterranean Basin and gave the Turks the foothold they needed to negotiate with the European powers. They also extended the rule of the Barbary corsairs across the entire Mediterranean region, playing a major role in politics and warfare. On paper, they may have been pirates, but the reality was that they were diplomats, merchants, warlords, and politicians, elevating the image of what a pirate truly could be. To the Spanish, they were nothing more than outlaws, but to the Islamic world they were hailed as heroes.

Under the command of the Barbarossa brothers, the Barbary pirates ruled the Mediterranean with an iron fist. Throughout the sixteenth century there was no question that the Ottoman corsairs were the most powerful force on the water, despite their oared galleys lagging behind the more sophisticated ships of the Spanish, French, and English. Eventually the reliance on those smaller vessels would begin to catch up with them, and by the dawn of the seventeenth century their unquestioned dominance of the seas began to falter. As the decades passed, heavier, faster, and better-armed European vessels began to outclass the Barbary galleys, who increasingly found themselves on the losing end of battles.

The Slow Decline of the Corsairs

Had the European nations focused on eliminating the pirate threat altogether, chances are that the Barbary corsairs would have gone away a lot sooner than they actually did. But as part of the political ploys of France, England, Portugal, Spain, and the Netherlands, they often paid the pirates to harass their rivals. For instance, at one point France and the Ottomans entered into a treaty that aligned them with one another against the Spanish. As these nations stayed focused on each other, the Mediterranean pirates were allowed to stay just off of France's radar, a useful tool that could be brought to bear when necessary.

By the 1700s, the British navy began to exert itself as the most powerful fleet in the world. By that time, piracy had gone from being a minor nuisance to a major problem for England, directly impacting the business of the Crown. This gave the Royal Navy the incentive it needed to begin hunting down and killing pirates anywhere that they could be found. Those efforts would prove to be so successful that the Brits were able to sign a peace treaty that forbid the North African states from attacking ships under British protection.

That treaty extended to American ships as well, which flew under a British flag at the time. However, once the thirteen colonies signed the Declaration of Independence in 1776, the British navy was quick to point out that those vessels were no longer off limits. A year later, Morocco became the first independent country in the world to officially recognize the United States of America as a nation, but it did not take long for the Barbary corsairs to recognize American vessels as prime targets either. With British protection no longer covering those ships, the corsairs attacked them with reckless abandon.

As word spread that sailing ships from the US were soft targets that were easy to seize, more and more pirates began raiding any vessel displaying the American flag. It wasn't long before numerous vessels, along with their cargo and crews, were captured and held for ransom. At the time, the fledgling US government was extremely low on funds and could not pay the sums demanded by the corsairs. Eventually however, the US and the pirates negotiated a peace treaty that saw the pirates promise to leave the US ships alone, in exchange for a hefty annual tribute from the Americans. That tribute amounted to about 20 percent of the government's total annual budget in the early years of its existence.

The treaty managed to secure peace for a time, but in 1801, the North African nations of Algiers, Tunis, Morocco, and Tripoli declared war on the US, citing late payments of the promised tribute as grounds for their actions. But much had changed since those early naval engagements that forced the Americans to sign the treaty in the first place. Following the adoption of the US Constitution in 1789, America now had provisions in place to collect taxes and use that money to build and maintain a navy. Their ships were able to hold off the assaults of the Barbary corsairs and delivered them a crushing defeat. Later, that naval victory was followed up by a ground assault led by the US Marine Corps, which attacked at "the shores of Tripoli." With victory at hand, a new treaty was signed in June of 1805 that allowed for the ransom of American prisoners, while also dropping all mention of paying an annual tribute.

The Barbary pirates weren't done with the Americans just yet however, and in 1812 the same North African states once again declared war on the US. The announcement was strategically timed to take place just as the British were also declaring war on their former colonies. Distracted by this move, the America did not have enough resources to properly deal with the Barbary corsairs. Instead, it focused its time, energy, and funds into fighting off the British threat.

Once the War of 1812 was over, the US turned its attention to North Africa. Now, with an even larger and more modern fleet, it sent an entire squadron of ships to confront the pirates. That fleet easily defeated and captured two corsair vessels and set sail for Algiers, where it found a new ruler who had recently ascended to power. He was much more willing to negotiate than his predecessor and the two sides soon agreed to exchange prisoners and end the conflict. The new treaty did away with all demands for tribute and the Algerians agreed to leave US ships alone. The American navy then moved on to Tunis and Tripoli to secure similar deals with the other Barbary states.

American sailors battling corsairs during the First Barbary War.

Despite remaining a major threat to merchant ships on the Mediterranean and Atlantic, it became increasingly clear that the Barbary corsairs were in serious decline. By the time they signed the peace agreements with the US, their pirate raids had dropped in frequency significantly. So much so that villages began to appear once again along the coast of the Iberian and Italian Peninsulas, something that hadn't happened in nearly three hundred years.

For a time, the corsairs continued to harass British ships and create chaos out on the water, even though their success rate had dropped significantly. The Royal Navy had mostly managed to curtail those efforts, bringing peace and order to the Mediterranean at long last. It had been nearly a thousand years since the Berbers took to the sea to pillage and plunder, but the dominance of the British fleet was such that even the other great powers of the world struggled to match them on the oceans. Something that pirates in other parts of the world would soon come to learn.

Still, the attacks from the Barbary corsairs did not end completely until the French conquered Algiers in 1830. That invasion, and subsequent occupation, lasted for more than 130 years, with strict French oversight for the majority of that time period. That conquest brought an end to all of the serious pirate activity on the Barbary Coast, which for ten centuries had been amongst the most dangerous places on the entire planet.

The Tale of the
Barbarossa Brothers

Throughout human history there have been tens of thousands of men—and to a much lesser extent women—who have heeded the call of the seas to become pirates. Most of those individuals were anonymous figures, serving on a ship in the hopes of acquiring enough wealth and status that they could potentially change their station in life. It has always been a rare thing for a pirate to break through the ranks, leave his or her mark on the world, and be remembered long after death. Rarer still is that two pirates from the same family could pull off such a feat, but that is exactly what Oruç and Hisir Reis managed to do, collectively making a name for themselves as the Barbarossa brothers.

Born on the island of Lesbos in the Mediterranean Sea during the 1470s, Oruç and Hisir were the sons of a potter and merchant named Yakup. Their father had played an instrumental role in helping the Ottoman Turks liberate the island from the Genoese in 1462 and he was made a local administrator for his service. In the years that followed, Yakup and his wife Katarina started a family that included four sons and two daughters.

When they were old enough, the four sons began helping Yakup with the family business, with Hisir assisting their father in making pottery. Meanwhile, both Oruç and the youngest brother, Ilyas, took up sailing in part to learn to operate a small boat that Yakup had purchased. The two young men eventually sailed the Aegean Sea, delivering goods to marketplaces not only on Lesbos, but to other nearby islands as well.

Eventually, all four of the Reis brothers became sailors of varying experience and skill. Oruç, a natural and gifted seaman, was the first to take up the trade. Over time, those skills allowed him to expand his trade routes, striking out across the Mediterranean to more distant ports of call. On those voyages he learned to speak several languages, including Italian, Spanish, French, Greek, and Arabic. This gave him the ability to not only barter effectively with foreign merchants, but also communicate with the sailors he encountered in his travels.

One of Oruç's voyages took him as far away as Tripoli in Lebanon, with brother Ilyas coming along as part of the crew. On their return voyage to Lesbos, their ship was attacked by another vessel under the command of the Knights Hospitaller, a Catholic military organization that fought against Islamic forces throughout the crusades. During the battle, Ilyas was killed and Oruç was taken captive and imprisoned in the Knights' castle on the island of Rhodes.

By that time, Hisir had also taken to the sea and had even purchased a ship of his own. Like his older brother, he had launched his career as a merchant, dealing not only in his father's pottery, but goods made by other artisans as well. When word reached him that Oruç had been captured and Ilyas had been killed by the Knights Hospitaller, Hisir was outraged. The Knights did not know it yet, but that seemingly innocuous raid of a merchant ship ignited a flame that had lasting implications not just for the Mediterranean, but for much of Europe, Northern Africa, and the Ottoman Empire too.

Oruç remained in captivity on the island of Rhodes for nearly three years, but eventually Hisir hatched a plan to spring him from prison. Sailing to the Knight's stronghold, he snuck inside, located his brother, and helped him escape. The two sailed off, happy to be reunited, but now galvanized in their hatred of the enemy. By attacking and imprisoning Oruç, the Knights Hospitaller had unwittingly unleashed a formidable enemy for the Christian kingdoms of Europe.

After gaining his freedom, Oruç decided to make a dramatic shift in his career. Previously, he had been content to sail the Mediterranean as a merchant, making a modest living selling goods throughout the region. But after three years in captivity, he was ready to exact a measure of revenge against those who had killed his brother and taken away a considerable portion of his life. Determined to make his enemies pay, he

AROUDĴ,

Illustration of Oruç Barbarossa.

sailed to Antalya along the coast of what is now Turkey. Once there, he convinced an Ottoman prince by the name of Şehzade Korkut to back him as a privateer, with the expressed mission of taking the fight directly to the Knights.

For more than three hundred years the Knights had been battling Muslims, both in the Holy Land and on the Mediterranean. For a time, they operated out of Jerusalem, but when that city was conquered during the First Crusade, they were forced to relocate, eventually settling on the island of Rhodes in 1310 CE. Since that time, they had been conducting raids on Muslim ships and had been particularly troublesome for Ottoman traders. The Catholic military faction operated under a direct mandate from the Pope himself and viewed their campaign as a holy war that was conducted in the name of God.

Eager to have a new ally against the Knights, Korkut gave Oruç eighteen galleys to use in his campaign in opposition of their shared enemy. And while Oruç had plenty of latitude when it came to conducting his raids, he also served his patron and took orders directly from the prince from time to time. This was especially true when Korkut became governor of the Ottoman city of Manissa, at which time his influence and wealth grew considerably. That afforded him the luxury of giving Oruç another six ships, which were then used to launch successful raids on the Italian Peninsula and throughout the Aegean Sea.

By 1503 Oruç had begun to make quite a name for himself operating as a privateer. His attacks on ships and coastal villages helped keep the enemies of the Ottoman Turks in check and allowed him to begin to build considerable personal wealth. More importantly, his deeds had earned him a great deal of renown, which helped him to amass a crew of hardened sailors who were steadfastly loyal to their captain. They also allowed him to establish a base of operations on the island of Djerba, which was located off the coast of Northern Africa near Tunisia.

Amongst those loyal followers was Oruç's own brother, Hisir, who had joined his sibling not long after Oruç had created his new outpost. The duo began plotting raids together and it wasn't long before they started to leave their mark on the Mediterranean. In 1504, they captured two Papal galleys and numerous other vessels, including a Sicilian warship with more than four hundred Spanish soldiers aboard. These impressive victories, along with an effective campaign of raiding European coastal towns, brought both men considerable fame. It even drew more Muslim corsairs to their cause, increasing their strength and reach considerably.

Over the next decade or so, Oruç and Hisir became the most successful and well-known privateers on the Mediterranean Sea. Not only did they capture countless enemy ships, but they also gained immense notoriety amongst the Ottoman Turks and other Muslim nations. From 1504 to 1510, the bothers helped transport Muslim Mudéjars safely out of Spain to North Africa, potentially saving thousands of lives in the process. By then, Christian forces had reclaimed the Iberian Peninsula, and the Muslims that still lived there were facing increasing levels of persecution. Thanks to Oruç's leadership in particular, many of those individuals were able to find their way across the Mediterranean and back into friendly territory.

Because of their continued successful raids against Christian outposts, the brothers quickly gained notoriety across Europe. There, they were branded as pirates and outlaws, with Oruç earning the title of

Corsairs defeat the Holy League.

"Baba Oruç," meaning "Father Oruç." Because of how those words were pronounced, the name evolved as it spread across Spain, France, and eventually Italy, where it was converted to "Barbarossa"—meaning "red beard." Both brothers came to be known by this name amongst their European adversaries. It was also the moniker that would stand the test of time, surviving across the centuries.

In 1512, Oruç earned another nickname, this time coming from his Muslim brethren instead. During an attempt to retake the port city of Bugia in Algiers, the privateer captain lost his left arm in a battle with Spanish invaders. Afterwards, he replaced that arm with a prosthetic made of bright metal, earning him the title of "Gümüş Kol," which means "silver arm" in Turkish. The loss of a limb hardly slowed him down, as he and Hisir soon launched a massive campaign along the Spanish coast during which they managed to capture twenty-three ships in a single month.

The next five years were a flurry of activity for the brothers, who engaged English, French, and Spanish fleets at various points, almost always prevailing in those engagements. The continued success of the Barbarossa brothers frustrated and confounded the Europeans, who struggled to anticipate where and when they would strike next. Over this span of time, Oruç and Hisir plundered dozens of enemy vessels and sacked nearly as many towns. Their reputation as fierce combatants, smart tacticians, and bold sailors earned them grudging respect from their Christian counterparts, most of whom fled in fear whenever the flagship of one of the two men approached.

In 1516, Oruç and Hisir made the bold move of recapturing the Algerian cities of Jijel and Algiers from the Spanish. They then held off a fierce counterattack that allowed them to consolidate their hold on the region by moving inland to take control of several other Spanish out-posts. Despite the fact that they now found themselves waging war against their old enemy in the heart of the North African desert, their ties to the sea remained. In order to move their heavy cannons at faster speeds, Oruç ordered his men to attach sails to the guns, allowing them to glide over the desert sands. This brilliant maneuver allowed the privateers to transport a considerable amount of firepower over long distances in a surprisingly short span of time, catching their adversaries off guard once again.

With Algeria now under their control, Oruç quickly declared himself sultan, taking command of the entire country. But he knew that if he and his men were going to hold onto their prize they would need a little help from some friends. Not long after declaring victory, the brothers offered Algeria to the Ottoman Empire, joining as a newly established province in 1517. In doing so, Oruç gave up the title of sultan, but was named governor of the region instead. Better still, the Ottoman sultan also declared him the chief sea governor of the West Mediterranean, with the promise to send ships and men to support Oruç's efforts.

A year after that important victory, the Spanish struck back. Determined to regain their foothold in North Africa, Charles V—the king of Spain and the Holy Roman emperor—arrived in Algeria with a major force in tow. With more than ten thousand troops at his disposal, plus another thousand bedouin fighters, he marched on the city of Tlemcen where Oruç awaited with his six thousand Turkish and Moorish soldiers. Charles laid siege to the city for three weeks, with Oruç and his men holding them at bay. Eventually, the overwhelming numbers of the invading army proved too much to hold back. When the walls were breached, most of the Muslim forces were killed, including their commander. Oruç was no more.

Devastated by the loss of his older brother, Hisir nevertheless knew that he had to continue his work. The Ottoman sultan declared him the commander and chief of the Algerian province and sent forces to aid in the war against Spain. The younger brother also inherited the mantle of Barbarossa too, assuming the famous name that had been bestowed upon Oruç. Over the years, his actions only enhanced that name, extending the legend of the two men even further.

The first order of business for Hisir was retaking Tiemcen, which he accomplished in fairly short order. From there, he held off a joint Spanish-Italian incursion into Algeria and launched a counterstrike of his own, attacking Southern France, the Balearic Islands, and targets along the Italian Peninsula. Most satisfying of all, the newly anointed Barbarossa also assisted in the Ottoman conquest of Rhodes, expelling the hated Knights Hospitaller in 1523, some three decades after they had imprisoned his older brother and killed his younger brother. Payback had been a long time coming.

Over the following decade, Hisir fought a never-ending war with the Spanish; he launched a constant stream of raids against enemy towns and ships. He proved to be every bit as formidable in battle as his brother, capturing enemy vessels at an astonishing rate. As he conducted raids against France, Spain, Tuscany, and Sicily, he continually kept the enemies of the Ottoman Empire on their heels, all the while maintaining his base of operations back in Algeria. As far as his European adversaries were concerned, Hisir's exploits continued the Barbarossa legacy, expanding it to new—and frightening—heights.

One of his more spectacular successes came in August of 1529, when Hisir and his troops helped liberate over seventy thousand Muslims living on the Iberian Peninsula. Most of those men, women, and children were descendants of the Moors who had conquered Spain more than eight hundred years earlier. For centuries, their families had lived in that region, but now they were under increasing pressure by the Holy Roman Empire to convert to Christianity. Those that did not were tortured, enslaved, and killed.

In just one month, Hisir and his fleet evacuated all of the Muslims who wished to leave Europe, making seven consecutive voyages across the Mediterranean to retrieve them all. Once again, this was continuation of his brother's work, but it solidified the family's place in Ottoman and Muslim history. It also brought more merchants, sailors, warriors, and workers to the Islamic states in Northern Africa, further fortifying Muslim cities.

In 1531 Hisir, who had now fully embraced the name of Barbarossa, met a worthy adversary in the form of the Italian admiral, Andrea Doria. A brilliant leader in his own right, Doria sailed out of Genoa at the behest of Charles V with orders to recapture cities and ports that had

Illustration of Hizir Barbarossa.

been lost to the Ottomans. Hisir turned Doria back in their initial encounter off the coast of Spain, but the Italian was dedicated and resourceful. Doria went on to win major victories for the Holy Roman Empire, recapturing the cities of Coron, Patras, and Lepanto along the coast in Greece.

Dismayed by these losses, Ottoman Sultan Suleiman the Magnificent summoned Barbarossa to his capital city of Istanbul. There, Hisir was given orders to retake the lost cities and attack European outposts along the way. Barbarossa embarked on his mission in August of 1532 and soon set about raiding Corsica, Elba, Sardinia, and various other cities on the coast of Greece and the islands in the Aegean Sea. Through conquest and shrewd negotiations, he added eighteen more galleys to his fleet before sailing to the town of Preveza to confront Doria directly. The two met in a brief naval skirmish that sent the Italian's fleet fleeing across the sea. During the battle, Barbarossa added a few more ships to his growing armada before returning to Istanbul victorious.

Once he arrived back in the Ottoman capital, Barbarossa was greeted personally by Suleiman. The sultan was so impressed and pleased with what Hisir had accomplished that he immediately named him "Kapudan-i Derya," essentially making him the grand admiral of the Ottoman navy. He also conferred upon him the title of "Beylerbey," which meant Hisir was also the chief governor of North Africa. As if that was not enough, Suleiman also put the provinces of Euboea, Chios, and—most importantly—Rhodes under Hisir's direct control. Barbarossa was now in charge of the island that was once held by the Knights Hospitaller, the men who were responsible for imprisoning his bother and sending them both down a path that turned them into the most feared sea captains in the entire Mediterranean.

Now in complete control of the Ottoman fleet, Barbarossa set sail in early 1534 with a flotilla consisting of more than eighty ships. He continued his marauding ways along the coasts of Greece and Italy, sacking and plundering dozens of towns. His armada even approached the mouth of the Tiber River, where the warning bells inside Rome itself could be heard ringing out in alarm. From there, he traveled across the

Mediterranean to retake the Tunisian port city of La Goulette, which was of particular strategic importance.

At this point, Barbarossa seemed nearly unstoppable, as even the vaunted Andrea Doria could not match him as a tactician. Wherever the Spanish made inroads in claiming territory from the Ottomans, the grand admiral eventually arrived on the scene and retook those conquered lands. The mounting frustration of always being bested by this single, remarkable man led Charles V to take drastic measures in the hopes of either winning over his foe or ending his life.

Following one of Barbarossa's rampages across the Mediterranean, the Holy Roman emperor sent an emissary to meet with Hisir directly. That ambassador carried a message from Charles V promising that the admiral would receive the title of "Lord of North Africa" if he abandoned the Ottomans and switched sides. Unsurprisingly, Barbarossa turned down the offer, as he was already the chief governor of that region anyway.

When Hisir refused Charles V's offer, the emissary lunged at him in an attempt to assassinate the admiral on the spot. However, that attempt failed, and once Barbarossa had composed himself, he decapitated the man on the spot using his own scimitar. The attempt on his life was a sharp reminder that his enemies would go to great lengths to hasten his demise.

A year later, the Holy Roman emperor and his allies showed just how far they were indeed willing to go. In an effort to hunt down and destroy Barbarossa once and for all, Charles V assembled a fleet consisting of more than three hundred ships and twenty-four thousand men from Italy and Spain. That powerful force descended on Tunis to reclaim the lands that had been lost there, only to find that the wily Ottoman commander had sailed away before the enemy could arrive. In doing so, Hisir gave up some ground in Tunisia, but he raided the Spanish islands of Majorca and Menorca just for good measure on his way back to Algiers.

The conflict between the Ottoman Turks and the European powers continued to deepen. Suleiman the Magnificent once again recalled his most trusted naval commander to Istanbul. Once there, Barbarossa was put in charge of a fleet consisting of more than two hundred ships. Suleiman's orders this time were to attack the kingdom of Naples, which was under Venetian control. Barbarossa's campaign was an incredibly demoralizing one for the Europeans, as Hisir and his men once again wreaked havoc across the Mediterranean. The defeat was so complete that the devastation to the island of Corfu included all of its agriculture being wiped out and the vast majority of its population being sold off into slavery.

The war with the Ottomans was so damaging to Venice that the city sent an ambassador to the Vatican to meet with Pope Paul III. The Venetians implored His Holiness to assemble a "Holy League" against the Ottomans, Suleiman, and Barbarossa. Sensing the threat that the empire posed to Europe and Christianity, the pope agreed, bringing together a unified force of nations designed to sweep their enemies off the face of the Earth.

The Holy League consisted of ships and men not just from Venice, but from Genoa, Portugal, Spain, Malta, and the Papal States as well. Its largest battle fleet, commanded by Andrea Doria, featured more than three hundred ships, all of which were swift and well armed. In contrast to the forces that were arrayed against him, Barbarossa had just 120 galleys, which were smaller and slower, but very sturdy and maneuverable. The Ottoman fleet also had its great admiral, and once again he proved to be the ultimate lynch-pin when it came to determining the outcome of the battle.

The two fleets gathered near the Greek city of Preveza and for a time it looked like it could be a rout in favor of the Europeans. But the tight cliffs and rocky shores along the coast of Greece reduced the wind to almost nothing, which soon rendered the multinational armada of the Holy League at a disadvantage. Without an ocean breeze to help them sail, the European vessels soon became slow and ungainly. Anticipating this potential problem, Barbarossa had brought galleys that relied on oars rather than sails. This gave his men a distinct advantage over the enemy and it did not take long before the rout was on in the opposite direction.

The Ottoman victory wasn't just decisive, it was so utterly complete and devastating that it took years for the European nations to recover.

Barbarossa had snatched victory from the jaws of defeat, prevailing over his enemies once again. Using smaller, more well-organized, and more disciplined boats, he was able to outmaneuver his adversaries. The Holy League was vanquished, with what few survivors remained sent back home in humiliation.

Les musulmans, armés de tout ce qui leur tombe sous la main, fondent sur les chrétiens.

Corsairs capture a galley.

The defeat opened up the city of Tripoli for the Ottoman Empire, who further advanced into Northern Africa and beyond. The Turks' dominance in the region went largely unchallenged for more than three decades, bringing on a new era of growth and expansion. Much of that was due almost solely to the strategic and tactical genius of Barbarossa.

Following his victory at the Battle of Preveza, Hisir went on another raiding mission across the Mediterranean. With little resistance, he swept the last remaining vestiges of Christian factions from the Aegean Sea, consolidating it firmly into the Ottoman Empire. Fearing for its own safety, Venice quickly signed a peace treaty with Suleiman, ceding all territorial gains to the Turks. They also agreed to pay a tribute of three hundred thousand gold ducats, the equivalent of about $40 million today.

Despite suffering serious losses to Barbarossa yet again, Charles V still was not ready to be done with his most vexing foe. In 1540, the emperor repeated his offer to make Hisir his chief admiral and give him control of all of North Africa. True to form, the aging seaman rejected the offer, which again prompted a major attack by the Spanish. This time, the Holy Roman emperor was on hand to oversee the operation

The bombardment of Algiers.

himself as a fleet of ships under the command of Andrea Doria lay siege to Algiers.

During the campaign, Charles V ignored the advice of his commanders and attempted a beach landing in inclement weather. As a result, many of the ships under his command ran aground, stranding them along the shore. In contrast, Doria took his own fleet out to sea to avoid the same predicament, with his vessels remaining intact. But now, the fleet had been reduced in numbers and scattered, reducing its advantage over the enemy.

Undeterred, the emperor attempted to march on Algiers, traveling overland along the coast. But his weary men were no match for the Ottoman forces under Barbarossa's command who harassed them along the way. With his army unorganized, outflanked, and shaken, Charles V had no choice but to withdraw back to Europe, suffering yet another humiliating defeat.

The following years saw the Ottoman Empire join forces with the French against their common enemy of Spain. Always the loyal and trustworthy servant, Barbarossa once again set sail at the request of the sultan. By 1543, his fleet had swollen to over two hundred ships and he had more than thirty thousand troops under his command. This was enough to capture a number of important targets in Italy, and even threaten Rome itself. He may have taken the city too, had his new allies not stepped in. Unable to allow the Vatican to be captured by a Muslim army, the French intervened, asking Barbarossa to turn back. Hisir obliged the request, leaving the seat of Catholic power unscathed.

From 1543 to 1545, the notorious Barbarossa once again brought a reign of terror across the Mediterranean. His fleet ranged far and wide, attacking outposts from Greece to Spain and back again. However, he was approaching the age of sixty and was beginning to slow down. A long life of travel, adventure, politics, and warfare had taken its toll and he was ready to finally be at peace. Upon returning to Istanbul after his final campaign, the great privateer who had risen to become grand admiral retired at long last. He built himself a palace in the city and took up residence there, enjoying a quiet and peaceful lifestyle until his death the following year.

The Barbarossa brothers are a prime example of privateers who were branded as pirates by their enemies. In terms of military victories, Oruç and Hisir might be the most successful pirates in history, sacking towns and enemy ships for more than fifty years. During that time, they became known as some of the most fearsome and bold sailors to ever take to the seas. They were rarely bested in combat and seldom forced to give quarter.

Their keen military minds not only served them well throughout their careers, but also benefited the Ottoman Turks greatly. The empire owed them a great debt of gratitude for not only helping it expand into Northern Africa, but also for serving as the first line of defense against their European adversaries for the better part of five decades. Without the Barbarossa brothers leading the way, it is possible that the Ottoman Empire would have been a very different place, both in geographical size and duration.

It is hard to imagine how the history of the Mediterranean would have played out differently had the Knights Hospitaller not attacked Oruç's ship and imprisoned him in their stronghold. It is possible that had that not happened, the elder Barbarossa brother may have been content to remain a merchant throughout his life. But by turning him into a privateer and later a conqueror, the Knights unknowingly reshaped the history of the region. And when Hisir picked up his brother's mantle after his untimely death, he proved to be an even smarter, shrewder, and more cunning enemy.

To say that two brothers rose up to become more than just privateers or pirates would be a vast understatement. Throughout the course of their careers, they commanded large fleets, sailed under the flag of the Ottoman Empire, and ruled over kingdoms of their own. Despite all of that, in the Western world they remain largely unknown. Unsurprisingly, amongst Muslims they are still seen as legendary heroes nearly five hundred years after their deaths.

That is a legacy that few figures in history—pirate or not—could ever hope to claim.

CHAPTER 4

The Pirates of the Caribbean Sea

If there is any place on Earth that is most closely associated with pirates, it is without a doubt the Caribbean. For more than three hundred years seagoing raiders prowled those waters, making life difficult for the European powers looking to establish a foothold in the New World. During that time, ruthless and daring buccaneers raided merchant ships, cargo vessels, and royal treasure fleets, creating havoc on the high seas in the process.

These exploits ushered in what would become known as "the Golden Age of Piracy," an era that latest roughly from 1650 to 1730. During that time, pirate activity was rampant throughout the Caribbean, as well as along the coasts of North and South America. This era also introduced the world to some of the most notorious and ruthless pirate captains to ever set sail, with names like Blackbeard and Henry Morgan echoing across the centuries, inspiring tales of heroism and villainy.

European Voyages
Unlike in the Mediterranean, where the exact origins of pirate activity have long been lost to the mists of time, we have a pretty good idea of when piracy actually began in the Caribbean. Christopher Columbus' arrival in the New World in 1492, and his three subsequent voyages to the region over the following decade, created quite a stir back in Europe. While Columbus himself was Italian, he sailed under a Spanish flag,

which gave his patrons—King Ferdinand and Queen Isabella—claim to anything that he "found." Naturally, the Spanish were quick to plant their banner in this newly discovered land, although England, France, Portugal, and the Netherlands were quick to follow.

When the Spanish began exploring the Caribbean, along with Central and South America, they were overjoyed to find that their newly claimed lands were rich in resources, particularly silver. It was not long before a steady supply of that metal, along with plenty of gold and precious gems, was being shipped back to Europe to fill the coffers of the Spanish Crown. Naturally, this influx of riches drew the attention of the other European nations, with the maritime powers soon setting out to stake their claims too. The vast new region of the Western Hemisphere offered opportunities for wealth that had not been seen in Europe in centuries, and none of the great powers wanted to be left out.

The English, French, Dutch, and Portuguese were not the only ones who caught wind of the vast amounts of treasure aboard those Spanish galleons either. Pirates and privateers sailing off the coast of Europe could not help but be tempted by those ships too. Rumors ran rampant regarding the size and contents of their cargo holds, which were said to be filled with untold treasures. Regardless of whether those tales were true or not, the seeds of temptation had been planted amongst a generation of sea captains who were already familiar with operating outside the law.

At the time, a voyage across the Atlantic took upwards of two months to complete and required a ship that was sturdy and dependable. Most importantly, the vessels needed a seasoned crew that was willing to set off into largely unexplored waters. In the years that followed Columbus's initial voyage, this was a combination that was not easy to come by. Most of the vessels setting sail for the New World were part of a royal fleet with experienced naval officers and a hardened, professional crew. After all, until an Italian explorer had arrived in the Caribbean, and safely navigated his way back home, no one had ever survived such a voyage before.

By the early 1500s, the Spanish had established a number of settlements across the New World, with Santiago in Cuba, Cartagena in Colombia, and Santo Domingo on Hispaniola amongst the most important. These places made up part of what was known as the Spanish Main, which was a term used to describe the country's holdings in the Caribbean, Mexico, and coastal South America. There, Spanish colonists established ports that were used to ship valuable resources back to Europe, with little fear of attack from marauders. At the time, there was not much pirate activity in the area.

This period of safety and security did not last for long however, as there were a number of factors that helped to give rise to pirate activity in the New World. First and foremost, the same improved ship designs that allowed Europeans to gain a leg up on the pirates of the Barbary Coast also allowed more ships to venture farther out into the Atlantic. The first vessels that reached the Caribbean may have been a part of royal fleets, but those that were chartered by private companies and even

Pirate with ships.

individual captains followed not long after. Amongst them were ambitious buccaneers looking for fortune and adventure far from the well-trodden shores of Europe and the Mediterranean.

The sailors who crewed those early trans-Atlantic voyages also happened to be seasoned professionals who had plenty of experience on the high seas. Many were privateers that had been commissioned by King Francis I of France to wage a proxy war against Spain and Portugal. In 1493 those two nations signed the Treaty of Tordesillas, which divided the world in half along a north-south line located 1,270 miles west of the Cape Verde Islands in the Atlantic. Essentially, the treaty divvied up the trade rights for any territories outside of Europe, giving Spain control over the majority of the New World and the Pacific Ocean beyond. Meanwhile, the Portuguese received the Indian Ocean and everything to the east, including Asia. Naturally, this was not a particularly popular proposal amongst the other European nations, who were left out of the agreement altogether. The situation was made worse when the treaty was officially endorsed by the pope, who gave his seal of approval in order to secure peace between Portugal and Spain.

To combat Spain's growing dominance in the Atlantic—and by default the New World—France issued letters of marque to any sailors looking to fight for the French cause. Officially issued by the French Crown, these documents made it legal for ships owned and operated by private citizens to attack and confiscate the vessels that flew the flag of an enemy nation. In other words, if France was at war with another country, privateers could raid the vessels sailing under that country's flag without fear of reprisal by French authorities. By creating incentive for independent ships to attack Spanish vessels, France dramatically increased its naval presence and granted the privateers the potential to reap significant rewards in the form of plunder.

During the first half of the sixteenth century, France was mostly alone in its campaign against Spain, although the English and Dutch eventually joined the fight too. By then, all three countries were encouraging privateers to raid Spanish ships, which were by far the richest targets on the ocean. That alone was enough to lure more sailors to become privateers and pirates, with the possibility for gaining enormous wealth awaiting them on the high seas.

Some of the earliest pirates to take to the waters of the Caribbean came from the island of Hispaniola. Known as Greater Antilles today, it was first settled by the French in 1625, with early colonists learning to survive off the land as hunters while exploring its rugged interior. As they became more established on Hispaniola, the settlers created small outposts on the island, much to the chagrin of the Spanish, who were not ready to cede any part of the New World to their European rivals.

From time to time, the Spaniards sent raiding parties to Hispaniola in an effort to drive the French off the island. If the colonists fled, they were allowed to leave, otherwise they were just as likely to be killed as taken prisoner. The Spanish hunting parties also slaughtered every wild boar that they came across, taking away a primary source of food for the French hunters. Over time, those tactics proved quite effective, as eventually the settlers abandoned Hispaniola for the nearby island of Tortuga.

Smaller and more defensible, Tortuga allowed the French to more easily withstand Spanish attacks. But unlike Hispaniola, the tiny island did not have much in the way of resources, which meant the colonists had to routinely sail to other nearby islands in search of food and other important materials. Over time, these sailors found that it was actually safer and easier to raid passing merchant ships for the things that they needed, rather than spend valuable time and limited resources on exploring the other islands of the Caribbean. Eventually, almost everyone living on Tortuga was involved in the pirate trade to some degree, creating one of the first thriving pirate coalitions in the New World.

Things grew even more interesting for the French pirates in 1655, when the English captured the island of Jamaica from the Spanish. It was not long before the inhabitants of that island were trading goods and services with those living on Tortuga, establishing a mutually beneficial relationship between the two colonies. The relationship was so friendly in fact that the British governor in charge of Jamaica began issuing letters of marque to the French pirates, as well as English privateers, essentially making it legal to wage war on their mutual enemy, the Spanish.

Curiously enough, the term buccaneer did not exist until the sixteenth century. Today, it is a well-known synonym for pirate, but it originally had a very different meaning. It is derived from the name of the smoke houses that the French used to smoke their meats. Known as "boucans," these little shacks were common on both Hispaniola and Tortuga, with "buccaneer" used as the term for those who worked inside these simple, but effective kitchens. But as more and more of the French set sail on pirate raids, the name continued to be applied to those who were once perceived as just simple hunters. Before long, the original meaning was all but forgotten, with "buccaneer" evolving into a colloquial term for a seafaring outlaw.

Despite its wealth and power, Spain simply did not have the resources it needed to defend and control the entirety of the New World. This, combined with the increasing economic and military power of England and France, caused the Spanish to work towards more friendly relations with its rivals. Thus, by the start of the seventeenth century all of the European powers, including Portugal, had colonies and outposts on the far side of the Atlantic, bringing an uneasy peace to the region.

However, the end of hostilities between the European powers caused a sharp rise in pirate activity, as most of the privateers operating under French, English, and Dutch flags saw their letters of marque revoked. With fewer opportunities to raid Spanish vessels, many ship captains and their crews found themselves out of work. Worse yet, most of these men did not have any other skills or prospects to fall back on, so they returned to the ocean and continued their marauding ways. The difference was that this time they were doing it as outlaws and not under the legal consent of one of the European monarchs.

The Golden Age of Piracy

This increase in the number of buccaneers on the high seas paved the way for the Golden Age of Piracy. This era represented an eighty-year period in which piracy had a direct impact on trade, politics, and warfare across the globe, but especially in the Caribbean and the Atlantic. During this time, Europe's maritime powers often found themselves battling pirates as much as each other, with the buccaneers displaying a new level of sophistication in terms of naval tactics and ship building that had not been encountered before.

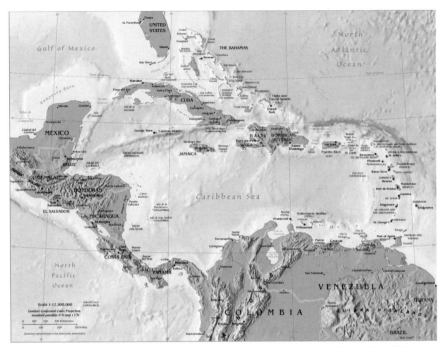

Map of the Caribbean.

Because they had most likely trained and served in the navies of one of the major European powers, these seventeenth-century pirates were far more skilled than earlier outlaws of the sea. They knew how to navigate over long distances, track the wind with great precision, and handle increasingly more agile and better-armed ships. They also had a good understanding of the most effective tactics for use during naval engagement, as they had trained in how to effectively use cannons to cripple their opponent and efficiently board their ship.

This combination of abilities and experience made this new breed of pirate a formidable foe, but they had one other trait that also made them dangerous—they were desperate. Many of the men who took to piracy as a way of life did so because they had no other way out of poverty. Born as peasants, and with few opportunities to improve their station, joining a crew of buccaneers at least gave them hope for a better future. With so little to lose, and the potential for earning a significant payoff, the pirates of the seventeenth and eighteenth centuries were more willing to put their life on the line if it could lead to an economic payoff.

As all of the major European nations established footholds throughout the Americas, the number of cargo ships and merchant vessels arriving in the New World rose significantly too. This meant there were more targets for the pirates who operated across the region, although Spanish ships remained their favorite quarries. While the French and English were emerging powers on the world's stage, the Spanish set the standard for wealth and resources, much of which was contained in their distinctive galleons that shuttled back and forth between Seville and the Caribbean.

The alarming rise of piracy in the Atlantic and the Americas forced Spain to look for new ways to protect its substantial assets while at sea. One of its solutions was to employ convoys of ships that traveled back together from the New World and back home to Spain, carrying cargo in both directions. When sailing west, those ships were filled with goods and supplies that would support the growing colonies in the Americas, and when those vessels sailed back to Europe, they were generally filled with not just silver and gold, but exotic spices, sugar, tobacco, and other goods.

These convoys—which often numbered fifty ships or more—became known as the "treasure fleet." With so much cargo onboard, they attracted plenty of attention from privateers and pirates alike. In order to keep those ships safe, they were accompanied by faster, more agile, and heavily armed Spanish galleons, which were amongst the most feared and impressive warships of their day.

The strategy of having ships travel together in large numbers, with support from military vessels to keep them safe, was mostly successful for the Spaniards. While pirates often targeted the treasure fleet, they rarely gained a favorable outcome when engaging the well-trained and well-equipped Spanish navy. As it turns out, far more Spanish ships were lost to bad weather than pirate attacks, with powerful hurricanes occasionally sending vessels to the bottom of the ocean. Those losses were often costly to the Spanish Crown, but they were ultimately viewed as acts of God that were almost completely unavoidable.

Piet Pieterson Heyn

That isn't to say that there were not some pirates that did manage to find a measure of success against the legendary treasure fleet. For instance, in 1628 the Dutch privateer Piet Pieterson Heyn launched a campaign against the Spanish with an eye on hitting them directly in their coin purses. To do that, he knew he had to strike at the treasure fleet and its lucrative cargo. He and his crew intercepted and raided as many as sixteen ships flying under the Spanish flag, plundering a king's ransom in cargo. But that number could have been much higher, and even more damaging to Spain, if it were not for a talkative young cabin boy who shared details of the raid with the Spanish ahead of time.

Thirty years prior to his attack on the treasure fleet, Heyn was already a seasoned sailor when the ship that he was serving on was captured at sea by the Spanish. Taken as a prisoner of war, he was pressed into service as a galley slave, manning the oars aboard an enemy boat for more than four years. During that time, he learned to speak Spanish fluently by observing and interacting with the crew. He also becoming intimately familiar with how their ships operated, which proved to be highly valuable information in the years that followed.

Eventually, Heyn was released as part of a prisoner exchange program between the Dutch and Spanish. Once free, he embarked on a successful career as a merchant captain, gaining wealth and status along the way. He was granted the title of vice-admiral for the Dutch West India Company in 1623, which sent him sailing for the New World the following year. Once there, he led several raids against the Portuguese in Brazil, where Heyn and his crew managed to not only sack the city of Salvador, but capture more than thirty enemy ships too.

The Dutchman's crowning achievement was without a doubt his successful attack and plunder of the treasure fleet. Knowing that the Spanish were about to ship their annual cargo of silver and gold from the

Americas back home to Spain, Heyn bided his time and waited for his opportunity to attack. Eventually, that patience paid off when his fleet engaged the Spanish as they sailed across the Caribbean with cargo holds filled with treasure being shipped back to Europe from Mexico.

It is estimated that thanks to Heyn's daring campaign, enough treasure was liberated from the Spanish to completely fund the Dutch army for eight months while they undertook some strategically significant campaigns in various parts of the globe. Perhaps more importantly, the shareholders of the Dutch West India Company were given a 50 percent dividend that year, with the organization's fortunes greatly bolstered by the influx of silver acquired on the high seas.

By successfully raiding the Spanish treasure fleet, Heyn also inked his name in the history books. He is generally recognized as the only ship captain to capture a sizable number of Spain's famous cargo vessels, bringing home a substantial amount of booty in the process. But had things gone a little differently, the amount of plunder that he captured could have been a whole lot larger.

As fate would have it, a young Dutch cabin boy got lost while traveling through Venezuela and ended up as a prisoner of the Spanish. While under interrogation, the boy was quick to give up the few secrets that he actually knew, which included some vague details about Heyn's plans to raid Spain's most prized vessels. That was enough to convince the Spanish to keep their Venezuelan treasure fleet in port, although it was too late to warn their compatriots in Mexico to do the same. When the flotilla of cargo ships set sail from there, it found the Dutchman and his allies lying in wait. Had the cabin boy not tipped them off, the number of ships sailing as part of that squadron could have been much larger—and Heyn's reward much greater.

A year after he raided the treasure fleet, Heyn returned home to the Netherlands where he was greeted as a conquering hero. His exploits had made him popular not only with the investors of the Dutch West India Company, but with the general population as well. To the Spanish, he was a notorious pirate who stole what rightfully belonged to them, but to the Dutch he was a man to be praised and honored. So much so that he was named the lieutenant-admiral of Holland, essentially making him the commander of the entire Dutch navy. Sadly, this was not a position he would hold for long, as he died that same year in a battle against the Dunkirk Raiders, an organized group of pirates that were disrupting Dutch trading routes.

There were a handful of other successful attacks on the treasure fleet over the years, but those generally resulted in substantial damage to the ships themselves, without much plunder exchanging hands. For instance, the famous British admiral Robert Blake engaged the fleet in battle in both 1656 and 1657, destroying a number of the Spanish vessels while they were in port at Cadiz and Tenerife. But Spanish crew members managed to unload the ships before the Royal Navy could close in on the vessels, leaving very little treasure behind. Later, at the Battle of Vigo Bay in Galicia, Spain, all of the naval ships designated to protect the fleet were either captured or destroyed by the British navy. But once again all of the goods and merchandise had been offloaded before a single cannon ball had been fired, leaving very little to plunder.

Letters of Marque

One of the defining factors of the Golden Age of Piracy was how quickly and easily the status of a pirate or privateer could change. Prior to that era, whether or not someone was viewed as a pirate was fairly narrowly defined. But in the sixteenth and seventeenth centuries those lines began to blur, creating a more fluid environment for seafaring men (and sometimes women) looking to operate both inside and outside the law.

Over the centuries, most pirates were fairly self-serving when it came to how they operated on the high seas, usually having their own best interests at heart when striking at ships and towns. From time to time, a country or faction might pay a notorious pirate to leave its ships alone, or to antagonize a rival nation instead, but usually those kinds of agreements were fleeting. It was highly unusual for a pirate to sail for any kind of cause, other than maximizing his own profits and increasing his status.

The use of letters of marque began to change that, allowing pirates to set sail in the service of a king or queen, while still pursuing wealth and fame on their own. Additionally, pirates who had been issued such a letter would always have safe harbors to return to when it was time to sell off plundered goods, make repairs to their ship, take on men and supplies, or just lay low for a while. Previous generations of pirates had to create their own outposts or come to an agreement with an existing town or village, while those with a letter of marque could safely sail into any port that was controlled by the country whose flag they were flying under.

Even during the era when Europeans were just starting to colonize the New World, the concept behind a letter of marque was an old one. It is believed that King Henry III of England was one of the first monarchs to actually hand out these documents, offering them to privateers as early as 1243 CE. Such a letter entitled a ship captain and his crew to legally attack vessels that belonged to the enemy of the king without fear of reprisal. In turn, governing powers could weaken their enemies and privateers were granted the right to keep half of whatever they confiscated from the ships that they raided, with the rest going into the royal coffers.

Later, a variant of the original letter of marque was introduced that was called the "letter of marque and reprisal." Essentially, this version of the document allowed a privateer to ask permission from a king or queen to wage their own private war against a specific person or faction. If the letter was granted, the person who received it could attack ships and other holdings of the specified individual or group while still operating within the law. Naturally, the Crown took half of any goods or treasure that was seized as part of that conflict.

The use of letters of marque was fairly limited for the first few centuries after their introduction, but by the sixteenth century they became far more common. This resulted in increased pirate activity, as more and more privateers took to the water in the service of specific nations. Early on, most of those letters came from the French, English, and Dutch as a way of increasing their naval presence in the Caribbean at a time when their navies were not large enough to compete directly with the Spanish.

Some of the most notorious pirates and privateers of the Golden Age of Piracy sailed under letters of marque at one time or another. For instance, Sir Henry Morgan made it his mission to undermine Spanish authority in the Caribbean during his career, raiding colonies throughout the region. He often did so with the official support of the English Crown, which granted him immunity from prosecution in British territories. Similarly, explorer William Dampier also sailed under a British letter of marque, which granted him the right to attack enemies of the Crown wherever he roamed. In Dampier's case, that included not just the Caribbean and the Americas, but also Australia, Papua New Guinea, and other remote locations around the globe.

Eventually the use of letters of marque began to fall out of favor, in large part because more young men were electing to set sail as privateers than were actually joining the Royal Navy. By the eighteenth and nineteenth centuries, the British fleet had risen to become the best in the world, but in order to find large enough crews to man those ships, the government needed to stop issuing the documents and rescind some of those that had already been granted. Sailors looking to stay on the proper side of the law began joining the navy as expected, although it did not have much of an impact on piracy. While most pirates saw the benefit of having a safe harbor to which they could escape, not to mention the protection from prosecution for their crimes, they were not about to give up their ability to raid ships at will in order to serve under an English officer.

It did not hurt that there were plenty of places for the pirates operating in the Caribbean to escape for a while if things started to get too dangerous. There are more than seven thousand islands spread out across the Caribbean, most of which are still uninhabited to this day. Those islands have countless hidden coves and inlets that made for perfect hiding spots for a ship looking to avoid detection. After spending days at sea on marauding missions, it was not uncommon for a pirate crew to sail into one of these makeshift harbors for a little rest and relaxation.

There were even certain port cities where privateers and pirates were welcomed. Places where they could come ashore to sell their plundered goods and purchase supplies without fear of being attacked or arrested.

Take Port Royal for example, an outpost that was originally founded by the Spanish, but later became a haven for those who were looking to avoid any unnecessary entanglements with the established European powers.

Port Royal

Located on the island of Jamaica, Port Royal was established as a colony in 1518, making it one of the earliest settlements in the Caribbean. Other than being a good place to grow sugar cane, the Spanish did not find much else of interest there. Still, due to its location, it became a strategically important outpost, which is why the Spanish maintained a presence there to ensure that it did not fall into enemy hands. That proved to be a wise decision, as by the middle of the sixteenth century, Port Royal had grown into an important center for commerce located along a bustling trading route.

For 146 years the Spanish held onto the city, using it as a place to collect goods from across the Americas before shipping them back to Europe. But in 1655, the English invaded Jamaica, capturing it from Spain and immediately turning it into a British colony. This was a turning point for Port Royal, which remained an important city in terms of mercantile trade but soon developed into a favorite stop for privateers and pirates too.

Under English rule, any ship operating with a letter of marque issued by the British or the Dutch was welcome in Port Royal. The location of the city made it a good base of operations for those looking to prey on Spanish merchant vessels and it did not take long for privateers to flock to its harbor. As a result, the city experienced an economic boom that led to dozens of new shops and warehouses being built to support the influx of plundered goods.

Over time, word got out that Port Royal was the place to go if you wanted to sell off anything that may have been acquired under less-than-proper circumstances. This attracted not just a constant flow of English and Dutch privateers, but also a fair number of pirates who were willing to risk coming ashore there. The city became a neutral zone of sorts where any ship, other than those operating under the Spanish flag, was welcomed. Merchants set up shop there to acquire merchandise, without asking questions about how it was actually obtained. This made the city the perfect place for anyone looking to fence Spanish treasures that had been seized out on the high seas.

The loss of Port Royal to the English, combined with the rise of pirate activity in the waters surrounding Jamaica, had a profound effect on the Spanish. The increased attacks on their cargo vessels disrupted trade routes and shipping schedules. This made it increasingly difficult to keep their colonies supplied with the goods that they needed, which only served to fuel the growth in trade that traveled in and out of Port Royal. It also gave rise to a unique economic symbiosis between the merchants who operated in the port and the pirates that frequented it.

Playing both sides of the coin, many merchants sponsored Spanish expeditions to deliver goods to the colonies in the Americas. But those same merchants frequently funded privateers who raided Spanish ships and settlements as well. This resulted in a constant flow of plundered booty into Port Royal, which became one of the wealthiest communities in the Americas thanks in large part to this high level of pirate activity. Before long, the amount of commerce that passed through the town far outstripped the revenue generated from growing sugar cane on the island—the main resource that Jamaica had to offer under Spanish rule prior to blossoming into an economic powerhouse.

The decision to embrace privateers and pirates brought more than wealth and trade to Port Royal, it also delivered a measure of security. The British knew that they didn't have a sufficient number of troops to defend themselves from either the Spanish or the French, should they choose to attack. But the large number of heavily armed ships that came and went from the port were enough to give even those European powers reason to pause. Capturing the city might have been possible, but win or lose, it would be a costly battle. That was too much of a risk for England's enemies to take.

By the 1660s, Port Royal had become the most notorious pirate stronghold in the entire Caribbean. The city had gained a reputation as a rough-and-tumble destination that was said to have one drinking establishment for every ten residents. The streets of the city were frequented not only by buccaneers and thieves, but by slave traders, prostitutes, and murderers too. Famous pirates like Henry Morgan, Edward Teach (aka Blackbeard), and Christopher Myngs were just a few of the famous pirates who became frequent visitors.

A combination of wealth and lawlessness made Port Royal a place to be avoided for most upstanding citizens. The city gained a reputation for drunken debauchery, bloody duels, gambling, prostitution, and all manner of seedy activity. Fortunes were made and lost in its markets and shops, while the pirate activity served as the engine that drove the Jamaican economy. That was good for business provided you were a pirate, privateer, or merchant who operated there, but it soon became evident that everyone else should stay away.

The uneasy peace between the British authorities and the pirates that frequented Port Royal did not hold forever. While it served the Crown's best interest to allow the buccaneers to have access to the city for years, eventually the Royal Navy grew in strength and stature, no longer requiring the assistance from privateers to keep Jamaica safe. This was especially true when the English signed the Treaty of Madrid with the Spanish in 1670, effectively ending hostilities between the two nations. As part of that agreement, all letters of marque were revoked, leaving hundreds of privateers out of work and scrambling for a new way to make a living.

In 1674, former privateer Henry Morgan became Sir Henry Morgan and was appointed the lieutenant governor of Jamaica. Part of his duties were to bolster the defense of Port Royal and end piracy in the region once and for all. Morgan had become a very wealthy man thanks to his own piracy, and despite his orders he remained a close associate and business partner of many outlaw captains. At that time, the city was still a popular port of call for privateers and buccaneers alike, even though they were not quite as welcome there as they once had been.

For his part, Morgan tried to find a balance between the interests of the pirates that had helped defend Port Royal and those of the British Crown. But the same treaty that forged a peace between the English and the Spanish also brought about a change in attitude towards privateers on the part of the English. Once seen as crucial allies, the Royal Navy now saw privateers as antiquated and unnecessary. With their services no longer needed, the buccaneers were eventually branded as outlaws, with British ships going to great lengths to hunt down and capture the seagoing raiders.

Jamaica declared piracy illegal in 1687, bringing an end to the days when Port Royal was seen as a safe harbor for buccaneers and privateers. Instead of being greeted with open arms as they had been in the past, pirates were attacked, arrested, and often hung from the gallows instead. Meanwhile, the steady stream of trade that those ships had brought into the city was replaced with a thriving slave market, which continued to bolster Port Royal's economic fortunes. The slaves who were constantly arriving from Africa were sold off at a rapid pace and sent to work on plantations, in mines, and at other locations across the New World.

In 1692 tragedy struck Jamaica when a massive earthquake—followed closely by a tsunami—struck the island. Port Royal took the brunt of the damage, with a large section of the city being reduced to rubble. It is estimated that about 6,500 people lived in the town at the time, with about two thousand permanent structures in place. But years of building on perilous ground and stacking too many houses, shops, and taverns into such a small space caught up with the residents of the city, many of whom were killed in the disaster.

In the years that followed, several attempts were made to rebuild the port, although numerous setbacks kept it from ever regaining its former glory. The longer the city was out of commission, the easier it was for other ports to lure away its merchants and ship traffic. By the middle of the eighteenth century the town had mostly become a curious footnote in the history of the Caribbean; a place that was once the most infamous and notorious pirate den in the entire world.

Nassau

Just as Port Royal saw its fortunes forever changed, another Caribbean city was about to take its place as a popular pirate stronghold. In 1696 the recently rebuilt port city of Nassau in the Bahamas played host to a famous pirate named Henry Every, instantly gaining a reputation as a place that was friendly to buccaneers. In the years that followed, it grew to become a notorious haven for brigands and outlaws, inviting in a cast of unusual characters.

When Every arrived in Nassau, he was one of the most wanted men in the entire world. He had reportedly raided dozens of ships throughout the Indian Ocean and claimed large amounts of plunder in the process. But just as the Royal Navy started to close in on his position, he fled to the Caribbean where he hoped to avoid capture. Once there, he used his enormous wealth to convince Nicholas Trott, the governor of Nassau, to allow him to safely sail into the harbor. Reportedly, Every not only offered up plenty of silver and gold, but his ship the *Fancy* as well. At the time that he arrived in port, it was said that the *Fancy* was loaded down with more than fifty tons of elephant tusks and a hundred barrels of gunpowder. That cargo alone was worth a small fortune.

Unfortunately for Every, he could not stay hidden from his pursuers, even in the Caribbean. Both the Royal Navy and the East India Company—whose ships he routinely raided—were still searching for him. The navy sent orders to Trott to arrest the pirate on sight, but the clever and resourceful Every managed to evade capture and slip out of Nassau. What happened to him next is anyone's guess, because the legendary buccaneer completely disappeared, never to be seen or heard from again.

When word got out that Every had been allowed to dock in Nassau, other pirates began to come and go from the port as well, covertly conducting business there. It would take another decade before it would truly transform into a true pirate stronghold, eventually developing into a base of operations for some of the most famous and infamous outlaws to ever sail the Caribbean.

The turning point for Nassau came in 1706, when France and Spain launched a major assault on the city. It was the second such bombardment in three years, and it was enough to drive out the British government and most of the citizens that had been living there. Soon, news spread amongst English privateers that the port had been mostly abandoned, which made it an even more attractive destination for those operating on the edge of the law. The port was severely damaged by the raid, but it was still an excellent place to launch counter attacks against French and Spanish ships.

As mentioned, England and Spain eventually made peace with one another, resulting in many privateers having their letters of marque canceled. Rather than give up their life as a buccaneer however, most turned to piracy instead. With few legitimate ports open to them, those renegade ships began to make their way to the open port in Nassau. It wasn't long before the city was almost entirely made up of pirates, with a few merchants, shops keepers, tavern owners, and other businessmen and women finding a way to make a living in that raucous environment.

At its height, it is estimated that more than a thousand pirates called Nassau home. Thus it was a difficult place to attack, even for Europe's most powerful navies. The men and women living there even appointed their own governor, along with a few other city officials, essentially creating an independent republic of pirates. The infamous Blackbeard himself served as the town magistrate for a time, dispensing justice as he saw fit.

Order was maintained throughout the city thanks to a strict code of conduct adhered to by the pirates. In the case of Nassau, this pirate code extended not just to the city itself, but to the ships that the citizens served on. All of the buccaneers living there agreed to a democratic approach to how their vessels were run, with captains voted into position by the crews themselves. They even agreed to split the plunder that they acquired evenly, giving each man aboard the vessel an equal share.

The community that developed in Nassau was extremely unique. In the past, pirates had occasionally joined forces with one another because it was mutually beneficial for all parties involved. But the newly established pirate republic was something new altogether, as its residents created their own form of government, along with laws and rules, to help maintain order. This resulted in something similar to the pirate states that had existed in the ancient Mediterranean Sea, although in this case the pirate republic grew out of common goals and enemies, rather than a shared ancestral history.

Nassau also happened to be home to two of the most well-known female pirates of all time, both of whom sailed with the infamous Calico Jack Rackham. Anne Bonny met Rackham in the pirate-infested city when she moved there with her husband at the age of fifteen. Intrigued by the charismatic buccaneer, it wasn't long before she abandoned her marriage and sailed off with him instead. Dressed as a man, she served as part of Calico Jack's crew, before eventually giving birth to his child.

In contrast to Bonny, Mary Read was already a pirate when she met Rackham. Dressing like a man at an early age, she joined the British military, serving with distinction in a number of battles. Along the way, she also met a man, fell in love, and got married. When her husband died, Read abandoned her domestic lifestyle and hopped aboard a ship bound for the West Indies. While en route, the vessel was attacked by pirates who came aboard to claim their booty. Seeing an opportunity, Read volunteered to join the crew and eventually became a privateer in the service of the King of England. This led her to sail to the port of Nassau, where she connected with Rackham and Bonny.

The three outlaws stole a ship and sailed out into the Caribbean together, along with a full crew. Reportedly no one onboard knew that Bonny and Read were women, save for Rackham himself. However, the sloop they were aboard didn't get far as they soon found themselves under attack from a pirate hunter. Most of the crew surrendered without much of a fight, but Bonny, Read, and Rackham attempted to defend their vessel. They were overwhelmed by their attackers and were whisked off to Jamaica to stand trial.

All three were convicted of piracy and sentenced to hang, which was the fate of Calico Jack. But Bonny and Read both told the magistrate that they were pregnant, and they were both imprisoned while they awaited the births of their children. Read died during childbirth, while Bonny remained in prison until she gave birth. What became of her after that is unknown, as no further records can be found.

Because Nassau was made up of so many former English privateers, most of the pirates in the city originally elected to not attack British ships. As the years passed, that sentiment began to weaken and any vessels that strayed within range of the outlaws were deemed fair game. This had the unintended consequence of drawing the ire of the Royal Navy, which up until that point had mostly left the city alone. As the attacks increased, the English decided to put an end to the pirate republic.

A British ship battles pirates.

When King George I of England appointed a former privateer by the name of Woodes Rogers as governor of the Bahamas, he charged him with stamping out piracy there. To that end, in 1718 Rogers sailed to Nassau with seven ships and a royal pardon for anyone who turned themselves in, renouncing their outlaw ways. Many of the city's inhabitants accepted the offer and gave up their life of piracy for good. Others fled the town and continued their marauding ways, although now they were being hunted by the Royal Navy.

By reasserting control over the city, the British not only dropped the curtain on the pirate republic, but hastened the conclusion of the Golden Age of Piracy as well. By the 1720s, the Royal Navy was growing into the greatest military force to ever set sail and its considerable might was routinely being directed to stamp out piracy wherever it could be found. All acts of piracy were outlawed in nearly every corner of the British Empire, with convicted pirates typically being hanged for their crimes.

It was about this time that the use of privateers was also quickly falling out favor. For centuries, private individuals who owned ships were given permission to strike enemy vessels and settlements without fear of legal reprisal from the country that commissioned them. But many of those privateers ended up turning to piracy over time, making them a threat to any ships they encountered out on the water. With established professional navies quickly becoming the norm for the European powers, the need for privateers had diminished greatly. This meant fewer letters of marque were being issued, which in turn led to fewer opportunities for independent sailors to transition to a life of piracy.

Piracy and the Slave Trade

Just as the Golden Age of Piracy was coming to an end in the Caribbean, an economic shift was starting to take place in the region. The demand for sugar was on the rise in Europe, particularly in Great Britain. In order to meet that need, sugar plantations popped up on a number of islands, as the climate there was perfect for growing the sugarcane plant. Sugar production was extremely labor intensive however, so in order for the business to be viable, slave labor was needed to work the fields. Slave ships began arriving in large numbers, bringing thousands of Africans to provide the workers that were necessary to keep the supply of sugar flowing.

Throughout history, the slave trade and piracy have always been linked closely with one another, and the Caribbean was no different. While most of the slave ships sailing out of Africa were owned and operated by legitimate merchants, those vessels often made tempting targets for buccaneers. Built to hold cargo rather than for speed, the slave ships often had small crews and were easily outgunned by the other ships that they encountered while at sea. This made them easy to capture, and since the slave markets of the New World did not care where their merchandise came from, it was easy for the pirates to sell the prisoners off for a large profit.

Some of the slaves who were captured in these raids volunteered to join the pirate crew. For them, living the life of an outlaw was much more preferable to the hard labor that they faced while enslaved on a plantation or in a mine. Therefore, it was not uncommon for ships to have a number of African crew members working alongside their European counterparts. It has even been said that one of Blackbeard's most trusted companions was a former slave named Black Caesar, and integrated crews were often the norm. But if a pirate ship carrying liberated slaves was captured by the authorities, the European buccaneers were hanged for their crimes, while the African pirates were sold back into slavery.

Of course, the Caribbean was not the only destination that saw an influx of slave ships in the early part of the eighteenth century. The US also began importing more African slaves at that time, while tens of thousands more were sent to Brazil. With piracy on the decline across the Americas, it became easier and cheaper for slave traders to transport more and more slaves to the New World. By reducing the number of pirates out on the water, slavery actually began to dramatically increase. The Royal Navy even played a role in that slave-trading process, as the English were committed to protecting their economic interests in the New World.

The downfall of Nassau and the end of the pirate republic was a massive blow to the brigands who were operating in the Caribbean. From that point onward, their numbers began to dwindle rapidly and it was not long before they found themselves to be a vanishing breed. But they did not disappear altogether—at least not at first. Some fled the region and headed to Western Africa, where they could more directly prey on slavers. Others remained but shifted their raiding activity to the Atlantic coasts of North and South America, leaving the West Indies and the rest of the Caribbean behind. By that point, the risks and rewards associated with piracy were quickly growing disproportionate, as the Royal Navy doled out justice on the open ocean with cold efficiency.

Pirate activity in the New World lingered on for another century, although at a greatly reduced level. The early 1800s saw a resurgence of piracy along the Atlantic and Gulf coasts of the United States, as well as in the Caribbean, although it never quite approached the same levels that it had during the pirate heyday. Those years were a mere shadow of the Golden Age, although a few buccaneers still managed to leave their mark on history.

Piracy after the Golden Age
Jean Lafitte

The most famous of the pirates to come out of this era was the French privateer, Jean Lafitte. Sailing in the Gulf of Mexico, and operating out of New Orleans, Jean and his brother Pierre began as smugglers, bringing contraband cargo into the US. Later, they launched their careers as full-blown pirates, building a quick and efficient fleet of corsair ships that raided other vessels along America's Gulf coast.

Despite building a small and prosperous smuggling empire in the Gulf of Mexico, Lafitte is probably best remembered for his role in the War of 1812. That conflict found the United States caught up in the Napoleonic Wars that were taking place in Europe at time, as bitter feuds between the English and French bubbled over into the New World. As a move to cut off trade routes and supply lines back to France, the Royal Navy moved into the Caribbean and the Gulf of Mexico. Naturally, this reignited the decades-long battle between the US and England.

The final battle of the War of 1812 took place in New Orleans, where the British fleet was advancing on the mouth of the Mississippi River. General Andrew Jackson was in charge of US forces there, which had confiscated eight ships belonging to French smugglers in an earlier raid. Recognizing that he needed Lafitte's help, Jackson met with the pirate and asked for his assistance against the British. In exchange, the American general offered pardons for any of Lafitte's men who were willing to fight and help man the vessels.

When the battle finally took place, both Jean and Pierre Lafitte, as well as their men, served with distinction, helping to defend New

Portrait of Jean Lefitte.

Orleans from the Royal Navy. In fact, Jackson later commended the pirates for their skill and bravery in combat, praising them for their accuracy and efficiency in using cannons to ward off the British. It was said that these former buccaneers were even better at handling their weapons than the vaunted Royal Navy, who were resoundingly defeated by the rag-tag American force and their allies.

Afterwards, true to his word, Jackson requested and received a full pardon for Lafitte and the men who had helped defend New Orleans. This did not end the Frenchman's career as a smuggler and privateer however, as he later went on to establish a pirate base on Galveston Island off the coast of Texas. From there, he served as a spy for the Spanish for a time, while he established his own colony of buccaneers. He even issued letters of marque to other privateers, authorizing them to attack and plunder the ships they encountered in the Gulf of Mexico.

It is believed that Jean Lafitte perished in an attack on two Spanish ships sailing off the coast of Honduras in 1823. The death of the handsome and charismatic buccaneer also signaled the end of pirate activity throughout the Americas, including the gulf and the Caribbean. By 1830, piracy was outlawed in most locations around the world, with every major naval power hunting down and killing any rogue privateers and buccaneers that remained. That included the United States, which was building a small, but formidable, navy of its own by that time. The US's fleet would eventually be tasked with securing the waters all along the American coast, where pirate activity of any kind was no longer tolerated.

Evolving Piracy

The 1830s ushered in another important change that hastened the end of pirate activity as well—engine-powered ships. By then, most of the new ships that were being built were converted over to steam engines, drawing a close to the Age of Sail. This made it increasingly difficult for pirates and privateers to continue to operate around the globe, as vessels with steam engines were more expensive and complex to build and operate. The old wooden sailing ships that had been used for generations were quickly outclassed in terms of speed, maneuverability, and weaponry. This left the few remaining buccaneers at a severe disadvantage, making them easy targets for the increasingly sophisticated modern navy.

Still, there were always a few individuals that continued pursuing piracy as a way of life, and from time to time they would stir up trouble on the seas. Pirates and smugglers played a small role during the American Civil War for instance, continuing to raid slave ships right up until the conclusion of that conflict. By then, the glory days of the pirate were well behind them, with only a handful of daring—some would say foolhardy—outlaws who were still willing to risk an encounter with a modern warship on the open water.

The latter half of the nineteenth century may have closed the book on the pirates of the Caribbean Sea, but the legacy that those larger-than-life characters left behind certainly remains. Today, most of the pop culture references regarding pirates, right down to how they look and speak, come directly from the Golden Age of Piracy as it played out in the Caribbean. Movies, television shows, books, video games, and countless other modern depictions of buccaneers use that era as a classic frame of reference, often romanticizing it along the way.

Yes, the pirates that sailed the high seas at that time were outlaws who operated on the fringes of society. But they were also free men and women who had control over their own lives and destinies. At that time, there were few individuals outside of the aristocracy who could make that same claim. The profession brought with it a sense of freedom and rebellion that continues to resonate with individuals today. It is not uncommon for start-up tech companies to fly the famous skull and crossbones Jolly Roger pirate flag for instance, while artists, hackers, counter-culturists, and others pay homage to the pirate way of life in other ways. The original pirates of the Caribbean would probably take some pride in that.

Blackbeard.

The Tale of Calico Jack

Throughout history there have been examples of individuals who were hailed as heroes by some and viewed as vile villains by others. Men like Sir Francis Drake, Henry Morgan, or even the Barbarossa brothers were richly rewarded for their service to their nation, with their exploits celebrated by their fellow countrymen. Meanwhile, their enemies branded them as thieves and murderers, often blurring the lines between whether these figures were legitimate sea captains or oceangoing outlaws.

Sometimes, a pirate is just a pirate. Such was the case with Calico Jack—a man who quickly rose to prominence in the Caribbean Sea during the Golden Age of Piracy, only to fall from grace just as quickly. But not before he left his mark on the history of pirates, becoming one of the more colorful characters to ever set sail.

As with many pirates of the era, not much is known about Calico Jack's early years. He is thought to have been born in England in December of 1682 with the given name of John Rackham. He later went by the more informal name of Jack, with his penchant for wearing bright, colorful calico clothing providing the rest of his famous moniker.

It isn't clear exactly when or how Rackham made his way to the Caribbean, but the first official reference to him comes in a ship's logbook dating back to 1718, which would have made him about thirty-five years old at the time. That log was from a sloop called *Ranger*, which was under the command of Captain Charles Vane. A well-known pirate in his own right, Vane operated out of the Nassau Pirate Republic in the Bahamas, patrolling the nearby trade lanes for merchant vessels to raid and plunder.

One such voyage took the *Ranger* as far north as New York City, where Vane and his crew raided and plundered several small ships. Then, on their return voyage to the Caribbean, they came across a large, well-armed, French cargo vessel known as a man-of-war. The ship likely carried a great deal of cargo, making it an enticing target, despite the fact that it was considerably larger than the *Ranger*. The ship's size and many guns gave Vane reason for pause. Ultimately, he made the decision to avoid engaging the man-of-war in combat, much to the chagrin of his men.

Rackham was serving as quartermaster on that voyage and was reportedly one of the most vocal critics of Vane's decision. He pointed out that the man-of-war was more than likely weighted down with cargo, making it less maneuverable and an easier target, despite its larger size. The French vessel was also likely to have enough plunder to make their trip a highly lucrative one not only for Vane, but for the entire crew. The larger vessel would even make a fine addition to their fleet, Jack pointed out, greatly expanding their cargo capacity and firepower at the same time.

As was common with the pirates of that era, the crew of the *Ranger* took a vote, with most siding with Rackham. The captain was able to muster up only a fraction of the crew to vote in his favor. Despite the outcome of the ballots, Vane made the decision to leave the man-of-war behind, saying that when it came to such matters, the captain's decision was not only final, but outranked everyone else's votes.

This did not sit particularly well with Calico Jack or the crew members who had voted for his plan of action. Over the next few days, discontent grew amongst the men, who felt that by letting the man-of-war escape they had also allowed a major opportunity to slip through their fingers. Rackham, sensing a shift in morale and opinion coming, called for a second vote. This time the men would cast their lots to determine their confidence in the captain to continue to command their ships and lead them into battle.

Once again, the vote was overwhelmingly against Vane, who still only had a handful of supporters in his corner. This time however, the

Calico Jack.

crew voted to remove him as captain and promote Calico Jack to that position instead. After assuming command, Rackham ordered Vane and his men—which included one Edward Teach, aka Blackbeard—into the second ship that was a part of their fleet. Giving his former mates the smaller ship, Rackham outfitted the men with food, supplies, and ammo before sending them on their way.

Now fully in command, Rackham took the *Ranger* and her crew back to the Caribbean where they embarked on several raiding missions. Not known as a great tactician or a bold buccaneer, Calico Jack nevertheless found success by sticking to simple tactics that were proven to work. For instance, he generally preferred to prey upon smaller ships that sailed close to shore, using the *Ranger's* superior firepower to frighten them into surrendering. During one such raid, the men managed to capture a wealthy vessel sailing out of Jamaica known as the *Kingston*. Rackham immediately took a liking to the vessel and turned it into his flagship.

Unfortunately for Calico Jack and his men, the raid that allowed them to capture the *Kingston* took place within sight of the city of Port Royal. The blatant display of aggression and disregard for authority angered many of the merchants who frequented the town. Those merchants pooled their money together and hired a Spanish pirate hunter to track down Rackham and either capture or kill him.

The pirate hunter gave pursuit, but Rackham and his men were not only fast, but clever. They sailed the *Kingston* into shallow waters that were difficult for the larger Spanish vessel to navigate. Under the cover of darkness, the pirate captain and his men abandoned their newly acquired ship and slipped away into the forests of Isla de los Pinos, a small island off the coast of Cuba. There, they found refuge away from the pirate hunters, who captured their ship and claimed its rich cargo but were not as successful in apprehending the outlaws themselves. Calico Jack and his team came up empty handed in terms of loot, but at least they were still free men.

A further demonstration of how clever Rackham could be came not long after he and his men had captured a small sloop and sailed it to Cuba to make repairs. While they were in the harbor, a Spanish galleon arrived on the scene with a small English ship in tow. The galleon had been sent to the Caribbean to hunt for pirates and protect the shipping lanes, which meant its crew was always on the lookout for brigands. Upon spotting Rackham, the Spanish crew made a move to apprehend the outlaw, but a low tide prevented the larger warship from entering the harbor. Instead, the galleon dropped anchor at the entrance to the port and decided to wait until morning when conditions would be more favorable.

Seeing that their escape path was blocked, Calico Jack waited for nightfall and then ordered his crew into a rowboat. Quickly and quietly they approached the captured English sloop, which was still securely tied to the stern of the Spanish galleon. Stealthily they climbed aboard, disarmed the guards, and captured the vessel. Not long after, they raised the ship's sails and snuck off into the night without the Spanish noticing.

The following morning, the crew of the galleon unloaded their cannons on Rackham's original sloop, blasting it to smithereens as it sat in the harbor. But by then there was no one onboard and Rackham and his crew were already miles away. Through the smoke and cannon fire, the Spanish had not even realized that their captured English ship had vanished without a trace, taking the pirate crew along with it.

In 1719 a change was in the air for the pirates of the Caribbean. The British Royal Navy had turned a blind eye to their activities for years, but back home in England public opinion was turning against buccaneers and privateers alike. The age of the seagoing scoundrel was nearing an end and there was now little tolerance for piracy in any form.

That year, the British parliament sent Woodes Rogers to the Bahamas to assume the role of governor. Rogers, who was a former privateer himself, came with an offer of general amnesty for any pirate who asked for a pardon. Those who did not take the deal would be hunted down and hanged for their crimes. Unsurprisingly, hundreds of sailors took him up on the offer, with many jumping at the chance to return to a normal way of life without fear of imprisonment or hanging.

Amongst those who asked for the pardon were John Rackham and his small band of pirates. Calico Jack told Rogers that he and his men never wanted to turn to a life of piracy but were forced to do so by their former captain, Charles Vane. There was no love lost between Rogers and Vane, who had crossed paths on more than one occasion in the past. Believing Rackham's story, Vane granted the pardon, making him a free man who was completely absolved of his crimes.

Anne Bonny.

Rackham quickly strayed from the straight and narrow once again. While in Nassau meeting with Woodes, he also met a young woman by the name of Anne Bonny. Before long the two became lovers, but there was one major obstacle that prevented the two from sailing off into the sunset together. Anne just so happened to be married to James Bonny, a man who worked for Governor Woodes Rogers.

The torrid affair was quite the scandal in Nassau, particularly when James Bonny discovered that his wife was cavorting with a former pirate. Upon learning this, he took Anne to meet with Governor Rogers, who ruled that she should be whipped for committing the crime of adultery. When word of that punishment reached Rackham he offered to pay James a handsome sum of money to buy Anne's freedom and give him a divorce. Bonny refused however, causing Anne and her outlaw lover to steal a small ship and escape together, leaving Nassau behind forever.

Despite the fact that he had just been pardoned by Rogers, Calico Jack was soon back to pirate ways, assembling a new crew in just a matter of days. Seeing no other way for he and Anne to be together, the two lived as fugitives in the Caribbean accompanied by a small band of outlaws. Within days of their escape from Nassau, Rackham was once again leading attacks on small ships and stealing cargo out on the Caribbean.

Although he did not know it at first, one of Rackham's new crew members was actually a woman named Mary Read. Disguised as a man, she joined his crew and soon earned her place within the band of pirates. Eventually, Jack and Anne came to realize that another woman was in their midst, but they kept that fact a secret from the rest of the crew. Having a woman serve aboard a pirate ship was extremely unusual under any circumstances, but two female crew members was a particular rarity. This only served to add to the legend of Calico Jack in the years to come.

Over the next few months, Rackham and his new crew made quite a nuisance of themselves in the waters off Jamaica. The group captured and plundered a number of ships, most of which belonged to local fishermen who rarely ventured far out to sea. Small in size, not particularly fast, and generally unarmed, fishing boats made for easy pickings. During the turbulent Golden Age of Piracy, those vessels were low risk, as well as low reward. Fishermen rarely put up much resistance to pirate attacks, but they also didn't usually carry much of real value either. Plundering those ships allowed Rackham to stay in business, but he and his crew were not going to grow wealthy preying on those small ships either.

The constant raids against the local fishermen eventually drew the ire of Nicholas Lawes, the sitting governor of Jamaica. In October of 1720, he issued a bounty for the capture of Calico Jack and the rest of his crew, charging them with piracy on the high seas. Over the course of the previous few months, Rackham and his men had stolen a ship and attacked boats up and down the shores of the island. They had also disrupted trade and harassed innocent people along the way.

The warrant for Rackham's arrest caught the attention of several prominent pirate hunters, who soon sailed out of Nassau to search for the buccaneer. They picked up his trail near Jamaica and went looking for his ship in the surrounding waters. Thanks to a distinctive flag that flew from his mast, it was always easy to identify Rackham's ship. While many pirates created and flew their own flag at the time, Calico Jack's was quite unique. His featured an all-black background with a white skull prominently placed in the middle and two crossed cutlasses underneath. The flag became so iconic that it served to enhance Rackham's reputation and status. In fact, that very flag has survived across the centuries and remains an iconic symbol for piracy even in the twenty-first century.

In October of 1720 Calico Jack's string of luck ran out. One evening, while his ship was at anchor, Rackham and his crew were celebrating their recent success with pirates from another crew that had stopped by to join them. They enjoyed music and dancing on deck, with copious amounts of alcohol consumed by all who were in attendance. Both crews were so intoxicated that they did not notice the approach of a well-known pirate hunter by the name of Jonathan Barnet, who was able to board Rackham's ship before anyone even realized that he was there.

The battle that broke out ended quickly, as most of the pirates were simply too drunk to put up much of a resistance. Reportedly, just Rackham, Anne Bonny, and Mary Read offered any defense of the ship, but they too soon found themselves subdued by Barnet's men. The entire fight was over within minutes, and the notorious Calico Jack, along with his young lover, had been captured at last.

A few days later, Barnet sailed into Spanish Town in Jamaica where he turned Rackham, and his band of outlaws, over to the authorities. Collecting his reward, the pirate hunter was soon on his way, although not before the court passed judgment on the brigands. All of the men were convicted of piracy and sentenced to hang for their crimes. During the trial however, both Anne Bonny and Mary Read revealed that they were pregnant, resulting in a lighter sentence for the two women. Both were sent to a nearby prison, where they were incarcerated while awaiting the arrival of their unborn children.

Anne Bonny and Mary Read.

Not long after the judge handed down his ruling, Rackham was transferred back to Port Royal where his sentence was carried out. On November 18, 1720, Calico Jack was hung by the neck until he was dead during a public execution. His body was then put on display as both a warning and a deterrent for other would-be pirates. The gruesome display was meant to give others a glimpse of the fate that awaited them should they take the same path as the notorious pirate.

Over the next few months, the rest of Rackham's crew were found guilty of piracy and mutiny. Most ended up hanging in the gallows in either Port Royal or the city of Kingston, Jamaica. Governor Woodes Rogers had initially come to the Bahamas with the goal of ending piracy in as peaceful and amicable fashion as possible. But when a private accepted his offer of a pardon, then went back on his word, Rogers was quick to extract vengeance for their crimes. Sentencing was swift and harsh, with most convicted buccaneers being put to death in a timely fashion.

As for Anne Bonny and Mary Read, both only escaped being executed along with the rest of the crew thanks to their pregnancies. Both were imprisoned in Fort Charles, Jamaica, where they could be kept under observation until their claims could be confirmed. Had either of them not been pregnant, they likely would have been convicted and hung alongside their male counterparts. Pirates—male or female—were viewed as equals in the eyes of the law.

As it turned out, both women were declared pregnant, which bought them a stay of execution, at least for a time. The two women were still kept under lock and key, and Read died in her prison cell in April of 1721. The exact cause of her death is unknown, but it is believed to have been the result of complications during childbirth.

What ultimately became of Bonny remains a mystery. No record of her release from the prison has ever been found, nor is there an indication of whether or not she died there. Medical records from the era do not reveal her giving birth either, so it is open to speculation as to whether or not she was pregnant at all. With her life potentially in jeopardy, she may have chosen to make that claim in order to avoid being sent to the gallows.

Calico Jack Rackham is the perfect example of a pirate who was far more famous than he was successful. All told, his career as a buccaneer only lasted for about two years, ending with his capture, conviction, and execution. His colorful name and clever personality helped to inflate his legend amongst the generations that would follow, but compared to some of his contemporaries, Rackham was not especially noteworthy.

During those two years of marauding, Calico Jack did manage to plunder numerous ships. But his penchant for attacking small, easily overpowered vessels meant that he was never able to acquire much in the way of plunder. A smart, charismatic man, he did inspire his crew to stand by him, even when they were not earning any serious wealth. Unfortunately for most of his crew, they also ended up paying the price for that loyalty once they were captured by Jonathan Barnet.

Despite his relatively modest successes as a pirate, Calico Jack does remain one of the few men from the Golden Age of Piracy who are remembered all the way into the twenty-first century. A large part of that is because of the two female buccaneers on his crew. By all accounts, Anne Bonny and Mary Read took their roles as part of the crew very seriously, with both standing out as bold outlaws in their own right. The women worked the ship just like the men and were always prepared to defend themselves and their captain. While female pirates were not completely unheard of, they were definitely few and far between. The fact that Bonny and Read were able to earn the trust of Rackham, and serve as his advisors and lieutenants, is a testament to what remarkable women they were.

The other legacy that Calico Jack has handed down through the ages is his famous pirate flag. During the seventeenth and eighteenth century, it was not uncommon for seafaring marauders to fly their own unique standard when going into battle. Most of those flags were simple, unremarkable, and utterly forgettable. But Rackham's distinctive design featuring a skull and two crossed cutlasses has managed to stand the test of time, becoming a part of popular culture. His banner, along with the equally iconic skull and crossbones, has become synonymous with piracy during the Golden Age, enduring through the decades that followed. Those same flags often adorn the walls of college dorm rooms and tech start-ups, where the pirate attitude is still celebrated to this day.

Unlike many of the other buccaneers who sailed the Caribbean, Calico Jack was not a privateer, merchant, or a slave trader. He was a pirate through and through, which was enough to cement a legacy that has lived on for three hundred years after his death. He may not have been the most successful outlaw to ever set sail, but he certainly had

Calico Jack's flag.

more style and panache than many of those who became extremely wealthy and famous by raiding enemy ships.

Most pirates of the Golden Age would probably have traded fame for fortune every time. But Calico Jack was not like most other pirates and it seems likely that he would be quite pleased with the legacy that he has left behind.

CHAPTER 5

The Pirates of the Persian Gulf and the Indian Ocean

Although there is a rich and storied history of piracy in the Mediterranean, Atlantic, and Caribbean, it should come as no surprise that pirate activity was not exclusive to those regions. In fact, nearly every ocean, sea, or gulf on the planet that has been used for maritime trade has experienced some level of piracy at one time or another. In some cases, that activity dates back thousands of years to the Age of Antiquity, while in others it ran parallel to the discovery of the New World. Ultimately, the proliferation of piracy to every corner of the globe serves as a reminder that no matter where humans go, human nature generally remains the same.

Persian Gulf Piracy
Mesopotamia and Onward

Sometimes referred to as the "Cradle of Civilization," the Middle East is credited as the place where the earliest organized communities began to take shape. The region where these civilizations first took root is referred to as Mesopotamia or the "Fertile Crescent" because it fell in a lush area located between the Tigris and Euphrates Rivers. Today, this part of the world is home to Iraq, Kuwait, Syria, and part of Turkey, with satellite kingdoms and city-states spreading out into what is now modern day Jordan, Israel, Lebanon, and Egypt.

Over time, some of the people living in Mesopotamia migrated west and settled along the Mediterranean basin, which as we already know turned into a hot bed of pirate activity. The history of piracy in the Mediterranean Sea is well chronicled, but not all of the tribes and kingdoms that sprung up across the Fertile Crescent traveled in that direction. Others formed around other bodies of water that bordered the Middle East, like the Persian Gulf and the Red Sea. Those turbulent waters played a significant role in opening trade routes and facilitating commerce amongst these fledgling kingdoms. Naturally, that meant seagoing raiders were not far behind.

The Dilmun were one of those groups of people who emerged out of the shadows of Mesopotamia. The civilization grew to prominence on the island that is now Bahrain, turning that location into an important center for trade sometime around 1000 BCE. Serving as a link between the Mesopotamians and the merchants from the Indus Valley, the Dilmun prospered thanks to a steady flow of luxury goods—such as silk, ivory, and gold—that passed through the city's marketplaces.

Thanks to its enviable location in the Persian Gulf, the Dilmun Kingdom soon grew in importance and wealth, although its stature was eventually threatened by marauders from the sea. The trade routes that connected through Dilmun were often targets of attack, with merchant vessels routinely being boarded and plundered. This made it unsafe and financially risky for traders to ship goods across the sea, so in order to circumvent the seafaring marauders, overland trade routes were adopted instead. While these routes took longer and were more expensive to maintain, they did keep the flow of goods moving. Sadly however, those same routes bypassed Dilmun altogether, causing the city-state's economy to collapse and Dilmun to become an obscure footnote in history.

By the eighth century BCE, Assyria was one of the most well-established and powerful empires in the Mesopotamian region, with a history that dated back more than a thousand years. Over that time, it too had established trading routes across the Persian Gulf, exchanging goods with other kingdoms both near and far. That included longer routes that extended all the way to the Indian subcontinent, where a number of other longstanding civilizations had emerged.

The details regarding pirate activity that took place during that era are somewhat scarce. Still, ancient records indicate that waterborne raiders were dangerous and disruptive enough that an Assyrian king by the name of Sennacherib launched a systematic campaign to wipe out piracy in the region. By all accounts, he found limited success and the pirates continued to attack ships traveling to and from India, which at the time were probably some of the most lucrative targets on any body of water on the planet.

Much like in the Mediterranean, pirate activity continued to be a significant challenge in the Persian Gulf for centuries, although it was never quite as prevalent there. While the civilizations that rose and fell around the Mediterranean were forced to deal with large pirate fleets and societies that embraced piracy as a way of life, there is little evidence that those activities were mirrored in the Persian Gulf. However, there were still plenty of outlaws to deal with out on the water, making the shipping of goods a risky, and sometimes costly, affair.

In the fifth century, the Sasanian Empire, the last of the Persian kingdoms before the rise of Islam, was harassed by pirates who raided ships coming and going from India. Centuries later, around 825 CE, Bahraini corsairs became the most feared force on the water just as trade activity was beginning to increase dramatically. By then, merchant ships were not sailing from just India, but China and Iran too. Accompanying that increased flow of traffic came more dangerous and organized marauders who were looking to profit off the plunder they took from merchant vessels.

Even Marco Polo made references to pirates in the Persian Gulf as part of his writings. He indicated that by the ninth century, the body of water was so dangerous to sail that Chinese ships would embark with as many as five hundred armed men to ensure that they would arrive at their intended port with their ships and cargo intact. Polo is known to exaggerate his numbers and stories from time to time, so the actual troop count may have been lower. But the mere fact that he mentions the threat, as well as how Chinese merchants dealt with it, provides some indication of how serious the challenges were for successfully navigating through the gulf.

One of the largest pirate strongholds in the Persian Gulf was located on the island of Socotra. Now part of modern day Yemen, Socotra was a thriving outlaw community between the eighth and thirteenth centuries, providing a sanctuary for the region's oceangoing rogues. The buccaneers who inhabited this island turned it into a market filled with illegally obtained goods. Whatever items they could plunder out on the ocean would go on sale there, with pirates and smugglers often trading the plunder that they had personally obtained for items that were better suited for their individual needs. Socotra was also a popular stopover for slave traders sailing back and forth between East Africa and Asia, proving that slavery was not just a lucrative business in Europe and along the Mediterranean Sea.

European Countries in the Persian Gulf

When Spain and Portugal signed the Treaty of Tordesillas in 1494, it supposedly cut the planet in half and gave each country control over a side of the globe. The treaty ceded most everything to the west of Europe to the Spanish, while the Portuguese received everything to the east. That meant that Spain gained control of most of the Americas, while Portugal claimed Africa, the Middle East, and the vast majority of Asia. Ultimately that treaty proved to be impossible to enforce and in time became obsolete. But for a while, it granted Portugal sole access to some of the wealthiest trade outposts in the entire world, including those stretching across the Persian Gulf to India and Asia.

Although Europe, Asia, and the Middle East all sit geographically close to one another, no European ships had ever ventured far enough east to establish trade with the nations along the Indian Ocean. In order for the Portuguese to exploit the access to the wealth of Asia as afforded them by the Treaty of Tordesillas, they needed to find a way to reach those distant ports. This proved to be a challenge, as it meant sailing south along the west coast of Africa, looping around the Cape of Good

A French ship battles corsairs.

Hope, and then proceeding north along the shores of East Africa—a long and difficult journey. As ship design, durability, and speed improved, that route eventually opened. Afterwards, Portuguese merchants were quick to capitalize on the opportunity to trade with Eastern nations, charting a course for what amounted to a new world of their very own.

With them came the first European pirates, although for a time Arab raiders remained the biggest threat to passing merchants. Those outlaws did not discriminate when it came to raiding and plundering ships, as they routinely attacked vessels from India, China, and Portugal with equal enthusiasm. Any boat that was loaded with the most valuable cargos, including gold, silver, silks, and spices was fair game. The Islamic corsairs also gained a great sense of satisfaction from attacking the ships of Christian nations, turning their illegal pirate activity into a holy war of sorts.

Increased merchant traffic created more opportunities for piracy, with hundreds of buccaneers taking to the Persian Gulf in the seventeenth and eighteenth centuries. So many seagoing raiders gathered along a 350-mile stretch of coastline between Khasab in modern day Oman and the island of Bahrain that it came to be known as the "Pirate Coast." The designation was so popular that it even appeared on maps and navigational charts of the time, signaling to ship captains to steer clear of the area at all costs. The raiders who operated along those shores were said to be greedy, bloodthirsty, and absolutely ruthless, making them foes to be avoided.

Over time, Portugal relinquished control of the region, while the British fleet stepped in as the preeminent navy on the world's oceans. As with elsewhere, the Brits launched a campaign to subdue the pirates who operated in the Persian Gulf, although those efforts met with only limited success. While it was true that the Arab ships and their crews' training tended to be no match for their English counterparts, many Muslim pirates saw their sea battles as a faceoff between Christianity and Islam, which only served to make them resist all the more.

Rahmah ibn Jabir ibn Adhbi Al Jalhami

During the nineteenth century, an Arab man known as Rahmah ibn Jabir ibn Adhbi Al Jalhami emerged as the Persian Gulf's most famous and notorious pirate. He was so successful and popular that at the height of his career he reportedly had more than two thousand followers, many of whom were former African slaves that Al Jalhami had freed who then joined his ranks.

Al Jalhami began his career by selling and trading horses. This provided him with enough money to purchase his first ship, which he immediately converted for use in piracy. Not long after he became a buccaneer, Al Jalhami scored his first major victory by plundering and stealing a much larger three-hundred-ton vessel. This ship allowed his crew to quickly swell in size to more than 350, turning the outlaw and his squad into a fearsome fighting force.

Unlike most of the pirates who operated in the Persian Gulf, Al Jalhami's motivations went beyond accumulating plunder and treasure. He was spurred on by his desire for revenge—as he felt that his tribe was slighted by the Al Khalifa, a regional ruler who maintained control of the region at the time. Al Jalhami fought alongside the Al Khalifa in a conflict with the Persians in Bahrain. But when that war was over, Al Jalhami and his allies believed that they did not receive the rewards that they deserved and had been promised. This created a struggle for power that ultimately resulted in Al Jalhami emerging victorious.

With his position of leadership secured, Al Jalhami turned the entire Al Jalahimah tribe to a life of piracy, with their actions directed squarely at punishing the Al Khalifa. He and his followers built a fortress that served as a base of operations in what is now Qatar and began conducting raids against merchant ships. They were so successful that they managed to capture dozens of vessels that were carrying goods and supplies to Al Jalhami's sworn enemy, soon negatively impacting his rival's economic state.

As a skilled diplomat and negotiator, Al Jalhami created alliances with other regional powers, including the Saudis and Omanis. This gave him allies in his fight against the Al Khalifa and allowed him to play a role in the politics of the region. He even managed to successfully broker a deal with the British, in which he agreed not to harbor fugitives provided the English vowed to leave his people and their stronghold alone.

One of the characteristics that defined Al Jalhami, and differentiated him from other pirates, was his strict adherence to rules and proper conduct in battle. He went to great lengths to ensure that he fought honorably and fairly when dealing with his adversaries. He also had the good sense to avoid attacking British ships so as not to draw the Royal Navy's ire. This good judgment allowed him to rally others to his side and helped turn him into a pirate lord who controlled large sections of the Qatari peninsula without drawing any undue attention from the European powers.

It is said that Al Jalhami met his ultimate end while battling the ships of the Al Khalifa on the waters of the Persian Gulf in 1826. In the heat of a pitched battle—and just as his enemy was closing in—he reportedly ignited the powder kegs on his own vessel, causing it to explode. This surprise maneuver not only claimed his life, but those of his crew, an enemy boarding party, and the pirate captain's own son, who was by his side at the time. It also cemented him as a legend amongst the Arabs whose exploits are still discussed to this day.

The British Royal Navy

Throughout the eighteenth and nineteenth centuries, the British Royal Navy attempted to quell piracy in the Persian Gulf on numerous occasions. For the most part, their efforts were fairly half-hearted, as the Arab marauders were rarely seen as a serious threat. The pirates who operated in these waters did routinely attack merchant vessels, but their actions did not cause any major disruptions to the trade routes. More often than not, the pirate activity was actually more focused on fighting other Muslim tribes, rather than attacking the ships that belonged to any of the major trading companies.

In order to establish and maintain order throughout the region, the British negotiated peace treaties with some of the more prominent local sheiks whose kingdoms lined the shores of the gulf. But the friction between the Christian and Islamic communities was difficult to avoid, and several conflicts arose during the early 1800s. The Royal Navy usually dealt with resistance with a harsh and swift response, often blockading ports and bombarding towns with their cannons. In 1853 however, the Treaty of Maritime Peace was signed, with the British Crown formerly recognizing some of the Arab kingdoms in exchange for a reduction in pirate activity and attacks.

The arrival of steam ships, which were faster and more agile than the traditional Arab vessels, hastened the downfall of piracy in the Persian Gulf as well. When those raiders no longer had anywhere to run or hide, they were much easier to chase down and capture. By the 1860s, the British had become much more serious about stamping out the slave trade around the world. This made it more difficult not just for pirates to operate in the area, but for smugglers and slavers as well.

Piracy in the gulf has always existed and is likely to always exist in some form or another. While pirate activity in the region never grew to quite the same scale as what was found in the Mediterranean Sea and the Caribbean, it has remained constant for more than three thousand years. Even now, in the twenty-first century, it is a fact of life in the Persian Gulf, even though it does not make headline news on a consistent basis.

This long and storied history of pirates conducting raids in and around the Persian Gulf indicates the possibility that the very first acts of piracy were conducted on this body of water. And since the gulf empties directly into the Indian Ocean, it is equally possible that piracy was first introduced to that ocean as a direct result of Arab raiders wandering farther abroad. But the history of piracy on the Indian Ocean is long and complicated in its own right, particularly when you consider the length of time that civilizations have existed upon its shore and just how massive that body of water truly is.

Pirates on the Indian Ocean

Covering more than twenty-eight million square miles, the Indian Ocean stretches from the shores of Eastern Africa and the Arabian Peninsula all the way to Australia, Indonesia, and the Malaysian Peninsula. To the north it is bounded by Asia and in the south it meets the Southern Ocean. Its waters touch the Atlantic at the southernmost tip of Africa and they flow directly into the Pacific Ocean far to the east. The Indian Ocean is massive in scope and size, bordering the two largest continents on Earth and serving as a waterway that has long connected distant parts of the world. It is home to some of the very first oceangoing trading routes and it has been a link between the earliest known civilizations on Earth. However, as with other parts of the world, piracy did not truly become a major threat until the European powers turned their attentions to India, Asia, and beyond.

That isn't to say that piracy did not exist in the Indian Ocean prior to the arrival of the Europeans. Historical records indicate that the Austronesian people, who lived on islands off the coast of Southeast Asia, were building trading routes as far back as 1400 BCE. The Austronesians were the first to build oceangoing vessels and used them to facilitate the exchange of goods with India and Sri Lanka. Over time, that network expanded to reach East Africa and the Arabian Peninsula, creating a vast merchant network that eclipsed anything that was happening in the Mediterranean at the time.

The Austronesians were not known for keeping detailed historical records, so evidence of pirate activity during this time period is scarce. That said, it is likely that as their trade routes grew in size, and the frequency of their voyages increased, their ships began to encounter hostile forces out on the water. Time and again the allure of plundering merchant ships has led to conflict on the high seas, which means that it is possible that pirates were operating in Southeast Asia more than 3,500 years ago.

Thanks to the historical records of the Chola Dynasty, historians know that piracy was an issue at least as far back as 400 or 500 CE. The Chola Dynasty in Southern India was one of the longest reigning empires in human history and established maritime trade with its neighbors across the Indian Ocean and along the Persian Gulf. Within the dynasty, pirate activity was deemed illegal, but any marauder who was captured and agreed to serve in the navy was eligible for a royal pardon. Those who took the deal then acted much like early privateers, protecting Chola's interest along the coast and combatting Arab pirates who were raiding ships and towns.

In the fourteenth century, Southern India split into two rival nations that were constantly at odds with one another. The Islamic Bahmani Sultinate was ideologically opposed to the Hindu Vijayanagara Empire. Capitalizing on this rivalry, war profiteers were willing to sell supplies to both sides of the conflict. Thus, a steady stream of merchant ships travel-led from the Arabian Peninsula and East Africa, bringing horses, which were needed by the mounted calvary, as well as an array of weapons for use in hand-to-hand combat.

Both the Bahmani and the Vijayanagara hired pirates and privateers to raid the trade routes, bolstering their own positions by capturing the incoming supplies for themselves, while simultaneously weakening their enemy. But there were also plenty of independent marauders who found that they could make a small fortune intercepting the merchant ships, plundering their cargo, and then selling off the goods to the highest bid-der themselves.

Timoji

The most famous pirate operating in the Indian Ocean at the start of the sixteenth century was a man named Timoji. In his younger days, he served as a privateer for the Vijayanagara, fighting against the Muslim sultanate. His orders were to intercept incoming merchant ships carry-ing fresh horses from Persia and divert them to his allies instead. His success in this role made him popular with the Rajas of the Hindu empire, who relied on a constant supply of Arabian steeds for use in their war with the Bahmani.

Later, Timoji made the switch from privateer to pirate and established his own base of operations on Anjadip Island off the coast of Goa in the Arabian Sea. From there, he launched raids against the fleets of wealthy trading ships that were sailing back and forth between India and the Persian Gulf. Over time, he amassed a small private army consisting of more than two thousand mercenaries and a personal fleet of nearly twenty ships—a force to be reckoned with on the Indian Ocean.

When the Portuguese began arriving in India, Timoji was one of the first to welcome them. He provided support, supplies, and intelligence to the Europeans as they established themselves in India, as well as other parts of Asia. The pirate even advised the Portuguese governors on how best to conquer the Indian province of Goa. To reward him for his service, the Portuguese gave Timoji an administrative role, serving as a liaison between local Indian factions and the European merchants. Later they even gave him command of his own military unit, as a sign of their trust. Ultimately, the sea called Timoji's name and he returned to a life of piracy, abandoning his role as a legitimate businessman and diplomat.

Zhen He and Chen Zuyi

Long before the Portuguese arrived on the scene, other merchants and explorers from distant lands as well as regional naval powers from across Asia traveled the Indian Ocean. Chief amongst them was a Chinese explorer and diplomat by the name of Zhen He, whose mission it was to make contact with other nations and open diplomatic relations. It is said that he sailed throughout Southeast Asia, Western Asia, and even East Africa from 1405 to 1433 CE. During these voyages, Zheng He used his large and well-trained crew to hunt down and destroy pirates wherever he found them, including the infamous renegade Chen Zuyi.

At the height of his power, Chen Zuyi had more than five thousand men and over a dozen ships under his command. Operating out of the island of Sumatra, he constantly raided merchant vessels as they sailed along the Malaysian Peninsula and through the hundreds of islands that are sprinkled across the region. These attacks became so effective that in the early years of the fifteenth century Zuyi had choked off all of the trade routes, effectively causing an economic collapse across the entire region.

The fateful showdown between Zhen He and Chen Zuyi took place in 1407, when the Chinese admiral was returning home with a fleet of ships filled with goods and treasure collected on his travels across the Indian Ocean. When the two first met, Zhen demanded the pirate surrender and, much to his surprise, Chen agreed to turn himself over to authorities. However, that act of conciliation was just a ruse, as the pirate was actually preparing a stealth attack. When Zhen received word of this deception, his armada attacked the pirate fleet, utterly destroying it in the process. During the battle, Chen was taken prisoner and sent to the capital city of Nanjing, where he was summarily executed.

The defeat of the pirate Chen Zuyi brought security and stability to the Strait of Malacca, where his fleet once preyed upon passing ships. That narrow corridor provides access between the Indian Ocean, the Pacific Ocean, and the South China Sea, making it of strategic importance in the years that followed. With pirate activity curtailed in that area, the Ming Dynasty used its fleet of ships to maintain control and facilitate trade across Southeast Asia, strictly enforcing its anti-piracy rules whenever necessary.

The Wokou

By early fifteenth century, China was no stranger to dealing with pirates. Its coastal cities and merchant ships had long been the target of seafaring raiders. Many of those marauders used the islands off Indonesia and the Malaysian Peninsula as bases of operations, routinely plundering passing vessels, then quickly retreating to safety before any naval vessels could track them down. With more than 1,700 islands in that part of the world, it was nearly impossible to discover exactly where the outlaws were hiding.

Perhaps the most troublesome of all of the raiders that the Chinese faced were the "wokou," which quite literally translates to "Japanese pirates." Despite what their name implies, these outlaws were not only of Japanese origin, but also Korean and Chinese. These bands of marauders typically operated from islands located in the Sea of Japan and the East China Sea, although they would occasionally sail farther abroad as well, sometimes going as far as the Indian Ocean.

The wokou were a constant menace for more than 1,200 years, beginning in the fourth century and remaining active well into the sixteenth century. Throughout that period, they raided the coastlines of Korea and China, although they were not above attacking Japan either. This made them a threat to all three nations, who all actively pursued and punished any pirates who were known to be operating within the region.

The Ming Dynasty routinely launched campaigns to hunt down and destroy any large groups of pirates, but the wokou remained elusive. Their downfall did not truly come until the early 1600s, when the Japanese themselves became more proactive in eliminating piracy. Under the reign of Toyotomi Hideyoshi, who was the Imperial Regent of Japan from 1585 to 1592, the wokou pirates were systematically hunted and killed. This served to finally remove them from the seas, opening up an era of improved trade and exploration, with Japanese ships sailing farther afield.

With piracy curtailed, Japanese vessels began appearing more frequently on the Indian Ocean around the end of the sixteenth and beginning of the seventeenth centuries. While these ships were built to carry goods to ports located across Southeast Asia and beyond, they were also quite heavily armed. They sailed under the red-seal system, which was not unlike the letters of marque issued by European nations. A red-seal letter came directly from the sovereign of Japan and granted merchants permission to sail abroad for trade and diplomatic purposes. It is believed that in the early 1600s, more than 350 Japanese ships sailed to foreign lands with permission from this elaborate permit.

European Countries on the Indian Ocean

When it came time for the Portuguese to make their appearance on the Indian Ocean, they faced much bigger challenges than either the Chinese or Japanese. As difficult as it was sailing through the South China Sea or the Strait of Malacca, it was nothing compared to finding a route around Africa. If Portugal wanted to take advantage of the trade rights granted to it by the Treaty of Tordesillas, it first had to discover a safe and efficient way to reach India and Asia. In order to do that, the king of Portugal—Manuel I—turned to sailor and explorer Vasco da Gama.

Setting out from Lisbon with four ships and 170 men in July of 1497, da Gama reached the most southerly tip of Africa in December of that year. Proceeding around the Cape of Good Hope and then turning north, he soon found himself not just in the Indian Ocean, but in waters that were completely foreign to any European. The route took the Portuguese ships along the east coast of Africa, past Muslim-controlled Madagascar, and all the way to what is now Kenya. Once there, they encountered merchants from India who had reached the same shores by sailing directly across the Indian Ocean.

In the African town of Malini, de Gama hired an experienced pilot who was familiar with the route across open water to India. Using the monsoon winds to their advantage, da Gama and his men continued into the unknown, arriving in Calicut, India, in May of 1498, more than ten months after they had set out from Europe. Once there, de Gama discovered that much of the trade at the time was controlled by Islamic merchants and sultans. Arab traders had been using established maritime routes to India for several hundred years at that point, shipping silk, spices, and slaves back to the Arabian Peninsula on a continual basis. Those Muslim traders eventually became Portugal's direct competition, although the Portuguese did not know it just yet.

Despite the long voyage and hardships they had faced while en route, de Gama and his men achieved their goal of finding an oceangoing route to Asia. It took many months for them to return home to Lisbon, arriving with just two of their four ships and less than half of the crew remaining. Still, their success opened the doors for others to soon follow and eventually introduced European pirates to the Indian Ocean too.

Curiously enough, the first act of piracy by a European in the Indian Ocean likely came from de Gama himself. While sailing north along the east coast of Africa, the explorer and his crew found themselves desperate for supplies, but the Muslim ports and merchants they encountered were unwilling to trade with them. With few other options to choose from, the Portuguese men attacked and raided several Arab merchant ships that were reportedly unarmed. Using the heavy cannons he brought with him on the voyage, da Gama subdued these vessels and commandeered their cargo. This provided him with the supplies he needed to proceed with his mission, which was his only goal. The fact that he had to resort to such tactics underscores not only the length and difficulty of the journey, but just how prevalent and acceptable piracy was at the time.

Those would not be the only acts of piracy that de Gama committed. A few years later, he returned with a much larger, more heavily armed fleet, attacking several ports and a number of Muslim ships along the way. Reportedly, the Portuguese explorer even attacked a ship carrying Muslim pilgrims from Calicut to Mecca, plundering the vessel while it was at sea. When he was done looting the cargo, de Gama is said to have lit the ship on fire with the passengers still alive and trapped onboard.

Upon completing his return trip to India, de Gama used the military might of his well-armed vessels and well-trained crew to force local sultanates and principalities to negotiate trade deals. These efforts to establish and defend a maritime trading route to India marked a distinct change in direction for Portugal itself. Prior to de Gama's sailing expedition—the longest ever at that point in history—the Portuguese were armed traders looking for opportunities to grow in stature and influence. After de Gama's historic voyage, the country had transformed itself into a colonial power with control over sea lanes that gave it a global reach.

De Gama's success opened the doors for other Europeans, although it would be decades before the Portuguese saw their dominance in the Indian Ocean seriously challenged. In the meantime, the country gained a virtual monopoly on the spice trade, growing extremely wealthy and powerful in the process. The route around Africa was a long and perilous one however, with plenty of opportunities for pirates to attack merchant vessels traveling to and from Asia. Most of these buccaneers did not actually sail all the way to India but would instead lie in wait at various points along the twelve-thousand-mile route.

Over the course of the next century, Portugal built a thriving empire along the Indian Ocean, colonizing India, Bangladesh, and other areas. In the early days of that expansion, the ships that made the trip from Europe to Asia were mostly sponsored by the Portuguese Crown or wealthy merchants who could afford larger, more durable oceangoing vessels. But later, as ship design and construction improved, others would undertake the voyage too, including some daring privateers, slave traders, and pirates. By the turn of the seventeenth century, those factions were often referred to as the "harmads," which was a colloquial reference to the Portuguese armada. These harmads were well known for being ruthless, relentless, and brutal in their assaults, raiding local merchant ships, pillaging towns, and taking prisoners to be sold in the slave markets.

Among the primary targets for Portuguese pirates were the ships of the Mughal Empire. The Mughals appeared on the scene in Asia at about the same time as the Portuguese, defeating the sultan of Delhi in 1526 to consolidate their power. In the ensuing decades, the empire grew to cover a large portion of the Indus Valley, stretching across Southern India into Afghanistan and Kashmir. The Mughals built a reputation as some of the greatest shipwrights in all of Asia, which in turn led to bustling trade with merchant vessels sailing as far away as Africa and Arabia to conduct business. Over time, this allowed the kingdom to grow wealthy and prosperous, which only served to make their ships even more popular targets.

Pirates from Portugal were responsible for a major international incident when marauders attacked and captured a ship named *Rahīmī* in 1613. That vessel, which was bound for Mecca with more than six hundred passengers, was owned and operated by Mariam-uz-Zamani, who was the Mughal empress at the time. Representatives of the empire demanded the return of the vessel and its passengers, but the Portuguese refused to comply. In retaliation, the Mughals attacked and captured the town of Daman, which was a Portuguese stronghold. This showdown served to fuel the flames between Portugal and the Mughal Empire, heightening the conflict between Muslims and Christians in the process.

As it turns out, the influence and power of the Mughal Empire far outlasted that of the Portuguese in Asia. While de Gama and those that came soon after him were originally able to subdue the locals with their superior firepower, it was not long before the aura surrounding their might began to wear off. The Muslim kingdoms on the Indian subcontinent quickly determined that the Portuguese were few in numbers and not as strong as they tried to portray themselves. A number of conflicts broke out that served to undermine Portugal's hold on the region, which was made even more tenuous when Spain established a stronghold in the Philippines and began making its own territorial claims on the Indian Ocean.

Dutch ship under attack from galleys.

The Dutch followed soon after the Spanish, bringing a strong navy, and more importantly a sense of organization and focus to the region. The English were not far behind, and with their appearance the Portuguese stranglehold over the trade routes to Asia was broken forever. By the early seventeenth century, ships representing all of the European powers were a common sight in the Indian Ocean, with pirate activity ramping up dramatically as a result.

At that time, the English and French were still issuing a large number of letters of marque, which sent privateers not just to the Caribbean, but also to the Indian Ocean. Many of these ships operated in both regions, raiding Spanish and Portuguese vessels with equal enthusiasm. Later, those letters of marque were revoked, and to make up for the shift in the political landscape, they turned to piracy instead.

Kanhoji Angre

The seventeenth century also saw the rise of the East India Company out of England and the Dutch East India Company from the Netherlands. Both corporations were formed around the same time in the early 1600s, and they came to control much of the trade flowing in and out of the Indian Ocean as the years passed. Their presence alone increased the number of ships operating in the regions significantly, including both those employed by the two companies and those looking to profit at their expense. Much like the wealthy Mughal boats, those owned by the East India Company were frequent targets of pirates and privateers, with a local admiral by the name of Kanhoji Angre going out of his way to prey upon the European ships.

Angre took advantage of British, Dutch, and Portuguese expansion into India and became a constant thorn in the side of all three nations. But it was the British that he preyed upon most regularly, routinely plundering the ships that operated under the flag of the East India Company. It was the official policy of the Maratha Empire, of which Angre was a privateer, that the corporation's ships should pay a tax anytime they passed through its waters. When company officials refused to comply with those fees, attacks against their ships increased substantially.

In the late sixteenth and early seventeenth centuries, Angre set up several bases of operation along the west coast of India and on islands located nearby. From there, he launched raids against passing ships, then escaped back to his stronghold for protection. During one of these raids, the pirate captured the private yacht of a high-ranking official and killed a businessman by the name of Thomas Chown. To make matters worse, Angre took Chown's wife prisoner and held her captive for three months before a ransom of thirty thousand rupees was paid for her safe return.

In the years that followed, Angre continued attacking and plundering the ships of the East India Company until the corporation became so exasperated that it signed a peace treaty with him. In that treaty, Angre agreed to stop harassing the company's ships in return for a hefty payout in cash. That agreement stood until a new company president arrived in India and put a reward out for the capture of the pirate. Unfazed by this change in course, Angre simply returned to his marauding ways, once again attacking East India Company ships. His success persisted throughout the rest of his life, as he evaded capture and died a wealthy and well-respected man.

Madagascar

With so much ship traffic coming and going from India throughout the seventeenth and eighteenth centuries, it is little wonder that so many pirates of various nationalities operated off that country's coasts. But that was not the only hotbed of piracy in the Indian Ocean at that time. The most prominent of those locations was the island of Madagascar, which had been colonized by Islamic settlers six or seven hundred years earlier. Despite having colonies on the island, it remained a largely wild and unexplored place. This, coupled with its strategic location off the coast of Africa, made it the perfect spot for conducting pirate raids. Enterprising buccaneers would lie in wait as European ships passed through the Mozambique Channel, where they were often easy targets for the experienced pirate crews.

Even before de Gama rounded the southern tip of the African continent, Madagascar was a hub for trade. The northern part of the island was home to several port cities that had been built by Arab merchants, as they shipped their goods across the Indian Ocean for hundreds of years before the Portuguese ever dreamed of sailing east. With the

Europeans arriving on the scene, the shipping lanes became far more crowded. This meant more targets of opportunities for the marauders who called Madagascar home.

Madagascar's hidden coves, dense jungle, and unmapped coastline proved to be the perfect hiding place for pirates, who saw a steady supply of Portuguese, Spanish, British, and Dutch ships sail past. The tiny tropical island of Ile Saint Marie, found off Madagascar's northeast coast, was an especially popular place for the brigands to set up shop. From there, they had the ability not just to prey on European ships to the west, but also to quickly sail north to the Red Sea to attack the Mughal Empire's pilgrim ships as they made their way to Mecca.

It is estimated that by the turn of the eighteenth century, as many as 1,500 pirates inhabited Madagascar, making the waters that surrounded the island some of the most dangerous on the planet. At that time, the country was not even on most maps of the world yet, remaining largely unknown even to experienced navigators. When it was added to atlases and charts later, it often bore the name "Pirate Island," a clear indicator of just how prevalent piracy was in the region.

During the Golden Age of Piracy in the Caribbean, Madagascar fell squarely in the middle of the "Pirate Round." This was a sailing route taken by English buccaneers who began their voyage in the western Atlantic or even as far away as the Caribbean. From there, they sailed down the coast of South America, then took the Cape Route around the southernmost tip of Africa. Many would stop to resupply on the island nation before pursuing hunting ships to plunder along the coasts of the Red Sea, Persian Gulf, and India. Typically, these opportunistic raiders followed the ships of the East India Company, which made annual journeys to and from England, heavy with booty in both directions. The oceangoing outlaws did not hesitate to attack Muslim ships that were caught out at sea either, as their cargo holds offered plenty of riches too.

Madagascar was such a haven for outlaws that it is said to have once been home to a pirate colony known as Libertatia. Historians remain split as to whether or not the place ever truly existed, but as the legend goes, a pirate captain by the name of James Misson founded the colony

Pirate attack.

under the guiding principle that everyone who lived there would be treated equally, regardless of color, nationality, or religious beliefs. This was a pretty open and unusual attitude for the seventeenth century, but it was in line with how pirates governed their ships, where they demo-cratically selected their captains, and crews were of mixed races and creeds. The level of acceptance aboard a pirate ship is generally seen as being well ahead of it time.

If the stories are to be believed, Misson sailed the coast of Madagascar until he found a hidden cove that would serve as a perfect place for his new settlement. The spot he chose reportedly had plenty of fresh water, good soil for growing crops, and friendly indigenous people with which he could trade. Many of the pirates who came to Libertatia were said to have renounced their marauding ways and settled down there to live a quiet life, enjoying the warm island weather and relaxed lifestyle that the tropics provided.

The problem is that there is no evidence that Libertatia ever existed, other than some vague reports by a few writers of the era. It is unclear whether or not the stories of the idyllic pirate colony were completely made up or simply passed on as second-hand accounts. Despite numerous searches over the centuries, no one has ever been able to locate the settlement nor find a connection with it to anyone living on Madagascar. Still, the ideals of the place were enough to create a legend that persists to this day, with some still holding out hope and belief that such a place was real.

One thing that historians do not dispute is the role that Madagascar came to play in the slave trade. As with the Mediterranean, Atlantic, and the Caribbean, the Indian Ocean saw slave ships frequently carrying their cargo to Europe or India to fulfill the growing need for workers on both continents. Many of those slaves came directly from Madagascar, with the local tribes often waging war on one another in order to sell the vanquished off to the Europeans.

Just like in other regions of the planet, pirates routinely raided slave ships in the Indian Ocean as they made for easy targets and a quick profit. As European interests in India grew, the need for slaves to work on plantations within the country increased steadily as well. Those looking for slave labor did not particularly care where they got it from, as long as they could get plenty of manpower to help fulfill their ambitions.

The island of Zanzibar was another one of the primary players in the slave trade of the Indian Ocean. Located off the coast of East Africa, the tiny island was rich in spices, but also served as a major slave market, supplying African men and women for use in India and to a lesser extent in China. First organized and maintained by the Portuguese, and later Arab traders, Zanzibar's slave market remained active even after 1873, when the ruling sultan caved to pressure from the British and signed a treaty banning the practice. Despite efforts to end the trade of African slaves, the market on Zanzibar remained active all the way up to 1909, when slavery was abolished in East Africa at long last.

From the time the Portuguese first opened the route from Europe to India, until the end of the Golden Age of Piracy in the 1730s, the amount of mercantile traffic on the Indian Ocean rose exponentially. The booming trade of spices and silks, coupled with a thriving slave market, made the waters off the coast of East Africa and Asia some of the most lucrative for pirates of the era. All of those factors played a contributing role in what is most likely the single biggest heist by any pirate in history.

Henry Every

In early September of 1695, the famed pirate Henry Every (mentioned in Chapter 4) was sailing the Indian Ocean and patrolling the Bab-el-Mandeb Strait, which separates the Arabian Peninsula from the Horn of Africa. Every knew that there would be heavy ship traffic as Muslim pilgrims returned home to India following the annual journey to Mecca. As he was known to do, the English outlaw joined forces with five other pirates in an effort to increase their chances of scoring significant plunder. While Every was ambitious and smart, he also realized that there was strength and safety in numbers.

At one point, this makeshift fleet of marauders spotted the Mughal treasure fleet as it was making its way back to the subcontinent, no doubt filled with an abundance of riches. Amongst those ships were the *Ganj-i-Sawai*—which was owned by the Mughal emperor—and its escort the *Fateh Muhammad*. With these vessels squarely in their sights, the buccaneers gave chase, eager to find what those two ships might have in their hold.

Henry Every selling his loot.

It took several days for Every and his allies to chase down the *Fateh Muhammad*, which reportedly offered little resistance when met with an armed bordering party. As suspected, the ship was indeed carrying plenty of treasure that was being shipped back to India. Historians estimate that the raiders made off with more than £50,000 worth of plunder. That equates to over $10 million today.

But Every was not satisfied with the size of that haul and elected to go after an even bigger prize—the *Ganj-i-Sawai*. Aboard his forty-six-gun frigate, the *Fancy*, the pirate captain gave chase, eventually catching the Mughal vessel out on the open ocean. Despite his formidable weaponry, Every found himself outgunned, as the *Ganj-i-Sawai* had more than fifty guns of its own and was carrying a force of nearly five hundred men, most of whom were armed with muskets.

The *Ganj-i-Sawai* resisted heavily, firing her cannons at her pursuers and attempting to outmaneuver Every and his crew. But in the opening minutes of the battle, one of the ship's cannons exploded on deck, killing several crew members and damaging the ship significantly. To make matters worse for the Mughals, the *Fancy* scored a direct hit on the *Ganj-i-Sawai*'s mainmast, severely crippling its ability to escape. Not long after, the pirate crew scrambled aboard and captured the vessel relatively quickly and easily.

Over the next few days, Every and his men tortured members of the *Ganj-i-Sawai*'s passengers and crew to get them to reveal the location of the ship's treasure. Many of the women onboard were raped and conditions grew so heinous that some of them even threw themselves overboard, preferring to drown in the ocean rather than be subjected to further suffering. Eventually, the crew of the *Fancy* did find the plunder they had been searching for and it likely exceeded even their wildest imaginations.

Historians say that the *Ganj-i-Sawai* was carrying an estimated five hundred thousand gold and silver pieces on its voyage back home. That alone was worth a fortune, but there were also plenty of other valuables amongst the passengers, including jewelry, precious stones, spices, and silk clothing. All told, the complete haul is believed to have been worth over £500,000, which works out to more than $105 million today. That was enough plunder to ensure that each and every pirate who took part in the raid was given £1,000 in cash, as well as some gems. That works out to roughly $200,000 in modern day value for each of them.

Every's daring raid earned him the nickname the "King of the Pirates," but also put a rather large target on his back. The Mughal emperor was outraged by the attack and demanded the British Royal Navy and East India Company bring the crew of the *Fancy* to justice or risk losing their operations in India.

With no other choice but to at least try to track down Every and his crew of outlaws, the Royal Navy gave pursuit, sparking a chase that continued halfway around the world. The clever pirate knew how to evade capture however and soon made his way back across the Indian Ocean, around the tip of Africa, and into the Atlantic. Once there, he sped towards the Caribbean, arriving in the Bahamas just ahead of his pursuers. As we already know, he managed to bribe the governor of Nassau to allow him and his men to come ashore, offering the *Fancy* as a gift. Not long after that, he disappeared from the history books altogether, never to be seen again.

What happened to Henry Every and where he ended up remains a mystery. Some historians believe that with the riches he claimed from plundering the *Ganj-i-Sawai* he booked passage back to England under an assumed name, where he lived out the rest of his days in anonymity, having acquired a vast fortune. It is possible that he used that wealth to buy another ship and continue his pirate ways under an alias as well, but with the Golden Age of Piracy quickly drawing to an end, it seems more likely that the treasure taken from the Mughal Empire was part of his strategy to exit the pirate business for good.

Just as faster and more agile steam ships were the beginning of the end of the pirate era in the Caribbean, those same innovations were impacting pirates half a world away. By the start of the eighteenth century, the Royal Navy had launched a crackdown on pirate activity across the British Empire—which by that time spanned the globe. His (or Her) Majesty's fleet had become the greatest military asset the world had ever seen and it now trained its considerable attention—not to mention very heavy guns—on pirates in every part of the world.

Rahmahlbn Jabit was one of the most feared
and successful pirates of the Barbary Coast.

With letters of marque quickly becoming a thing of the past, and piracy outlawed across the globe, the sun was setting on the pirates that operated in the Indian Ocean. But unlike in the Caribbean, where buccaneers would become nearly extinct by the middle of the nineteenth century, piracy found a way to persist in the Indian Ocean. While the number of pirates who raided ships and plundered coastal towns dropped off dramatically over time, they never quite disappeared altogether. In fact, piracy remains an issue in parts of the Indian Ocean to this day, maintaining an unbroken legacy that dates back to when the first trade routes were opened between Mesopotamia and India.

The Tale of Captain Kidd

Throughout history the difference between a pirate and a privateer has always been separated by a thin gray line. Both sides offered plenty of adventure, risks, and rewards, but one provided protection under the law, while the other put the buccaneer squarely outside of it. Savvy sailors would often learn to operate in both realms, finding ways to profit from shifting politics, changing alliances, and nebulous borders. But on occasion, a privateer might find himself on the wrong side of that line, leaving him in an unexpected position. Such was the case with Captain William Kidd, who just might be the unluckiest pirate in history.

Born in the Scottish town of Dundee in 1654, Kidd was the son of a sailor who aspired to follow in his father's footsteps. He was not much more than a teenager when he joined the crew of a privateer ship and set sail in defense of the Crown.

His early years as a sailor taught him the nuances of commanding a ship, navigating the ocean, and managing a crew. Even though he was young, he was also a very quick study, and soon managed to distinguish himself amongst the other men. Kidd moveed up the ranks quickly, all the while garnering a reputation as a knowledgeable and trustworthy member of the crew.

Eventually Kidd took command of his own ship—the *Antigua*—and set sail for America. Once he reached the New World, he settled down in New York City for a time, finding the British colonies to his liking. Not one to stay settled for too long, Kidd routinely served as a privateer in the Atlantic Ocean. As friend to several colonial governors, the experienced captain was often asked to sail out to intercept a pirate ship or enemy vessel that had strayed too close to shore. With each successful defensive raid, the reputation of Captain Kidd grew, both with English officials and the general public. The tale of his exploits entertained the aristocracy and peasant class alike, turning William into a local celebrity.

In 1689, Kidd joined the crew of a ship bound for the Caribbean. That vessel was commanded by French privateer Jean Fantin, although his days as captain did not last very long. At some point during the voyage, the men mutinied against Fantin, taking control of the vessel. Before long, the crew—which included known pirate Robert Culliford— appointed Kidd as captain and the ship continued on its course for Nevis, a British colony in the Caribbean. Even though they were members of the same crew, Culliford and Kidd were not fond of each other. As fate would have it, the two men crossed paths many times throughout their careers, with the opportunistic Culliford becoming a nemesis of sorts for the more good-intentioned Kidd.

Upon arriving in Nevis, Kidd and his men set about making repairs and upgrades to their newly acquired ship. That included changing the name to *Blessed William*. The Scotsman also met with Christopher Coddington, who was serving as the governor of the island at the time. Coddington told him that England and France had gone to war and that he needed good ships to help defend the nearby trading routes. Not one to deny the English Crown, Kidd accepted a commission as a privateer, and enlisted in the governor's small fleet.

The commission with Coddington did not provide pay for Kidd and his men, but they were allowed to keep any plunder they took from the French. That was enough incentive for the crew of the *Blessed William*, who went on the offensive against the enemies of the Crown. One of their first targets was the island of Marie-Galante, which had only one small town. The English privateers were able to subdue the village in short order, burn it to the ground, and sail off with more than £2,000— roughly equivalent to about $400,000 today.

Throughout his campaign against the French, Kidd once again displayed outstanding leadership and initiative. He and the crew of the

Captain William Kidd.

Blessed William helped to keep the shipping lanes open between England and her colonies in the Caribbean and America. This allowed vital supplies to continue to flow in, even during a time of war. Later, Kidd's outstanding service earned him a citation from the British government, further enhancing his reputation as a captain who could accomplish great things.

After fighting the French in the Caribbean, Kidd sailed back to the New England colonies, where he continued operating as a privateer. By that time, the conflict between England and France had grown into what would eventually be called the War of the Grand Alliance, with England, Spain, the Netherlands, and Austria joining forces against France, which was under the leadership of Louis XIV at the time. Most of the fighting was contained to Europe, but some spilled over into the Atlantic Ocean. To help protect English interests in the New World, Kidd accepted a commission from both the colonies of New York and Massachusetts, squaring off against French privateers in the waters off North America. At the time, there were no large Royal Navy fleets to defend the coast-lines, making reliable and loyal privateers a valuable asset.

Despite sailing up and down the coast of North America and across the Caribbean, Kidd still found time to court a young woman, fall in love, and get married. He met Sarah Bradley Cox Oort while traveling through the aristocratic social circles of New York City. By all accounts,

Captain Kidd in New York Harbor.

Sarah was bright, beautiful, and charming. Twice-widowed at a young age, she also happened to be quite wealthy, providing a very comfortable life for her and her new husband.

Wedded bliss did not slow Kidd down much, as he continued to set sail on a regular basis. Not long after he and Sarah were wed, the Scottish seaman once again set out for the Caribbean under his commission as an English privateer. Once there, he and Robert Culliford were reacquainted while in port on the island of Antigua. Never one to let an opportunity to needle his nemesis go by, the pirate stole Kidd's ship and made off with it, leaving his rival stranded in the West Indies.

The loss of his ship was just a temporary setback for Kidd, who booked passage back to New York. Once there, he was summoned to meet with Richard Coote, who was not only the new governor of that colony, but also the governor of Massachusetts and New Hampshire. By that time, Kidd's reputation for being an outstanding privateer was well known, and Coote needed a man that he could trust. The governor relayed a request from King William III himself, asking Captain Kidd to not only continue to pursue French ships on the ocean, but to hunt down and capture pirates as well. Considering the source of the request, the Scotsman could hardly refuse.

Upon accepting this new role, Kidd was issued a letter of marque that had been personally signed by King William III. It not only provided Kidd and his crew with the legal protection that they needed, but also made provisions to provide cash to support a prolonged operation to hunt pirates in the Indian Ocean. At the time, the East India Company was continually under attack from hostile ships while sailing to and from Asia, and Kidd's new orders granted him permission to carry out the King's justice no matter where he sailed. This was fairly unprecedented for that era, as it provided him with far-reaching powers and responsibilities that few other ship captains had been afforded.

In order to pursue pirates and the French to the far corners of the globe, Kidd knew that he would need a new ship. Using some of the money earmarked for his expedition, the Scotsman ordered construction of a vessel that would be larger, faster, and more sophisticated than any he had commanded before. The vessel, which Kidd dubbed the *Adventure Galley*, combined both sails and oars, which was an incredibly unusual design decision for the time. This would allow it to maneuver in tight space and make headway against the wind should the need arise, although few ships bothered using both forms of propulsion in that era. Kidd felt that this level of versatility could prove useful when attempting to out-maneuver his pirate adversaries.

The *Adventure Galley* was also heavily armed, setting sail with thirty-four cannons on her decks. That was enough firepower to easily outgun the small sloops that most pirates favored during that era, as pirates usually preferred speed and maneuverability over heavy guns. The ship, and its many cannons, were manned by a crew of 150 men, each handpicked by Kidd. In his years as a privateer he had come to know a number of very good sailors and he wanted the best of them onboard his vessel on this globe-spanning adventure.

While publicly the purpose of Kidd's expedition was to hunt pirates and French merchants, behind the scenes his wealthy sponsors had ulterior motives. They wanted to profit from this venture, with the King claiming 10 percent of the plunder right off the top. The other sponsors would get a cut too, which meant Kidd was expected to deliver a good return on their investment. The Scottish privateer was tasked with destroying England's enemies and then sailing home with a hold full of silver and gold—an immense amount of pressure. Eventually this charge came to feel like an anchor around his neck, weighing down on his every decision.

The voyage got off to a bad start before the *Adventure Galley* had even left London. As the story goes, when the ship was preparing to depart, it sailed past several ships in port, including a yacht that was part of the Royal Navy. At the time, tradition dictated that as a sign of respect, any passing vessel would salute the yacht on its way out to sea. Whether by accident or on purpose, Kidd failed to issue that salute, angering one of the officers onboard the naval ship. Things went from bad to worse when some of Kidd's crew allegedly dropped their trousers and patted their backsides, displaying a complete lack of respect for authority.

In retaliation, the yacht's captain stopped the *Adventure Galley*, reprimanded Kidd, and drafted a large number of his men into the Royal Navy. This not only left Kidd scrambling to recruit new sailors at the last minute, but also had a demoralizing effect on those that remained in his original crew. In addition, it meant that the men that he was now setting sail with were not the trusted, experienced seamen that he thought he'd have under his command.

In September of 1696, Kidd and his new crew departed for the Cape of Good Hope at long last. Their plan was to sail south along the western coast of Africa, round the cape, then travel north into the Indian Ocean. Even though this route had become much more commonly used in the two centuries since Vasco de Gama had first charted the course from Europe to Asia, it remained a long, difficult, and arduous journey.

Once at sea, Captain Kidd's problems continued to mount. His new ship proved to be problematic from the start, springing several leaks not long after it left England. In the rush to prepare the *Adventure Galley* for the expedition, the shipwrights apparently cut corners, producing a vessel that never lived up to expectations. The ship proved seaworthy enough, but it was not as durable and dependable as Kidd would have liked, creating unnecessary stress over whether or not it would see him and his men through their long journey.

After weeks of sailing, the *Adventure Galley* arrived in Madagascar without capturing a single pirate ship while en route. They had hoped to encounter at least a few buccaneers traveling between the Indian Ocean and the Caribbean, but they had not come across a single vessel. Even more perplexing was the absence of pirates near Madagascar, which had long been a favorite refuge for the outlaws. Having sailed so far without capturing any plunder seemed like an ominous sign to the crew, who were growing restless.

Worse yet, by the time the *Adventure Galley* reached the Comoros archipelago off the coast of East Africa in February of 1697, a cholera outbreak had ravaged the crew's health. Kidd decided to stop off at the tiny island nation with the hopes of allowing his men to take some time to recover. While they were there, a third of the sailors died. This only

Captain Kidd and members of his crew.

served to further cement the idea within the remaining sailors that the voyage was cursed and that they were all doomed.

Desperate to gain a victory and squelch any grumblings of mutiny, Kidd ordered his men to attack several smaller ships that they came across on the Indian Ocean. Even those efforts proved fruitless however, as a pair of cargo vessels carrying coffee out of Yemen were able to elude capture and escape. Later, they found some success in taking a few small Indian ships, but the plunder was meager at best.

Challenges to Kidd's command renewed in late 1697, more than a year after the *Adventure Galley* had set out from London. The vessel had come across a Dutch ship out on the open ocean and Kidd's men urged him to attack. But the English and Dutch were not hostile to one another at the time, so the captain refused. This sparked an argument between the officers and the men that resulted in Kidd accidentally killing one of his gunners.

By January of 1698, it was all that Kidd could do just to keep his crew together. The men, sensing the voyage was not going to be profitable, had begun fighting amongst themselves and plotting the forcible removal of their captain. The ship was in need of a major victory if there was any hope of salvaging the expedition. Kidd had proven to have little talent for pirate hunting and at times it seemed that fate itself was stacked against them. After weeks at sea they had little plunder to show for their efforts, despite suffering heavy losses.

Just when things were at their darkest a ship known as the *Quedagh Merchant* appeared on the horizon. The vessel was owned by Indian traders, but had been hired by Armenian merchants to ship gold, silver, silk, spices, and other valuable items back to Europe. In an attempt to ensure safe passage, the merchants had also purchased special passes from France that would allow them to sail unmolested by French ships, even though the vessel did not sail under the French flag, nor was it even aligned with the country in any way.

Heavy with cargo, the four-hundred-ton ship was slow and ponderous. One look at the vessel and Kidd knew that it was weighted down with enough treasure for him and his crew to salvage their entire operation.

That was all of the encouragement the crew needed, particularly after they had spent nearly a year and a half at sea without acquiring any booty to fill the ship's hold. Kidd ordered the men to attack and the *Adventure Galley* bore down on the merchant vessel. Within minutes, its thirty-four guns had easily overpowered the *Quedagh Merchant,* its captain quickly surrendering. The fortunes of Kidd and his crew had dramatically changed, although not necessarily in the way they thought at the time.

After taking the *Quedagh Merchant,* Kidd discovered that the captain of the ship was actually an Englishman, and he immediately felt pangs of regret. He tried to order his men to return the vessel, explaining that they had made a major mistake. But the crew was hungry for success and plunder and refused to give up their prize. Some argued that because the merchant boat had French papers allowing for safe passage, the taking and plundering of the ship was completely legal. After all, they argued, those special passes were akin to sailing under the French flag.

Not completely convinced, but fearing total mutiny, Kidd acquiesced. He ordered his men to take possession of the merchant ship and all of its cargo. By that point of their voyage, the *Adventure Galley* was practically falling apart and he and his crew were eager to have a seaworthy ship under their feet once again. It didn't hurt that the *Quedagh Merchant* was full of highly valuable goods too, completely turning around the fortunes of the captain and his men.

It didn't take long for word to reach England of Kidd's raid on the *Quedagh Merchant.* The attack on the ship was immediately condemned by both the king and the expedition's benefactors, signaling a turn of fortunes for a captain who had once been held in high regard. Word was sent out to several ships of the Royal Navy, ordering them to hunt down and capture Kidd and his accomplices. To make matters worse, in the nearly two years since they had left London, public support for pirates had waned significantly. Now viewed as despicable outlaws, anyone charged and convicted with piracy faced harsher punishments for crimes committed out at sea.

After capturing the *Quedagh Merchant,* Kidd renamed it the

Adventure Prize, a nod to its value and wealth. In its cargo hold, he found plunder worth tens of thousands of pound sterling, enough to make him and his crew, along with their sponsors, very wealthy men. He was also careful to hold on to the French passes of safe passage, already formulating a defense for his actions. By presenting them to the Crown, he hoped to use the documents as an excuse for attacking the ship.

His job in the Indian Ocean done, Kidd set sail for the Caribbean, stopping in Madagascar while en route. Once there, he ran into his old nemesis Robert Culliford, who was in command of a small pirate ship and a crew of his own by that time. This time they met as friends, with Kidd even gifting his former shipmate a few cannons and an anchor for his new boat. However, the meeting was not completely without difficulty, as the majority of Kidd's remaining men jumped ship and joined Culliford's crew instead.

When Kidd resumed the voyage to the Caribbean, the *Adventure Prize* is said to have had a crew of just thirteen. By then, he knew that he was a wanted man and that his easily identifiable merchant galley was a liability. Once in the West Indies, he sold off his remaining portion of the plunder, scuttled the *Adventure Prize,* and bought a new ship that he named *Antonio.* His plan was to set sail for New York, where he hoped he would not only arrive safely, but also receive an audience with Governor Richard Coote. Kidd felt that if he was given the chance to plead his case he could somehow gain a pardon, returning to the Crown's good graces.

For the governor, Kidd's turn to piracy had become an embarrassing affair. It was he who had vouched for the Scottish captain in the first place and helped him earn his letter of marque from the king. Fearing that any further association with Kidd could prove dangerous to his own status and career, Coote invited the sailor to join him in Boston under false pretenses. When Kidd arrived there in July of 1699, he was arrested on the spot and thrown into prison pending a trial for his crimes.

It took more than a year for Kidd to be shipped back to England, where he faced intense scrutiny from parliament. Members of that governing body pressed the sailor to share the names of his backers on his ill-fated voyage, hoping to use the affair as a way to discredit their political rivals. Loyal to a fault, Kidd refused to divulge any of the names of the men who helped finance his expedition. The English government proceeded with his trial on charges of piracy.

Nearly another year passed before Kidd stood before the High Court of Admiralty to tell his story. When that day finally came, he was shocked to discover that a charge of murder had been added to his list of wrongdoings. The death of the young gunner during the attempted mutiny on the Indian Ocean had come back to haunt him at the most inopportune time. A ship's captain was given a lot of leeway in how he doled out punishment and discipline amongst the crew, making it almost unheard of for a commanding officer to stand trial for harming one of his men. In this case, the Crown was looking to make an example of Kidd, and adding another heinous crime gave them an even stronger case against the Scotsman.

Despite having good legal representation, Kidd stood little chance of ever being acquitted. The trial took place on May 8 and 9 of 1701 and ended very quickly. When it was over, Captain William Kidd was found guilty of five counts of piracy and one count of murder. He was sentenced to death by hanging for his crimes, with the sentence to be carried out as swiftly as possible.

On May 23, 1701, Captain Kidd took the long walk to the gallows. But the former privateer had yet another string of bad luck on that day. On the first attempt to hang him, the rope broke, sending him sprawling roughly onto the wooden platform. Some of the individuals who had gathered to watch the proceedings saw this as a sign from God and called out for mercy on the convicted pirate. But the rope was reconfigured, the noose returned to his neck, and he was hanged once again, this time losing his life in the process. Afterwards, his body was hung over the Thames River at a place called Tilbury Point. It remained there for three years, a warning to all others who might be tempted to follow in his path.

In the aftermath of Kidd's trial, many questioned his actual guilt. Some of the evidence that could have potentially cleared him of the

Hanging of Captain Kidd.

charges—most notably the French passes found aboard the *Quedagh Merchant*—were missing. Those documents remained lost for more than two hundred years, eventually being rediscovered after they had been misfiled amongst various other paperwork.

Today, historians often debate whether or not William Kidd was ever a pirate at all. It seems that for the bulk of his career he went to great lengths to avoid sailing down that path, even holding pirates in great disdain. Whether or not the attack on the *Quedagh Merchant* was legitimate or piracy remains open to discussion, with some feeling that the use of the French passes brought a degree of legitimacy to the Scotsman's capture of the wealthy cargo boat. Others point out that the evidence at the trial was very thin, with some of the charges trumped up just to make an example out of the famous privateer. The prevailing notion is that piracy had dramatically fallen out of favor and the High Court of Admiralty had already made up its mind long before the first gavel fell. Kidd just happened to have the misfortune of falling on the wrong side of public opinion and legal standards at the time.

As with other notorious pirates, Captain Kidd's legacy lives on well into the twenty-first century. Prior to his Boston arrest, the seaman had traveled to Gardiners Island and buried some of his treasure there. This loot was later recovered and sent to England as evidence in the trial. But there are some who believe that there is still a chest of gold or other pirate booty waiting to be discovered there. To this day, treasure hunters will still visit the place hoping to find Kidd's lost gold, although so far they have all come up empty.

Kidd's ship, the *Adventure Prize*—formerly the *Quedagh Merchant*—was discovered in 2007. The ship now rests just off the coast of the Dominican Republic in water that is no more than ten feet deep. It sits a mere seventy feet from shore, hidden in plain sight. Yet somehow the wreckage managed to elude discovery for more than three centuries, helping to maintain the lore around Captain Kidd.

CHAPTER 6

The Pirates of the Pacific Ocean

It is difficult to believe in this day and age, but up until the start of the sixteenth century, the Pacific Ocean was virtually unknown to European and Arab explorers. Obviously the people living in Eastern Asia, specifically Japan and other islands sprinkled across that vast body of water, were well aware of its existence, but for the Western world it was just one giant blank spot on the map. Therefore, piracy was late in coming to the Pacific and when it did arrive, it never took hold at the same level as elsewhere around the planet. That said, several merchant trade routes were eventually established on the ocean, which meant pirate activity eventually followed.

Early Explorations

The first contact with the Pacific by any European explorers is believed to have come in 1512, nearly fifteen years after Vasco de Gama opened his trade route to India. The Portuguese navigator António de Abreu is credited with finding the western edge of the ocean while mapping the "Spice Island" along the tip of Indonesia. To Abreu, the Pacific looked like a never-ending sea that stretched past the horizon.

The eastern edge of the Pacific was actually discovered a year later when Spanish explorer Vasco Núñez de Balboa crossed the Isthmus of Panama on foot and came to its soft, sandy beaches along the western side. He too saw only a massive body of water spreading out in front of

199

him, but because it fell away to the south of his position, he called it the *Mar del Sur*, which means the South Sea.

Balboa had no way of knowing it at the time, but the Mar del Sur actually stretched over ten thousand miles to the west and spread out across more than sixty-three million square miles. Its edges run from the Arctic Ocean in the north to the Southern Ocean in the south, with North and South America serving as boundaries to the east, and Asia, Australia, and the Malaysian Peninsula forming its westernmost border. To put that size and scope into perspective, the Pacific is more than twenty million square miles larger than the Atlantic and it is over seven thousand miles wider too.

The ocean's massive scale made it difficult to explore, which is why it took much longer for the European Powers to find ways to exploit it. This also meant that pirates saw little reason to travel there, as there were few merchant vessels, colonies, or established trade routes to raid. There simply was not any incentive for anyone to go there for quite some time.

The Pacific officially received its name in 1519, when Portuguese explorer Ferdinand Magellan and his crew became the first Europeans to sail around Cape Horn, the southernmost tip of South America. The region's notoriously difficult seas are known for their rough waves, high winds, and sudden, violent storms. Even today, in the twenty-first century, "rounding the Cape" is still seen as a unique and sometimes dangerous challenge. Five hundred years ago it was a terrifying journey into the unknown that offered little certainty of survival.

When Magellan and his men were finally able to pass through that difficult stretch of water, they found nothing but calm seas awaiting them on the far side. This prompted the explorer to declare that the ocean they sailed into was "Pacifico"—meaning "peaceful" in Portuguese. The name stuck and it has been the official title of the Pacific Ocean ever since.

Despite the fact that he was Portuguese, Magellan was actually sailing under a Spanish flag. The explorer had proposed a voyage to India and the Spice Isles to King Manuel of Portugal on several occasions, but each time his request was denied. So, out of frustration, he went to Spain's King Charles I with a new proposal instead. Because the Treaty

A Spanish galleon.

of Tordesillas ceded control of everything east of Europe to the Portuguese, Magellan proposed taking a new route to the west. His voyage led to the European discovery of the Philippines, along with numerous other island chains, and opened up an alternate route to Asia.

Magellan ultimately died in the Philippines while confronting an indigenous tribe that he was attempting to convert to Christianity. But his dwindling fleet of ships continued on without him, eventually reaching the Spice Islands they had so desperately been searching for since setting sail from Europe. Once there, they loaded up on precious cargo and the remaining crew pressed on for home. Under the command of a captain named Juan Sebastián Elcano, the loan surviving ship—the *Victoria*—sailed across the Indian Ocean, rounded the Cape of Good Hope, and arrived back to Spain, completing the first circumnavigation of the planet. Of the 270 men who had set out with Magellan three years earlier, fewer than twenty survived the entire voyage.

In the decades that followed, the Spanish and Portuguese were the first to launch serious efforts to explore the Pacific, although other European nations followed. Expeditions sponsored by Portugal were the first to reach the Caroline Islands, Aru Islands, and Papua New Guinea in the 1520s. In 1542, the Portuguese were also the first outsiders to visit Japan. Meanwhile, the Spanish launched their Pacific voyages out of Mexico and Peru, and eventually focused on establishing a colony in the Philippines. Spain's navigators added places like the Cook Islands, Solomon Islands, and Tahiti to the map. The Spanish were also the first to spot Australia, while the Dutch discovered Hawaii many years later.

Pirates on the Pacific

Due to its immense size, and the inherent dangers that came with crossing vast open seas, most pirate activity was confined to the western fringes of the Pacific for quite some time. For the most part, there was little reason for any buccaneers to wander out into the ocean, where only a few scattered islands—most lacking in any kind of wealth or resources—had been found. It would also take some time before any lucrative trade routes opened, which helped to keep pirate activity to a minimum.

That isn't to say that there was not piracy in the Pacific before the Europeans arrived on the scene. Much like in other parts of the world, seagoing raiders had been active for hundreds of years, routinely attacking merchant vessels and coastal villages in Korea and China. At first, those attacks were relatively small and unorganized, but—as usual—they became more focused and effective over time.

The first use of the word "wokou" occurred in 414 CE in reference to Japanese invaders who attacked the coastline of Korea. At the time, the word literally translated to "dwarf pirate" and was meant to be a derogatory insult to the stature of the raiders from across the sea. But those outlaws were so persistent, and became so common in the Sea of Japan, that over time the term wokou evolved to simply mean "Japanese pirate" instead. This name lasted even years later, when the crew of wokou ships were made up of members of multiple ethnicities.

Korea and Wokou

In the ninth century, piracy had become so prevalent in East Asia that a wealthy Korean merchant and warlord proposed creating a garrison just to fight off the growing number of marauders. In 825 CE, a man by the name of Jang Bogo asked permission from the local ruler—King Heungdeok of the Silla Kingdom—to build a fortress on the island of Wando in the Yellow Sea. The Yellow Sea sits between China and Korea and grants access to the East China Sea and the Sea of Japan, all of which sit peripherally on the Pacific Rim. The strategic location of Wando made it easy to defend and supply, while also offering quick access to the pirate-infested waters.

During his travels, Jang had gone to China and saw firsthand the impact that piracy was having not just on merchant ships, but also on the towns that sat along the coast. Not content to just haul off plunder taken from seafaring traders, the marauders would often attack villages as a means of capturing supplies and other valuables. These raids also allowed the brigands to kidnap locals who were later sold off into slavery as well.

When Heungdeok gave Jang his blessing to build an outpost on Wando, Jang immediately went to work constructing a fortress and a port that could house his large private navy. Impressed with Jang's work, the king then committed ten thousand men to the cause, giving the warlord permission to hunt down and punish pirates on the open seas.

In a sense, he had become a Korean privateer when that concept was still only beginning to take hold in Europe.

For the next two decades Jang maintained direct control over the Yellow Sea, dictating trade routes and the exchange of goods throughout the region. He also used his considerable forces to stamp out piracy wherever it appeared, delivering swift justice to any outlaw that was captured. His efforts helped to bring order to the seas off the coast of Korea and China, allowing merchant ships to safely sail between these two countries once again. The enhanced level of security that Jang's forces brought to the Yellow Sea even allowed Japan to improve relations with its neighbors too. But after he was assassinated in 846 CE, Jang's fleet and army grew unorganized and began to break apart, allowing piracy to return in force.

The wokou had never really gone away, although their activities were sharply curtailed while Jang waged his campaign against them. With the Korean warlord gone, they returned in even larger numbers, growing steadily in the decades that followed. As the centuries rolled on, they became an ever-present threat out on the water. So much so that trade routes routinely broke down and entire villages were forced to move farther inland in order to avoid the ongoing attacks.

The number of raids conducted by the wokou seem to have reached their peak sometime around 1350. After that, the Korean military turned serious about stamping out the pirates, although it took them nearly eighty years to truly get piracy under control. In 1380, a hundred warships were dispatched to strike at a major pirate stronghold along the coast of what is now South Korea. Armed with gunpowder, which the wokou lacked at the time, the Korean troops quickly gained the upper hand on their adversaries, sending them scrambling to escape. This offensive pushed the outlaws from of their outposts, but it only slowed them down temporarily.

In 1419, a much more concerted effort was launched to completely destroy the wokou. In the five decades that followed the first campaign against them, the outlaws had set up a base of operations on Geoje Island, just off the coast of Korea. From there, they continued their raids and their ranks once again began to grow in numbers. To combat this returning threat, the Koreans sent more than two hundred ships and seven thousand men to destroy the pirate outpost. Using captured wokou as guides, the Korean forces took their enemy completely by surprise, destroying 130 boats, burning nearly two thousand houses, and killing or capturing 135 marauders, while others made their escapes. The Korean forces also rescued over one hundred wokou prisoners and freed two dozen slaves.

From that time forward, the number of wokou attacks on Korean targets fell off sharply. The pirates continued to operate in the East China Sea and Yellow Sea for many years, but their bold assaults on merchant ships and seaside villages waned dramatically. For a time, they mostly disappeared from the sea, although by the sixteenth century they staged a comeback, thanks in part to shifting Chinese political policies.

China and Wokou

During the 1500s, China's Ming Dynasty actually banned private maritime trade, in effect pulling all merchant ships off the water. The move had more to do with Ming leaders consolidating control rather than combatting pirates, but the decision gave rise to wokou activity once again. With no merchant fleets to protect, the Chinese navy was severely neglected, quickly falling into disrepair. Fewer ships were sent out to sea, which meant there was less of a military presence to patrol the nearby waters. Unsurprisingly, this resulted in a rise in piracy as there simply were not enough ships to keep the East China Sea or Yellow Sea safe.

By the sixteenth century the wokou were no longer primarily made up of Japanese pirates, with their ranks now consisting of mostly Chinese sailors instead. Feeling repressed and exploited under Ming rule, the disenfranchised members of the lower class—both men and women—abandoned their lives in China and joined roving pirate bands instead. Smuggling and marauding offered them more of a chance to improve their station in life than staying back home, even if it meant sacrificing their safety and security.

With maritime trade banned altogether, the wokou soon found themselves in the unique position of being able to obtain overseas goods and deliver them to the Chinese mainland, albeit at greatly inflated prices. With only a reduced and dilapidated navy to try to stop them, the Ming rulers had almost no way to stem the tide of illegal goods that were suddenly flowing into its coastal cities. An entire economy sprang up for the sale of these goods, turning some pirate captains into wealthy smugglers almost overnight. In some cases, these captains became respected citizens in the towns that they supplied with goods and it was not uncommon for pirate bands to hold sway over local governments, influencing political and economic decisions in coastal regions.

Chinese junk ship.

In addition to supplying communities with hard-to-obtain goods from other countries, some pirate groups provided protection to seaside towns and villages as well. Naturally, these services came at a price as the smugglers found a new source of income to supplement their regular visits to overseas ports to collect cargo. In this way, the wokou evolved into opportunistic businessmen, albeit ones that were participating in some shady practices.

Piracy was not necessarily a permanent way of life for the wokou either. Members of a pirate band tended to come and go, sometimes spending just a few months as part of the crew, then leaving to pursue other avenues. Wokou captains sometimes made their fortunes and then quickly retired. The opportunities to become rich abounded, particularly since some of the more connected captains also worked directly with Ming administrators. While the official policy of the dynasty was to outlaw overseas trade and maritime merchant traffic, some of the well-placed bureaucrats still had a taste for the contraband goods.

It was during this time that wokou managed to establish a pirate colony in the Philippines and created their own trade routes to that far-off chain of islands. The modern day Filipino city of Aparri can actually trace its roots all the way back to the sixteenth century, when it was established to serve as a center for trade for merchants traveling across the region. The outpost was under the direct protection of the pirates, who maintained control over the town until Spanish soldiers finally expelled them in 1582.

Wokou Captains

Perhaps the most audacious of the sixteenth-century wokou was a man named Limahong, who was well known for frequently raiding the Chinese coast. But the pirate captain also earned a living as a smuggler, transporting illegal goods in from Japan and the Philippines back to China. His activities often led to showdowns with prominent Chinese generals who had been tasked with putting an end to the growing pirate menace.

On one of his voyages back to the Philippines, Limahong attacked and captured a Chinese ship that had recently traded with the Spanish. Aboard the vessel he found a surprising amount of silver and gold, with a crew member of the captured vessel telling him that there was plenty more to be had in the city of Manilla. The outlaw reveled in the idea of filling his hold with even more Spanish treasure, so he set sail for the city with visions of vast wealth dancing in his head.

Upon arrival, Limahong sent seven hundred of his men ashore to launch a ground attack on the Spanish outpost at Manila. The European forces fought valiantly however, maintaining good defensive positions throughout the encounter. The Spaniards repulsed the first attack using standard defensive tactics, with the Chinese suffering heavy casualties as a result. This did little to deter the wokou captain, who returned a few days later with his entire fleet. This time, he used cannon fire from the ships to help soften up the Spanish positions, but when his crew made a second assault on the fort by land, they once again met with heavy resistance. The pirates were turned back yet again and Limahong retreated out to sea. When the battle was over, the Chinese had suffered over two hundred casualties, while the Spanish lost just seventeen men.

Wang Zhi was another well-known wokou captain who sailed the far reaches of the Pacific in the sixteenth century. He famously guided the first Portuguese ships to Japan in 1543, allowing the two nations to interact and sign trade agreements with one another for the first time. Later, Wang Zhi launched an extensive and powerful crime syndicate centered on smuggling illegal goods into China. Over time, this venture became so profitable that he became one of the wealthiest men operating in the region, with thousands of pirates sailing under his banner.

The wokou captain Lin Daoqian was a contemporary of Limahong and Wang Zhi, and became quite the powerful pirate lord in his own right. It is said that at one point in his life more than five thousand men were under his command, with hundreds of ships at his disposal. He earned his riches by raiding the Chinese coastline, but later sailed to Thailand to escape Ming forces that had been sent to quell the growing pirate threat.

By 1555, wokou activity in the East and South China Seas had grown so prevalent that Ming officials finally decided that something had to be done about it. The Chinese general Yu Dayou was given a strong fleet and a well-trained army to help end the pirate activity and ensure the safe passage of ships sailing to and from China. Over the next few years, he hunted down and defeated more than two thousand wokou raiders, driving them away from the Chinese coastline. Later, he helped liberate the city of Putian, which had been taken over by pirates years earlier and had become a base of operations for the outlaws to launch their raids.

Yu Dayou's campaigns against the pirates were so successful that a little more than a decade after he initiated his attacks against the wokou, he had driven virtually all of them away from the Chinese coastline. This brought a much-needed level of safety and security back to the seas, allowing merchant traffic and passenger ships to sail between China, Korea, and Japan once again. But more than that, Yu Dayou's efforts—combined with a crackdown on piracy in Japan—essentially put an end to wokou activity in the East China Sea and the Sea of Japan, closing the book on one of the more infamous pirate groups to operate in the Pacific.

The Dutch in the Pacific

Vanquishing the wokou was only a temporary solution to the pirate nuisance that had been so rampant in the East and South China Seas, as well as the Sea of Japan. The dawn of the seventeenth century sent more Chinese raiders out onto the water, just as European influence in the

A Spanish galleon battles a Dutch ship.

region was starting to take hold. In fact, the new generation of Asian buccaneers found an unexpected ally in the form of the Dutch, who were looking for ways to facilitate trade with the isolationist Ming Dynasty.

The ban on the import of foreign goods to China remained in place, but Dutch merchants saw a chance to make a profit if they could find a way to break into that market. To that end, the Dutch East India Company partnered with several influential pirates in the hope that it would not only provide access into China, but open trade routes to Japan as well. All previous efforts by merchants from the Netherlands to influence Ming dignitaries had been rebuffed, but the company was willing to explore all options, and remain patient, if it meant access to Chinese harbors.

The relationship between the Ming Dynasty and the pirates that operated off its shores had always been a complicated one. Official policy was to ban all private maritime trade with other nations, providing the government with complete control over the flow of goods in and out of the country. But in order for the Ming elite to continue receiving the luxury goods that they wanted, the aristocracy often worked with buccaneers directly, circumventing their own rules and regulations in the process. It was perfectly fine for them to use and own contraband goods in a clandestine manner, but those items were not meant for regular Chinese citizens.

Sometimes the pirates were even used as diplomatic tools, being paid to attack the ships of rival nations or to leave certain trade routes open. On occasion, they were hired to help create a beachhead in a new region that was ripe for colonization. Ming Dynasty officials found the pirates to be highly useful under the right circumstances and would often turn a blind eye to their activities, provided they did not interfere with the interests of the emperor or the kingdom as a whole.

That said, if pirate groups began to grow in power, and became more organized, the Ming rulers would strike out in an effort to maintain control. Such was the case when it launched a military campaign against the wokou in the late 1550s. The Ming Dynasty had no qualms about using force against the marauders, even if they were once allies. Behind the scenes, Ming administrators knew that if left unchecked, piracy could be a disruptive force that threatened the security of the nation and its mercantile interests, but when controlled and directed it could be a powerful tool.

Zheng Zhilong

That was the environment that the Dutch East India Company found itself operating in at the turn of the seventeenth century. The corporation saw the benefit of working with powerful pirate lords, particularly those who had inside connections with Ming Dynasty administrators. Those pirates essentially became privateers for the company, helping it to pursue its goals in Asia. One of the more influential of the privateers was a Chinese pirate captain named Zheng Zhilong, who began working with the Dutch not long after the Europeans had colonized the island of Chinese Taiwan.

Zheng served as an interpreter and ambassador of sorts between the Dutch East India Company and the Ming Dynasty. He also worked with his European allies to undermine other pirate lords that had gotten in the way of Dutch expansion in the region. In return, the Chinese privateer was given access to European ship designs and weaponry, which proved to be significantly more advanced than the Chinese junk ships, which were large and stable, but lacked speed and maneuverability.

Soon Zheng found himself rising in status and power, becoming one of the most dominant forces on the South China Sea. So much so that he would sell special diplomatic passes to local merchants and fishermen that granted them protection from other pirates. This protection racket made him even wealthier and brought security and safety to the region. With Zheng's fleet patrolling the waters, other marauders elected to move on to greener pastures rather than face off against the pirate lord.

Most of the ships that traveled the high seas at the time payed Zheng for his diplomatic passes and as a result, were granted safe passage. Any ship that did not have a pass was either fair game for the other pirates or was attacked by Zheng's forces directly. This left most merchants and fishing vessels little choice but to pay up.

Always the opportunist, Zheng later partnered with seventeen other major bands of pirates that were working in the East and South China Seas, creating a pirate super-group of sorts that was known as the Shibazhi. Their combined forces allowed the marauders to attack the royal fleet of the Ming Dynasty itself, which surrendered when faced with such an overwhelming onslaught. But in a move that showed just how accepting and pliable the Ming and the pirate factions actually were, Zheng switched sides and officially joined the dynasty after the battle. In doing so, he was named the admiral of the coastal seas and was given command of an armada that consisted of more than eight hundred ships.

This new position put him in direct opposition with his former employers, the Dutch East India Company, which paid a group of pirates and privateers to make an unprovoked attack on Chinese ships. Zheng led his armada against the mercenary fleet in an all-out battle to determine who would control the Chinese Taiwan Strait. When the Chinese claimed victory, it brought a huge morale boost to the Ming navy, as up until then there were few showdowns with the Europeans that had gone in their favor. After the battle, Zheng reopened the trade routes with the Dutch and negotiated a peaceful agreement to both sides of the conflict.

The Spanish in the Pacific

The seas off the coast of China and Japan were not the only places where pirates operated in the Pacific, particularly as the Europeans continued to spread out across the ocean. The Spanish were forced to deal with seafaring marauders on a regular basis, particularly as their colony in the Philippines expanded in size and scope.

After defeating the Chinese pirate Limahong at the Battle of Manilla, the Spanish turned their focus towards building the Philippines into a major trading hub. The goal was to create a colony that could collect spices, silver, gold, and other goods collected in India and Asia, then ship them across the Pacific to a Spanish-held outpost in Acapulco, Mexico.

That route was known as the Trans-Pacific Trade Route or the Manilla Galleon Route—so named for the ships that were built in the Philippines and sailed the vast distance to reach the Americas. Once there, the cargo was offloaded and transferred via mule to train to the city of Veracruz, where it was then added to the Caribbean treasure fleet for transport back to Spain.

The exact route across the Pacific was kept well hidden to prevent English, Dutch, or Portuguese pirates from discovering it. This helped keep the galleons safe while at sea and resulted in almost no pirate activity out on the open water. The chances of two ships randomly encountering one another in the middle of the ocean were incredibly small, so most of the time pirates did not pursue the Manilla galleons out to sea. Instead, they would lie in wait along the coasts of the Philippines themselves or far across the Pacific along the shores of North and South America.

The waters that surrounded the Philippines were filled with the usual suspects in terms of pirates. In addition to Chinese and Japanese marauders, there were plenty of raiders from England, the Netherlands, and Portugal. Those buccaneers took every opportunity to plunder Spanish ships and over time those raids began to have a significant impact on the colony. Because it is located so far from Spain, the Philippines required a substantial investment to build, maintain, defend, and operate. Ongoing piracy only served to drive those costs up further, eating into profits and wealth at a steady pace.

Pirates and the Philippines

While Spain's old enemies in Europe were an ongoing challenge, and Asian marauders often made things difficult, it was a new adversary that created headaches for the Spanish in the Philippines. Muslim pirates operating out of Indonesia took to raiding Spanish ships, capturing treasure and slaves to haul back to their island kingdoms. This revived the recurring conflict between Muslim and Christian factions, which played out much the same way as it had in Europe and the Middle East during the crusades. Despite its growing empire, Spain never expected to be fighting a holy war on the far side of the planet.

When the Spanish arrived in the Philippines in 1565 their goal was not just to establish trading routes into Asia. The devoutly Catholic country had been converting indigenous people in the Americas to Christianity for decades and it saw no reason to not do the same on the Pacific Rim. At the time, the Spanish missionaries had no idea that some of the oldest Islamic countries in the world existed in nearby Indonesia, but once those sultanates became aware of the spread of Christendom on their doorsteps, they immediately launched a campaign against Spain's ships and settlements.

Many of the raids against Spanish targets originated in the sultanates of Ternate and Tidore, both of which supported pirate activity against their newly arrived enemy. Many of the raids were backed by the wealthy Sultanate of Brunei, which led to Spain launching the Castilian War in an effort to overthrow the country's leader. Because the conflict involved Christian and Muslim forces squaring off against one another, the show-down took on a greater meaning than just squabbling over valuable goods.

The war was brief, with Spain being forced to withdraw its forces back to the Philippines. But, the Spanish did succeed in reducing the number of Muslim privateers that were attacking its ships, bringing a measure of increased security to their operations on the edge of the Pacific.

However, Spain's trouble with piracy in the Philippines was far from over, as an indigenous people known as the Moro continued to create challenges for the Europeans for the many decades that followed. Like their Indonesian cousins, the Moro were also Muslims and viewed the arrival of the Christian Spaniards as an invasion of infidels. There were frequent Moro revolts over the years, which created unrest in the Spanish colony that routinely required the use of force to put down.

Eventually, the Moro took to the Sulu Sea to engage Spanish galleons and merchant vessels. That body of water, which was sailed by the Moro for hundreds of years prior to the arrival of the Europeans, is located to the southwest of the Philippines, flowing directly into the Pacific. Using large, surprisingly maneuverable ships, the pirates would send fifty to a hundred men out on the sea to prey upon passing shipping traffic. Using quick-strike tactics, they would overwhelm the opposition, plunder their cargo, and take the passengers and crew as captives. It is said that over the course of two years, these marauders sold thousands of Christians into slavery from these raids alone.

The Moro continued to challenge Spain for more than three hundred years, although—as with other parts of the world—technology, improved ships, and better weaponry eventually gave the Spanish the upper hand. The arrival of steamships allowed the Europeans to seize control over the Sulu Sea and put the Moro pirates on the run. The boats built by the Islamic forces simply could not compete with the faster, more powerful vessels that were brought to bear by the Spanish.

Still, the Moro refused to give in and took any opportunity that they could to disrupt Spanish trade in the Philippines. These activities continued until 1898, when the Spanish-American War ended and the US took charge of the islands. The Moro simply found themselves fighting the same war, just against a new enemy. This conflict extended well into the twentieth century.

Sir Francis Drake and John Coxon in the Pacific

While it was rare, the Spanish occasionally had trouble on the opposite side of the Pacific as well, most notably when Sir Francis Drake made his foray into that ocean. The former privateer was a valuable asset to the British, having served the Crown in a number of capacities over his long and distinguished sailing career. But to the Spanish, whose ships he frequently attacked, he was little more than a common pirate who was wanted for numerous crimes.

After Drake became the second person to ever lead an expedition around Cape Horn, he immediately began sailing northward along the west coast of South America. When he and his men neared the country of Peru, the Englishman came across a Spanish ship traveling along the same route. Never one to miss a chance to strike out at his old nemesis, Drake attacked and raided the vessel. Onboard he found over twenty-five thousand pesos made of gold, which would hold a value of roughly $9 million in modern day currency.

An English galley.

This was quite a haul for the explorer and his crew, but while searching the ship's logs Drake discovered that it had recently encountered another Spanish vessel named *Nuestra Señora de la Concepción* (Our Lady of the Immaculate Conception) just a few days earlier and it too was sailing north off the coast of South America. Better yet, the second ship was reportedly carrying an even richer cargo—a target too enticing to pass up.

Aboard his ship the *Golden Hind*, Drake gave chase and soon caught up with the *Nuestra,* which was not originally alarmed at the sight of another ship. Pirate activity on the eastern side of the Pacific was nonexistent at the time, so the Spanish captain assumed it was just another friendly vessel that was approaching. Much to his surprise, Drake and his men called for the Spanish crew to surrender. When they refused, a battle ensued, during which the *Nuestra* was soon subdued.

When the Spanish vessel was raided, Drake and his men took possession of a great deal of plunder. In addition to carrying twenty-six tons of silver, the *Nuestra* also had eighty pounds of gold, thirteen chests of other treasures, a golden crucifix, and various other valuables. That alone was enough to make his voyage profitable, even though he still had to sail halfway around the world in order to reach his home port back in England.

Drake was not the only one who managed to find a way to strike at the Spanish in the Pacific either, although other pirates had to find more creative ways to safely and quickly reach that body of water. During the late seventeenth century, a buccaneer by the name of John Coxon was one of the most feared men on the Spanish Main, raiding ships and towns across the Caribbean and along the coasts of the Gulf of Mexico. Over the course of about five years, he pulled off some of the most daring and successful raids of any buccaneer in history.

One of Coxon's biggest successes came sometime around 1680, when he and his band of loyal men trekked across the Isthmus of Panama—the thin stretch of land that separates the Atlantic and Pacific Oceans where North and South America meet. Their goal was to conduct a raid against the unsuspecting Spanish, who they rightly believed had become complacent and lax in their security.

Upon reaching the Pacific, the group of buccaneers captured two small Spanish sloops, then used them to launch a raid on the main Spanish fleet. After a pitched battle, Coxon and his men took control of those ships too, much to the embarrassment and anger of the local Spanish garrison.

Once again, surprise played a significant role in the success of the attack, as the Spanish were not expecting anyone to raid their vessels. This allowed Coxon and his crew to capture a significant number of ships, although later the pirate fell out with some of his allies and left the Pacific behind to return to the Caribbean on foot.

Drake's and Coxon's exploits were extremely rare examples of pirate activity on the far side of the Pacific. At the time, no buccaneers were willing to risk sailing around Cape Horn or crossing the vast distances needed to sail directly from Asia to the Americas. If they had, they probably would have been greatly disappointed, as other than a few Spanish ships, there was not much to find there. The west coasts of the North and South American continents were not even extensively mapped yet, let alone developing any kind of trade. That made such a voyage fruitless, with little plunder to be found.

A Continued Lack of Pirates

This remained the state of affairs for decades to come, particularly since trade routes across the Pacific took more than two hundred years to truly develop. Once the Panama Canal opened in 1914, merchants no longer needed to sail around the southernmost tip of South America, giving them a more viable and profitable way to ship goods across the globe. Of course, by then, the age of the pirate had long since come and gone from the Atlantic, Pacific, and the Caribbean, making such ventures much safer to conduct.

By the time the nineteenth century arrived, the British navy ruled the high seas, including the Pacific. Its powerful fleet was unmatched and the Brits used its considerable strength to not just hunt down pirates, but also to locate and eliminate slave traders. These efforts prevented piracy from ever gaining a serious foothold on the far side of the Pacific, with only a handful of rare exceptions.

For similar reasons, piracy was not a major issue in Australia either. While the continent was much easier for pirates to reach when sailing from Asia, it too had little to offer seafaring raiders. The Dutch were the first to definitively spot the landmass back in 1606 and later made the first charts of its coastline. They even named the place "New Holland," although there were never any serious attempts to colonize it or explore its vast interior.

Both the Spanish and English also visited Australia at various times, with Captain James Cook famously claiming the new continent for the British in 1770. Not long after that, it was declared a penal colony, with prisoners being sent from Europe to settle the wild, unexplored land. Vast, remote, and isolated, Australia seemed like the perfect destination for cast-offs and convicts.

Colonization continued at a steady pace, although—as with the west coasts of North and South America—it took some time for trade to develop, leaving little for pirates to raid. This kept the extensive, and barely charted, Australian coastline safe from marauders for decades.

Black Jack Anderson

That isn't to say that Australia did not see occasional pirate activity, most commonly in Tasmania, previously known as Van Diemen's Land. The island is located to the south of the main continent and was settled by former prisoners just like the mainland. At times, a group of prisoners would cooperate with one another long enough to seize a ship and make an escape from the penal colony. The vast majority of those cases did not involve the prisoners actually becoming pirates that raided ships on the high seas however. Instead, it was all about making their escape and trying to create a new life for themselves somewhere else.

Australia's sole known pirate—at least in the traditional sense—was a man named Black Jack Anderson. The African American sailor, who was born in Massachusetts, arrived on the continent in 1826 aboard a whaling vessel. Despite being a legitimate and competent crew member, Anderson later turned to piracy after being accused of murder following a drunken brawl. In order to avoid being sent to prison, he and some men stole a ship and escaped, eventually setting up camp on Middle Island off the coast of Western Australia. For a time, the outlaws hunted seals and traded furs to settlements along the coast, but later, they took to attacking and raiding passing ships making their way from Sydney to Hobart.

Anderson gained a reputation as a ruthless buccaneer who held life in low regard. He and his men often raided the coastal villages of aboriginals, brutally killing the men and kidnapping the women. Those abducted females were later sold into slavery, a practice that remained common throughout Australia despite the British outlawing the practice in 1833.

For more than a decade, the pirate crew preyed upon merchant ships, amassing a small fortune in treasure and goods. But eventually, Anderson's difficult demeanor and callous attitude towards the lives of his crew caught up with him. The pirate was reportedly murdered by his own men and buried somewhere near their outpost on Middle Island, bringing an abrupt and ignoble end to the only real pirate Australia ever saw.

Iron Jim Sallow

On the opposite side of the Pacific—about as far away from Australia as you can get—there are similar tales of a few mysterious pirates that once roamed America's Pacific Northwest. One of the more famous of these men was Iron Jim Sallow, who reportedly became friendly with the Native Americans who lived in the area and often traded goods and supplies with them. Sallow found the rocky shores, hidden coves, and numerous islands in that part of the world to his liking, as it was an ideal place for a pirate ship to hide from the authorities.

As the legend goes, Sallow managed to accumulate a sizable amount of treasure and decided to bury it in the Puget Sound area, not far from what is now Seattle. As pirates were known to do, he drew a detailed map that would help him reclaim his riches when he was ready to return for the hidden booty. Later, the map was stolen by a disgruntled crew member looking to claim that treasure for his own. The angry Sallow reportedly gave pursuit, chasing the thief in an effort to retrieve his map and ultimately return for his hidden gold. But both the pirate himself, and the man he chased, disappeared from history completely, without anyone ever knowing what became of them. This tale has survived the passage of time and continues to inspire fortune hunters looking for Sallow's lost gold to this day.

Pacific Coastlines

Considering the nature of the terrain in the Pacific Northwest, it is surprising that few other marauders seemed to have operated out of the area. Just as the concealed bays and towering cliffs were viewed as an asset to the Cilician pirates of the Mediterranean hundreds of years earlier, the topography of the shoreline in the northwestern Pacific seems tailor made for bands of buccaneers. A few ships did occasionally use that place as a base of operations, but the remote nature of the area and the slow-to-develop economy, along with the lack of wealthy trade routes, prevented it from becoming a true pirate haven.

As it turns out, that was the case with much of the eastern Pacific in general. Eventually the coastlines of North and South America included large cities, thriving ports, and harbors that became rich with mercantile traffic. But by the time that happened, naval ships diligently patrolled those waters, helping to hunt the few remaining buccaneers to near extinction.

By the mid to late nineteenth century, few pirates remained anywhere on the planet. On occasion, small bands of bold sailors desperately clinging to a bygone era sprang up here and there across the globe, usually only to be swatted out of existence when they grew to become too much of a threat. But the days of the swashbuckling buccaneer were clearly numbered, crushed under the relentless tread of modern technology and an international community that had matured to the point where the mere existence of those men and women was no longer tolerated.

The romantic ideals of sailing the high seas in search of grand adventure were over. The sun had set on the age of the classic pirate. But the twentieth century would introduce a new kind of oceangoing outlaw—one that was more dangerous and disruptive than those that had come before him, with a set of motivations that were both different, and yet eerily familiar to pirates of the past.

Jang Bogo.

The Tale of Sir Francis Drake

The life of a privateer was rarely black and white, but was instead composed of many shades of gray. The ultimate capitalists, a privateer captain might set sail in defense of king and country one day, only to find a more lucrative offer waiting for him the next. At times, he might make a living as a smuggler, a merchant, a slave trader, and, yes, even a pirate.

Having a slightly fluid moral compass often proved to be a valuable asset to a sailor, as it made it easier to shift allegiances or pursue other objectives whenever it served his best interest. After all, loyalties and alliances were always tenuous, but finding a way to survive, or even thrive, was the first order of business.

This was not necessarily the case with Sir Francis Drake, a privateer and explorer who was viewed as a national hero amongst the English but derided by the Spanish. His travels took him the length and breadth of the world, sailing distant seas, and broadening the scope of how we understand our planet. Along the way, he also found fame and fortune, while still staying loyal to queen and country.

Born circa 1540 in Devon, England, to a farmer and preacher named Edmund and his wife Mary, Francis was the oldest of twelve sons. When he was ten years old, the family moved from Devon to Kent, where they took up residence aboard a small ship while Edmund became the minister for sailors serving in the Royal Navy. At about that same time, young Francis was apprenticed to a family friend who operated a small merchant skiff that ran goods and supplies to and from France. Working aboard that vessel, Drake acquired the skills necessary to become a sailor and a merchant, setting him on the path to future glory.

By the time he was eighteen, Drake was already a seasoned sailor, who had traveled up and down the coast of England and France. He was so hardworking and valuable to his crew in fact, that when the ship's master passed away without a family of his own, he left Drake his ship as part of his last will and testament. It was around that same time that Drake joined a shipping company owned and operated by his second cousin, Sir John Hawkins. Working with that organization, he began to sail farther abroad, traveling to West Africa and eventually to the Americas.

John Hawkins was an extremely capable ship's captain, a successful merchant, shipbuilder, and navigator. He was also the first English slave trader to operate in the New World, delivering African slave labor to the newly established colonies there. Hawkins and his fleet would begin their journey by first raiding Portuguese ships and towns in West Africa, collecting loot and slaves along the way. After that, they would sail for the Americas, bringing vital goods and supplies—along with an ample supply of slave labor—for the desperate colonists.

Drake served alongside his cousin on three such voyages, becoming a slave trader himself for a time. This gave him the chance to sail across the Atlantic to the New World, where economic opportunity awaited both the bold and those willing to bend the law here and there. If a ship's captain had no issues with buying or kidnapping other human beings, then selling them off to wealthy landowners, it was possible to become quite rich in a relatively short span of time. Drake did not seem to have any qualms about the practice, putting coins in his pouch at the expense of other human beings.

It was on one of these voyages that Drake encountered the Spanish—which would leave a long and lasting impression on him. So much so, that for the rest of his life he would take just about every opportunity that came his way to seek revenge on his sworn enemy. In time, he came to make Spain regret the day it had ever crossed paths with Francis Drake, who would go on to fundamentally change that country's fortunes, dramatically reducing its stature and standing on the world's stage.

The fateful encounter occurred in 1568, with Drake serving on his second voyage to the New World with John Hawkins. Badly in need of resupply and repairs, the Hawkins fleet arrived in the port town of San Juan de Ulúa along the Mexican coast. While still negotiating the logistics of purchasing the needed supplies and scheduling maintenance, a

Sir Francis Drake.

bevy of Spanish ships attacked the English vessels, destroying all but two of them. Both Drake and Hawkins were able to escape, but only by diving overboard and swimming to safety.

From that point onward, Drake held the Spanish in very low regard and would dedicate his career as a seaman to exacting revenge. But not one to make rash decisions or rush into a conflict, he bided his time and waited for his opportunity to strike back. He was so patient, that as a young sailor he made several voyages to the West Indies simply to assess Spanish military strength and wealth in the region, taking detailed notes that would prove useful later.

The first chance to strike back against his enemies came in 1572, which is when Drake took command of two ships and sailed for the Isthmus of Panama under a letter of marque issued by Queen Elizabeth I. His goal was to attack and capture the city of Nombre de Dios, which is where much of the silver and gold from Peru was funneled in preparation for shipping back to Spain. With a crew of just seventy-three men, he accomplished his task, but suffered a serious wound in the process. Fearing for their captain's life, the crew grabbed Drake and spirited him away back to his ship, leaving the town—along with its treasure—behind.

A year later, Drake was finally able to gain a measure of payback against the Spanish by capturing the legendary Silver Train. Mainly consisting of mules traveling overland along an established trail, the train was used to transport precious metals and gems from Peru to Nombre de Dios. Once there, the commodities were loaded up on ships and sent back to Europe, filling the coffers of the Spanish monarchy. At the time, the New World was a source of enormous wealth and income for Spain, which relied on regular shipments of treasure to keep its vast empire, not to mention its army and navy, in operation.

Joining forces with a French privateer named Guillaume Le Testu, as well as a contingent of escaped African slaves, Drake and his crew set out to intercept the Silver Train on the trail while it was en route to its destination. While hiking through the steamy jungle, Drake would frequently stop to climb a tree in hopes of catching a glimpse of his quarry in the distance. During one such stop he climbed high enough above the ground that he caught sight of the Pacific Ocean gleaming in the distance. In doing so, Drake became the first Englishman to set eyes on that body of water, which remained the sole domain of the Spanish during that era. As the legend goes, Drake reportedly expressed his hopes that another Englishman would get the chance to sail those waters one day, never once considering that he would be the one to do so.

It is believed that the mules that made up the Silver Train were carrying roughly twenty tons of silver and gold when Drake and his men attacked and captured them. That would make their haul worth hundreds of millions of dollars by today's standards. Unfortunately, the raid yielded so much plunder that Drake was forced to order his men to collect as much as they could carry and bury the rest with the hopes of returning for it at a later time.

Hauling their heavy cargo back to the beach was not easy. Drake and his crew had to pass through miles of hot and humid rainforest just to reach the boats they had used to launch their raid. By the time they returned to the shore, they were exhausted, dehydrated, and reaching the end of their endurance. Much to their surprise and dismay, the men soon discovered that the boats that would safely allow them to return to their waiting ship were nowhere to be found. To make matters worse, Spanish forces had been tracking them for days and were closing in on their position, eager to reclaim their lost treasure.

The always resourceful Drake quickly came up with a plan. He ordered his crew to bury the remaining silver and gold and get to work on building a raft. It took some time, but they were able to engineer a makeshift boat that allowed them to push off from the beach and escape the clutches of their pursuers. The raft allowed them to travel the ten miles back to their ship, where the rest of the crew was anxiously awaiting their return.

For Drake, the raid on the Silver Train was a bittersweet victory. On the one hand, he had dealt a significant blow to his rivals, but on the other he and his crew came away with very little treasure to show for their efforts. A few pieces of jewelry and other items made it back to the ship, which prevented the voyage from becoming a total loss. But considering how much treasure had to be left behind, buried in the ground, it was a demoralizing loss.

After plundering the Silver Train, Drake and his men returned to England, where their exploits earned them a hero's welcome. While there, they learned that England and Spain had signed a truce, putting an end to their hostilities. Drake could no longer legally make raids against his sworn enemy, nor would his actions in the Caribbean be publicly acknowledged. As beneficial to the Crown as his raids had been, they were now seen as a source of friction with the Spanish.

With no foreign enemy to sail against, Drake joined a small fleet that was sent to Ireland in 1575 to put down an insurrection. During an attack on Rathlin Island off the Irish Coast, he and his allies captured a castle that contained two hundred Irish soldiers and four hundred civilians. After accepting the stronghold's surrender, one of the other admirals ordered the execution of all the men, women, and children that had taken refuge inside the fortress. The massacre was carried out in a swift and brutal fashion and remains a controversial historical event to this day. It could also account for a two-year gap in Drake's history, where little is known about his whereabouts. It seems likely that he was laying low in order to avoid being caught up in the scandal.

Unsurprisingly, the truce with Spain did not hold for long and by 1577 the queen had new orders for Drake. Knowing that he had achieved great success against the Spanish in the past, she asked him to take a fleet of ships around Cape Horn and into the Pacific Ocean—something that had only been done on one occasion prior to that time. Drake was given free rein to conduct raids against their mutual enemy, destroying and plundering any enemy ships or outposts that he came across. It was both an extremely dangerous charge and a potentially lucrative one, with the promise of plenty of silver and gold to be plundered along the way. Naturally, Drake eagerly accepted this charge, seeing it as not only a great honor, but a chance to continue doling out retribution to his old adversaries.

In December of 1577, Drake set sail from Plymouth, England, with five ships in his fleet. Commanding from his flagship—the *Pelican*—he ordered the flotilla to sail south along the west coast of Africa, where he picked up another ship by capturing a Portuguese vessel. All six ships then turned across the Atlantic, targeting the coast of South America as their eventual destination.

Crossing the Atlantic proved problematic however, with numerous men taking ill and perishing while at sea. The number of losses were so high that Drake ordered the abandonment of two of his ships and then burned a third upon reaching Argentina. His once large and promising fleet was rapidly diminishing in size before it had even reached the Pacific Ocean.

Worse yet, during the voyage Drake tried and convicted his co-commander Thomas Doughty of mutiny, treason, and witchcraft. The two men had openly argued about the best course of action for weeks and Drake—claiming full authority of the Queen—had Doughty beheaded. Historians question whether or not the sea captain actually did have the authority to order such an execution or if he fabricated his authority in an effort to eliminate a rival.

Morale was low and the prospects of the fleet looked dim when Drake and his men elected to winter in Argentina before attempting the perilous Magellan Strait—the route that would take them around Tierra del Fuego and Cape Horn, the southernmost point of South America. Pioneered by Ferdinand Magellan on his attempt to circumnavigate the globe more than fifty years earlier, the path was one of the most treacherous sections of water on the planet. It was so dangerous that when Drake braved the passage he emerged in the Pacific for the very first time, but found that he had lost two more ships in the process. One of those vessels was completely destroyed by the turbulent waters, while the other suffered so much damage that it had to turn back into the Atlantic and return to England.

Drake pressed ahead aboard the *Pelican*, becoming the first Englishman to sail into the Pacific Ocean. To commemorate the achievement he renamed his one remaining boat the *Golden Hind* in honor of Sir Christopher Hatton. Hatton was one of Drake's patrons and helped sponsor the voyage. He also famously had the mythical golden hind displayed on his family's coat of arms. In Greek tales, that creature was sacred to the goddess Artemis and was said to be so swift it could outrun an arrow.

Once safely around the horn, Drake's fortune finally began to take a turn for the better. Not only did he find smooth seas and good weather, but also plenty of Spanish ships and settlements to begin preying upon. Not expecting an attack from the ocean, many of those Spanish outposts were caught completely unaware, making them easy targets for the Englishman and his crew, who were eager to collect some plunder at long last.

One of the first ships that the *Golden Hind* captured was filled with Chilean wine, much to the surprise and delight of Drake and his men. More importantly, they also managed to capture detailed charts of the South American coastline and the waters that fell just off its shores. This made navigation much easier and helped the crew locate important points of interest along the way. The charts also prominently displayed the Spanish trade routes in the region and revealed the wealthy city of Valparaiso. Drake sacked that outpost on his way up the Chilean coastline.

Sailing north to Peru, the English privateer seized a Spanish vessel that reportedly carried twenty-five thousand gold pesos and an additional thirty-seven thousand Spanish ducats, which would be worth nearly $10 million today. That paled in comparison to the second treasure ship he plundered however, as Drake got heed of a vessel known as the *Nuestra Señora de la Concepción* that was sailing west on its way to the Philippines. Giving chase, the *Golden Hind* soon overtook the unsuspecting galleon and captured it as well. Aboard, the crew discovered a small fortune in silver, gold, gems, and other rate materials. It was enough to pay for the entire voyage and make Drake and his benefactors very wealthy men.

Continuing north, the *Golden Hind* made its way up the coast, transitioning from South America to North. Upon reaching what is now California, Drake sailed into a protected cove, disembarked from his ship, and declared the land that he found there for the queen. He left a few men behind to set up a small colony, with the promise of reinforcements and additional supplies to come. That colony floundered and disappeared as it was years before another English ship passed that way.

Deeming his mission complete in the Americas, Drake turned his ship west and set sail across the Pacific Ocean in July of 1579. His route took him past Palau and the Philippines before intersecting with the Moluccas, a chain of remote islands located on the western edge of the Pacific near modern day Indonesia. There, he accidentally ran his ship aground, but was able to get it unstuck without suffering any major damage simply by waiting for the tides to rise and by offloading excess cargo.

Safely back on the ocean, Drake set a course for more well-charted waters. Cutting across the Indian Ocean, he reached the eastern edge of Africa, then sailed down the coast to the Cape of Good Hope. Making his way along those frequently trafficked waters, the *Golden Hind* returned to the Atlantic Ocean in July of 1579. More than two years had

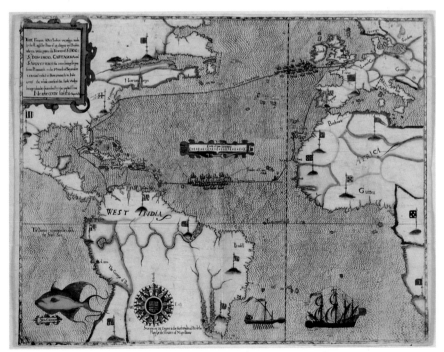

Map of Sir Francis Drake's circumnavigation.

passed since Drake and his men had sailed around South America. Now, only about half of the original crew still remained.

It was another two months before the ship sailed back into Plymouth harbor. Counting Drake, sixty men were aboard the vessel, which now had a cargo hold full of Spanish silver and gold. The vessel had also acquired a number of rare spices and other luxury items during the voyage, some which were plundered from enemy ships, while others were acquired from trading in Asia and Africa.

Drake's safe return once again made him a hero with the queen and his fellow countrymen. Not only had he managed to sack two Spanish treasure ships, and numerous other vessels and towns, he had also become the first Englishman to circumnavigate the globe. His voyage was only the second to complete the dangerous round-the-world journey, a point of significant pride for the Crown. For his service, Drake was knighted aboard the *Golden Hind* in April of 1581, an honor that was rarely conferred on anyone during that era.

Now bearing the title of Sir Francis Drake, the seaman had evolved into quite a villain as far as the Spanish were concerned. They had come to refer to him as "El Draque," which meant "The Dragon," and had put a substantial reward on his head. From their perspective, his criminal acts now spanned the entire planet, with substantial damage being done to the Royal Treasury. It is said that King Phillip II of Spain was so enraged and frustrated by the Englishman's raids that he personally issued the bounty for Drake, offering a reward of twenty thousand ducats, the equivalent of roughly $8 million today.

After his two-year journey around the globe, Drake was content to spend a bit of time back home in England. He dabbled in politics by first becoming mayor of Plymouth and later serving as a member of the British Parliament. But his heart belonged to the sea and even while fulfilling those duties, he still found himself returning to the ocean in some capacity or another. Often those voyages were for his own profit or for that of the queen.

In 1585, the English entered into a treaty with the Dutch, which saw both nations join forces against the Spanish. Once again, Drake was pressed into service, this time leading an attack on his lifelong enemy on three different continents. In September of that year, El Draque set sail with twenty-one ships and 1,800 soldiers to lead an attack on the city of Vigo along the coast of Spain itself. After capturing that objective, Drake and his men held it for two weeks before moving on to sack Santiago on the Cape Verde Islands off the coast of Africa.

From there, Drake and his men sailed across the Atlantic and on to South America, where they captured the cities of Santo Domingo in the Dominican Republic and Cartagena in Colombia. The raids did not end there however, as the fleet proceeded north to attack the Spanish outpost located at San Augustine, Florida. And just for good measure, the benighted admiral then sailed to Virginia to resupply Sir Walter Raleigh's fledgling colony in Roanoke.

Two years after his globe-spanning raids on Spanish garrisons, Drake launched yet another round of attacks. This time, he raided the port cities of Corunna and Cadiz along the coast of Spain, occupying the harbors of both towns for a time. In the process, he destroyed more than thirty ships, which inflicted serious damage on the Spanish navy and merchant vessels alike. The incursion was a tipping point for King Phillip II, who ordered the construction of a massive fleet that was designed to spearhead an invasion of England itself.

When the famed Spanish Armada set sail in 1588 it consisted of 130 ships which had been purposely built to escort an invading army to the shores of England. The animosity between the two countries had been raging for years and Phillip II was ready to do away with his greatest foe. The force he sent against the English was meant to not only overthrow Queen Elizabeth I and bring Catholicism to Britain, but also end the costly attacks by English and Dutch privateers. Men like Sir Francis Drake had inflicted great harm to the Spanish Crown, and the King of Spain was ready to dish out some retribution.

Fully aware of the armada's approach, the English sent a fleet of its own to intercept the ships in the English Channel. Serving as vice-admiral of the Royal Navy during the battle, Drake played a crucial role in the eventual English victory. One of his most important contributions was the capture of the Spanish ship *Nuestra Señora del Rosario* as it cruised up the channel. The vessel was carrying substantial amounts of silver and gold, which was to be used to pay the mercenary army that was awaiting the armada in the Spanish Netherlands. Those soldiers were meant to make up the bulk of the invasion force, but without those funds to pay them, the invasion was over before it even started.

Sailing northward, the armada dropped anchor off the coast of Northern France near the city of Calais. It was there that the mercenary troops were assembling, and the Spanish fleet's orders were to transport those soldiers across the channel to the shores of England. While the Spanish ships awaited the arrival of the army, Drake led a small fleet of fireships into their midst, setting a number of vessels ablaze as he went. Packed with tinder, kindling, and barrels of gunpowder, these fireships exploded in a startling flash of fire and smoke that damaged both hulls and sails.

Having engaged the enemy on the English Channel and off the coast of France, Drake and the other captains soon realized that while they were outnumbered and outgunned, but knew that their smaller, faster ships were far more maneuverable. Using that speed and agility to their advantage, they pressed an attack on the armada, which seemed to have fate working against it at every turn. Strong winds caused the Spanish ships to spread apart and have a difficult time maintaining their formations. This ultimately prevented the armada from operating at peak efficiency or bringing its formidable firepower fully to bear.

Using hit-and-run tactics, the English fleet was quickly gaining confidence against their more powerful foes. Drake and the other commanders sailed close enough to lure the Spanish into firing their powerful—but slow to reload—cannons, and then quickly darted out of range before those bombardments could hit. Just as the Spanish scrambled to reload, the English sailed in close enough to perform a broadside maneuver, inflicting heavy damage using a barrage of cannon fire of their own. These tactics confounded and frustrated the Spanish, who were also being picked apart by musket fire.

The battle raged for over eight hours, and near the end the English ships were beginning to run low on ammo. By that point, they were firing just about anything they could find at the enemy, who were floundering badly. The direct attack on the armada had destroyed, or severely damaged, dozens of ships, causing the Spanish to retreat back to their harbors. It also prevented the fleet from ever connecting with its ground forces, completely preventing the planned land invasion.

The English defeating the Spanish Armada.

It was a major military victory for the English against their long-time rivals and marked the beginning of the end of Spanish dominance out on the ocean. A year later, the English launched a failed attempt to counterattack the Spanish, and two other Spanish Armadas eventually took to the seas as well. But, the military might of King Phillip II was clearly in decline and the two countries formalized a peace treaty in 1604, easing decades of tension at long last. With Spain no longer the preeminent power in Europe, the British Royal Navy began its rise to prominence, ruling the seas for the next three hundred years.

Drake's role in the defeat of the Spanish Armada further cemented his place in history. By the start of the seventeenth century, his reputation was already legendary, and he was viewed as one of the greatest naval commanders to ever take to the seas. But that massive win against his old enemy was the peak of his career, as several significant defeats would soon follow. One of the most notable came in 1589 as part of England's counterattack against Spain. During that conflict Drake led an attack against the port city of A Coruña that sunk numerous enemy vessels. But Drake's forces suffered heavy losses too, including the sinking of twenty ships and the deaths of more than twelve thousand men.

Drake continued the campaign against the Spanish in the New World, attacking a number of important and wealthy targets there. While he earned some minor victories, most of his raids ended in defeat. That includes losses at the Battle of San Juan in 1595, during which the English had hoped to invade Puerto Rico. Later, he attempted to lead an overland assault in Panama, just as he had done years earlier when he captured the Silver Train. That too was met with defeat, sending the now aging admiral back to his ship in frustration.

During his incursion into Panama, Drake contracted a case of dysentery which ultimately led to his demise. While anchored off the coast of that country in January of 1596, he succumbed to the disease and perished. He was in his mid-fifties at the time and despite military losses late in his career, he was still held in extreme high regard by the queen and his fellow countrymen.

As per his request, Drake was dressed in full battle armor and given a burial at sea. His body was placed inside a lead-lined coffin and dropped overboard close to where his ship was anchored when he died. His passing brought great sorrow to his men, who returned home to England following the loss of their captain. He was a man who could not easily be replaced and who cast a long shadow for many years after he was gone.

While he had served as a privateer to the English throughout his career, and occasionally conducted raids with both Dutch and French allies, to the Spanish Sir Francis Drake was worthy of only scorn and contempt. It is safe to say that those feelings were mutual, as the sea captain never forgave, nor forgot, the unprovoked Spanish attack that resulted in thirty years of animosity.

It is hard to imagine what the world could have looked like had the Spanish not attacked Drake on that fateful day. It is possible that he would never have taken up arms against them and would have been content to live out his life as a merchant and slave trader. Instead, that attack sent him down a path that quite literally saw him span the globe to hunt down his enemies. Perhaps more importantly, the part he played in the defeat of the Spanish Armada hastened Spain's decline as a world power, setting the stage for Great Britain to become the greatest empire of its age with a fleet that ruled the seven seas.

Drake's legacy also demonstrates how challenging it is to reconcile the differences between a pirate and a privateer. While he was a hero to the English, there is no question that he made more than a few dubious moral choices throughout his career. Engaging as a slave trader, raiding defenseless ships, stealing the cargo of Spanish vessels, summarily executing crew members, and tacitly standing by while hundreds of innocent people were massacred makes him a complex historical character to reconcile.

That said, there is still much to admire about Sir Francis Drake, such as his patriotic loyalty and superior naval tactics. He was an individual who was a product of his age, and all of the shades of gray that came with it.

CHAPTER 7

The Pirates of the Modern Age

The Major Decline in Piracy

By the dawn of the twentieth century, piracy was mostly a profession of the past. Thanks to the rise in prominence of the British Royal Navy, the vast majority of pirate activity had come to a halt in all but the most remote corners of the globe. From time to time there were still occasional attacks by seafaring brigands in some out-of-the-way locations,

French ship attacking Algiers.

but those incidences were becoming increasingly rare. In fact, it had gotten to the point that the very idea of piracy had been almost completely relegated to the history books, a leftover concept of a bygone era.

There were a number of factors that contributed to the swift decline of piracy in the latter half of the nineteenth century. For instance, the growing might and reach of the British Empire meant that most shipping lanes and maritime sailing routes were now actively patrolled by sophisticated, well-armed, and well-crewed military vessels. This provided fewer targets of opportunity for marauders and made it increasingly more difficult for them to successfully attack a merchant ship and safely make their escape.

Later, other nations used their navies to protect shipping lanes and civilian vessels too. Countries like the United States, France, Germany, and Japan all had ships patrolling large stretches of ocean around the world, while most other nations protected the territorial waters that were under their jurisdiction. This gave pirates far fewer places to hide or trade their ill-gotten goods, which was also a contributing factor to their demise.

The nineteenth century also brought other changes to the world that hastened the end of piracy. Larger merchant ships became much more difficult to attack and plunder, while local administrative governments began to spring up on islands and along coastlines across the globe. This meant that there was more direct local oversight by the European powers in parts of the world that had long been governed from afar. It also meant a higher level of organization and improved communications, all of which worked against the increasingly anachronistic pirates.

But perhaps most importantly of all, there was a major shift in attitude towards pirates and piracy across the globe. In the past, nations had often used privateers and pirates to conduct proxy wars or to disrupt commerce with their enemies. But the world's oceans were playing an increasingly important role in maintaining diplomatic relations and conducting business, which simply left no room for government-supported roving bands of outlaws to interfere with emerging global economy.

Although there were still a few self-styled pirates who cropped up from time to time, piracy was an obsolete profession by the early years of the twentieth century. There were still men like Boysie Singh, who ran an organized crime racket in the Caribbean during the 1940s and '50s, operating as both a smuggler and pirate near the islands of Trinidad and Tobago. And American Dan Seavey, who was a smuggler, human trafficker, and timber pirate operating on the Great Lakes at the turn of the century. But the number of these cases decreased as the decades rolled on, to the point where most people around the world never thought about piracy still being an actual threat in the modern age.

The Return of Piracy

But just as there were a number of factors that helped bring about the end of piracy, there were also some important changes to maritime trade, geopolitics, and technology that contributed to its return during the 1990s and early 2000s. Not the least of those factors is the way that merchant ships have evolved in the more than one hundred years since pirates were last viewed as a serious threat out on the ocean.

Prior to the end of the nineteenth century, merchant ships were relatively slow and ponderous, but they were also outfitted with powerful cannons and carried large crews of armed men. The crews were entrusted to safely deliver the ship to a distant port of call, often at risk of not getting paid if it did not arrive in one piece. To that end, it was not unusual for them to defend the vessel and its cargo to the death rather than see it fall into the hands of buccaneers looking to plunder its holds.

Today's modern freighters operate in sharp contrast to the merchant ships of old. A twenty-first-century cargo vessel generally is not armed at all and is often manned by a crew of twenty-five or fewer. Additionally, those individuals are not usually all that well versed in the use of weapons of any kind, including firearms. This makes capturing such a ship a much more viable option than it had been in the past, increasing the likelihood of success should pirates decide to attack. This has turned commercial ships into tempting targets of opportunity once again, with the potential for a tremendous upside in terms of rewards.

But large, automated, and unarmed ships have been a staple in the commercial shipping industry for decades, and their presence alone did not contribute to the growth in piracy in the years leading up to the turn of the twenty-first century. A number of other factors played a role as well, including the end of the Cold War and a dramatic increase in global trade. The destabilization of an entire country in East Africa did not help either, creating a disenfranchised generation of desperate young men who would become the face of modern piracy.

Somalia

When the civil war in Somalia broke out in 1991, it threw the entire country into chaos. For more than twenty years the Supreme Revolutionary Council had been in power, but its leadership had grown more dictatorial over time. Members of the SRC controlled the flow of important resources, restricted public demonstrations, limited travel for Somali citizens, and imprisoned those who spoke out against them. Inflation was out of control and the country's economy was in shambles, prompting numerous local clans to revolt.

It did not take long to remove the ruling party from power, but the various factions that had helped liberate Somalia failed to come to any kind of consensus on how to govern the country moving forward. In the SRC's absence a power vacuum appeared, with armed militias battling it out with one another for control. Innocent civilians were often caught in the crossfire, with thousands killed or displaced by the ongoing fighting. With no official government taking charge of the country, Somalia became a failed state. This prompted an international peacekeeping force to intervene in the hopes of bringing some semblance of order and control to the region.

It took years for that to happen, but in the meantime the daily lives of the Somali people were severely disrupted. The country became one of the most dangerous places on the planet and a haven for outlaws, smugglers, mercenaries, radical Islamic factions, and other unsavory types. In general, it was a lawless country that had fallen out of step with the rest of the modern international community.

Out of this chaotic environment the modern day pirate was born. Hardly a ruthless killer or calculating thief, the first Somali pirates were actually simple fishermen who were defending their turf. As the civil war intensified back on land, commercial fishing ships from other countries invaded Somalia's territorial waters in an effort to catch schools of fish found just offshore. With no military or government to protect those waters, the local fishermen felt they had no choice but to take matters into their own hands, violently attacking ships that did not belong there in an effort to drive them away.

Eventually those attacks against rival fishing ships turned into raids on other vessels that wandered too close to Somali territory. Sometimes these new-age buccaneers focused on massive cargo vessels carrying petroleum or other important goods out of the Red Sea, the Gulf of Aden, or the Persian Gulf. At other times, they raided small sailing vessels with only a handful of people onboard. Either way, their goal was not necessarily to capture the ship or its cargo, but to instead grab small, easy-to-carry valuables such as jewelry, cash, and other items that could be quickly sold on the black market.

Later, as the success of these raids grew, the operations expanded in size and scope. Some of the more ambitious Somali pirates began capturing oil tankers and cargo vessels, then offered to sell them back to the corporations that owned them for hundreds of thousands of dollars. These oceangoing raiders even took a page out of the playbooks of their pirate ancestors, routinely kidnapping individuals from the boats and holding them for ransom. It is estimated that in 2010 alone, more than $230 million was paid out to pirates across the globe for the recovery of vessels, cargo, and people, with the majority of that money being funneled into Somalia.

That was not the only tactic that they learned from the buccaneers that roamed the high seas in centuries past. Pirates had already recognized that speed and surprise could be major assets when it came to overcoming their adversaries. The Somali pirates learned this too, often launching their raids at night and aboard small, fast, and agile motorboats rather than from larger, less nimble ships. This allowed them to pull up alongside a target, board the vessel, and begin grabbing valuables before the majority of the crew even knew they were there.

Over time, the Somali pirates grew increasingly bolder and more sophisticated with their raids, frequently employing multiple small— but fast—attack craft that operated in conjunction with one another. These speedboats typically launched from a much larger "mothership" that played a supporting role, providing a place of refuge to refuel and rearm between missions. Following a successful outing, the smaller boats would cruise back to the support vessel with plundered loot and hostages in tow, offloading their ill-gotten plunder. These tactics gave the pirates a floating base of operations from which to launch their attacks, while still being able to take advantage of their speedier motorboats on the open water.

The use of a larger mothership in combination with smaller attack craft served as a template for emerging pirates to use in other parts of the world as well. This approach proved highly efficient and effective, allowing the faster and more nimble speedboats to operate farther from shore than would typically be possible on their own. The mothership also acted as a floating safe house that could be hidden away, making it more difficult to find the outlaws after they sped off with the stolen goods and kidnapped victims.

The effective use of various types of ships and boats is not the only tool that these modern day pirates employ in their line of work. They also happen to be well armed, using automatic weapons, knives, explosives, and rocket-propelled grenades, RPGs. And while most lack formal training in how to use those weapons, they are proficient enough to be successful when conducting a raid on a modern cargo ship with a crew that typically lacks combat training of its own.

When the pirate attacks first began off the coast of East Africa, they were most often conducted against targets that were generally unarmed and operated by crews that did not carry any type of weapons. But as those raids became more frequent, and the loss of human lives, ships, and valuable cargo mounted, more and more shipping companies began hiring personal security teams to protect their vessels traveling on the

Indian Ocean. This resulted in more firefights between the Somali raiders and the security squads, which were often made up of former military personnel. This level of resistance eventually had an impact on the number of pirate attacks, reducing their numbers significantly. But it took some time for that to happen, and in the interim the seas off the Somali coast became more violent rather than less.

It was also about this time that the general public started to become much more aware of the modern pirate activity that was occurring in certain sections of the planet. While the majority of attacks went unnoticed or even unreported, a few high-profile cases made headlines around the world. This helped to raise awareness not only of the attacks that were occurring, but of the plight of Somalia and its people in general. The mere fact that they had resorted to using violence and piracy as a way to earn a living hammered home the point that the country was a struggling nation where lawlessness ran rampant. It did not take long for outside observers to realize that these pirates were not anything like the charming and quirky Captain Jack Sparrow, the character played by Johnny Depp in Disney's *Prates of the Caribbean* film series.

The MV Maersk Alabama

Without a doubt, the most well-known and well-publicized hijacking of a ship by Somali pirates was the attack on the *MV Maersk Alabama*. This particular incident was the subject of the 2013 motion picture *Captain Phillips*, which starred Tom Hanks in the title role. The film was instrumental in educating the public about the dangers of piracy in the Indian Ocean, particularly along the Somali coast.

The incident started on October 8, 2009, when four Somali brigands boarded the *Maersk Alabama* and quickly took several crew members—including Captain Richard Phillips—hostage. Unbeknownst to the pirates however, most of the crew were able to evade capture and take refuge in a secure room deep inside the ship. From that room, they were also able to take control of the vessel, locking out the controls on the bridge. This prevented the ship from being diverted into a Somali port, where it would have been ransomed back to the owners.

The hidden crew members were also able to capture one of the Somali men and negotiated with his compatriots to make a prisoner exchange. The two sides came to an agreement, but the pirates backed out of the exchange at the last minute, and instead took Phillips hostage again, dragging him onto a lifeboat that they used in their escape. Their plan was to use the captain as a human shield while they waited for more of their Somali friends to arrive, at which time they would return to the cargo ship in force.

In an effort to curtail pirate activity in the Indian Ocean and the Gulf of Aden, the US and the UK had increased their naval presence in the area a few years prior to the attack on the *Maersk Alabama*. Thus two American warships—the *USS Bainbridge* and the *USS Halyburton*—were quickly able to lend assistance to the cargo ship. The two vessels arrived on the scene the following day and tracked down the pirates, who still held Captain Phillips hostage.

Over the next few days, a tense standoff ensued, with the US Navy attempting to negotiate the release of Phillips. The Somalis were not interested in giving up their primary bargaining chip, so he remained in custody while they waited for reinforcements to arrive. Those reinforcements were not particularly excited by the prospect of confronting a US guided-missile destroyer however, so they never came.

Two days into the standoff, members of the US Navy SEAL Team Six arrived on the scene, having flown eight thousand miles from their base of operations in Virginia. Avoiding detection from the pirates, the SEALs stealthily made their way aboard the *Bainbridge*, where the SEAL snipers took up position. Watching the Somalis from a distance, they slowly observed them to understand how they moved and interacted with one another. The hope still was to deescalate the situation and bargain for Phillips' release, but the SEALs were there in case those negotiations proved fruitless.

On the fourth day an altercation broke out aboard the lifeboat between Phillips and his captors. Fearing that the Somalis were about to murder their hostage, the SEAL snipers fired three simultaneous shots from their rifles, instantly killing the pirates and bringing an end to the situation. The American captain was rescued unharmed and a fourth pirate, who was aboard the *Bainbridge* receiving medical treatment while serving as a negotiator, was taken into custody. Later, that individual stood trial for piracy in a US court and was sentenced to thirty-three years in prison.

The attack on the *MV Maersk Alabama* was eye opening for a number of reasons. First, it put modern day piracy center stage as observers from around the globe watched the events unfold almost in real time. The story made nightly news for several days and the Somali pirates were even conducting interviews with news agencies while they were still aboard their ship. In the past, it would have taken days, or even weeks, for the news of such an attack to spread, and yet this one played right before the eyes of the general public, shining a spotlight on modern pirates.

At the time, piracy in the Indian Ocean and the Gulf of Aden was rising at a rapid rate, with the *Maersk Alabama* becoming the sixth ship attacked in that region over the course of a single week. For the mainstream public it suddenly seemed as if Somali pirates were everywhere and no ships were safe from their marauding ways. The reality was, the raids had been occurring for years; it just took a high-profile attack on American citizens to get the attention of the media.

The taking of the *Maersk Alabama* also marked the first time that an American-flagged ship had been captured since the Second Barbary War in 1815. For nearly two centuries, no adversary had ever been able to successfully raid an American vessel. Yet four audacious Somali pirates—teenagers no less—were able to board a ship and take an American citizen hostage. This event enraged many US citizens who called on their government to do something about the rapidly devolving situation.

Attacks on Private Boats

It was not just attacks on large cargo ships that were making headlines either. Small, private boats were also frequently targeted, with the marauders ransacking the vessels for valuables and routinely kidnapping the passengers. Those unlucky individuals would usually find themselves being forcibly taken back to shore and held prisoner in a compound in Somalia with dozens of other captives, sometimes waiting months—or even years—for release.

Such was the case of Paul and Rachel Chandler, who set out to sail from the Seychelles to Tanzania in October of 2009. Their thirty-eight-foot yacht the *Lynn Rival* was boarded by hostile Somalis at night, but the Chandlers were able to send out an emergency distress signal before they were captured. That signal was mostly ignored for several days before authorities finally followed up on the alert. In doing so, they discovered the ship drifting off the Somali coast, with Paul and Rachel nowhere to be found.

The couple were taken hostage by the pirates and whisked away aboard the *MV Kota Wajar*, a container vessel that had been captured by the same raiders just a few days earlier. The Chandlers were then held captive in Somalia, where they remained prisoners for more than a year. Eventually, friends and family members raided about $800,000 to pay the ransom demanded by their Somali captors and secure their release.

In February 2011, Americans Jean and Scott Adam were sailing with friends Phyllis Macay and Bob Riggle in the Indian Ocean off the coast of Oman. The Adams, who were experienced sailors, had been traveling around the world over the course of the previous seven years aboard their fifty-eight-foot yacht, the *Quest*. During that time, they had visited numerous countries, often handing out bibles to those that they met. Macay and Riggle had only recently joined them onboard the *Quest* on what they thought would be a leisurely voyage.

One night, the *Quest* was boarded by nineteen pirates striking from a mothership that was active in the region. Quickly seizing the vessel and its passengers, the pirates planned to sail for the Somali coast where they could secure the ship and ransom the prisoners. But before they could reach the safety of those shores, the US Navy arrived on the scene with an aircraft carrier, a guided-missile cruiser, and two guided-missile destroyers in tow.

American naval officers opened negotiations with the Somalis almost immediately, with two of the pirates coming aboard one of the destroyers to discuss terms. Those talks went well into the night and extended into the following morning with little progress. But before the two sides could come an agreement, tragedy struck.

For some unknown reason, one of the Somali outlaws who remained aboard the *Quest* decided to fire an RPG at the destroyer where the officers and their companions were discussing terms for the release of the four Americans. By some stroke of luck, the rocket missed its target, exploding harmlessly over the ocean instead. Within seconds, gunfire broke out aboard the yacht, which prompted the US forces to send a boarding party to investigate the situation.

Upon reaching the *Quest*, a brief battle ensued, resulting in the death of one pirate by gunshot wounds and another by knife. The thirteen other Somalis that were onboard surrendered immediately, quickly bringing an end to the standoff. Unfortunately, the bodies of Jean and Scott Adam, as well as those of Phyllis McCay and Bob Riggle, were found aboard the ship—all four were killed by their captors before help could arrive.

The taking of the *Quest* and the killing of the four Americans onboard only served to underscore another growing realization amongst the general public. Thanks to countless films, television shows, books, and video games, we have clung to a romanticized view of piracy for decades. The bearded, swashbuckling rogue with a patch over one eye and parrot on his shoulder was an established archetype. But the pirates that arrived on the Indian Ocean in the late 1990s and early 2000s were nothing like that. They were ruthless, cunning, and greedy. They were also quick to attack helpless, innocent civilians who happened to be sailing in the wrong part of the world.

The reality is, the pirates from history behaved in very much the same fashion, they have just been portrayed differently in modern popular culture. Thanks to a twenty-four-hour news cycle, not to mention the speed and connectivity of the Internet, we now get much better insights into just how dangerous and deadly actual pirates can be. Had that same technology existed during the Golden Age of Piracy in the Caribbean, the buccaneers of that age would have been viewed in a much different light.

By the end of the first decade of the twenty-first century, the novelty of the return of piracy to the Indian Ocean had pretty much worn off. While many were amused by the idea of modern pirates roaming the seas at first, the reality of the situation was that Somali pirates were stealing hundreds of millions of dollars' worth of goods and resources, while also killing and kidnapping hundreds of innocent people. These marauders were attacking dozens of ships each month, successfully boarding and capturing quite a few.

To combat the growing tide of piracy in the waters off East Africa, a coalition of international naval vessels began patrolling the area. For a while, these ships found themselves in conflict with the pirates on a regular basis and were even attacked themselves from time to time. But gradually, the superior firepower, training, and technology that those modern navies brought to bear began to take their toll on the Somalis, whose tactics and weapons may have been effective against unarmed civilian vessels but were extremely outmatched by modern naval ships.

It is believed that in their heyday, Somali pirates operating in the Indian Ocean off Africa were making roughly $120 million per year by ransoming prisoners and selling stolen goods. To make matters worse, their attacks are estimated to have cost the shipping industry anywhere between $900 million and $3 billion annually. But by 2012, the peak days of piracy were over thanks to the presence of US, British, and other allied vessels patrolling the region.

Pirates in the South China Sea

In the years that followed, the number of attacks that occurred off the Somali coast began to drop sharply. In 2013, the US government issued a report saying that pirate attacks had fallen off by more than 90 percent over the previous year, and by 2015 pirate activity was almost nonexistent. The proposition of engaging with a high-tech, modern naval ship seemed far less enticing than boarding and looting a cargo vessel or sailing yacht, but those soft targets were no longer easily accessible. This created a substantial deterrent for the young men who had previously viewed piracy as a viable way of life, but now found it to be an extremely dangerous pursuit.

While the Indian Ocean may have become safer for civilian and commercial shipping after military vessels began patrolling those waters, things have not gotten dramatically better inside Somalia itself. The country has made some progress in its attempts to become more stable and to rejoin the international community, but it is still a very dangerous place to visit. Most experts believe that if those patrols were to stop, piracy would quickly return. For that reason, the US and its allies continue to maintain a strong naval presence throughout the area.

Considering just how much attention the Somali pirates received throughout the early 2000s, it's easy to understand why so many people are under the impression that the waters off the coast of East Africa remain the most dangerous in all of the world. As it turns out however, there are other places where piracy has gained a significant foothold and has become a serious problem. So much so that at times these other parts of the world have rivaled—and even surpassed—Somalia in terms of overall danger.

Just as piracy off the Horn of Africa was starting to take off in the early 1990s, so too did the number of attacks on cargo ships in the South China Sea. It was almost as if the brigands in both parts of the world were working in parallel with one another, striking dozens of ships using very similar tactics. But while the Somali pirates were eventually subdued, it has taken longer to curtail their Asian counterparts, some of which remain extremely active to this day.

While not particularly large in size when compared to some other bodies of water, the South China Sea remains a strategically important stretch of water. More than a third of the world's shipping traffic passes through the area on an annual basis, often in the narrow confines of the Singapore Strait and the Strait of Malacca. This includes vast amounts of goods sent back and forth between China and Europe, as well as almost all of the petroleum that is shipped out of the Persian Gulf to places like Japan, South Korea, and China each year.

With more than a hundred thousand ships coming and going from Singapore alone, it's easy to see why the area is popular with pirates. The sea is also bounded by the Malaysian Peninsula and Indonesia which offers up countless islands for the outlaws to hide out on. This makes tracking down missing ships and cargo nearly impossible, let alone finding the men and women responsible for taking them.

One of the tactics that separates the pirates of the South China Sea from those found in East Africa is that they almost never take hostages. Whereas the Somalis often made hundreds of thousands of dollars ransoming their captives back to friends and family, the Asian raiders prefer to remain focused on stealing valuable cargo from large container ships or oil tankers. This also runs counter to the Somali approach, which was to grab as many easy-to-carry valuables as possible, rather than getting bogged down with larger, harder-to-unload cargoes.

For the pirates of the South China Sea, stealth is an asset. The marauders often approach a cargo vessel in smaller, faster boats, and board it as quickly and quietly as possible. From there, they overpower the small crew, lock them safely in a room, and get on with looting the ship. This usually involves bringing a (most likely stolen) cargo vessel of their own alongside the one they are plundering and quickly offloading the goods. By the time the local coast guard or navy arrives on the scene, the modern day brigands are already long gone.

Of particular interest to these pirates are tanker ships carrying crude oil. Petroleum is a bankable commodity that is both in constant demand and nearly impossible to trace. These are two qualities that make it highly coveted amongst marauders who will go to great lengths to procure the liquid loot.

Usually, that entails assaulting a ship by first pulling alongside it in small attack craft. Then, using grappling hooks and ropes, the pirates scale the side of the vessel, climb onboard, and subdue the crew quickly and quietly. Once the tanker is secured, the pirates will send a signal to a nearby tanker of their own, letting their accomplices know that they have successfully taken the ship. The smaller tanker will come alongside the captured ship and begin siphoning off the oil within a matter of minutes. Once the pirates have gotten their fill, they escape into the twisty maze of islands that is the Malaysian Peninsula or Indonesia.

The waters of the Strait of Malacca are so thick with shipping traffic that it is a common sight to see two vessels parked directly alongside one another. Some boats do this in order to exchange cargo while out on the ocean, particularly if they are owned by the same shipping company and are sending goods in opposite directions. But this has made it even more challenging for passing ships to spot pirate activity even while it is taking place. Because so many ships link up in this fashion, a naval patrol ship could sail past an attack in progress and not even notice it.

A modern day pirate ship in the Strait of Malacca.

Of course, not all attacks on cargo ships in the South China Sea follow the same template, nor is their goal just to capture crude oil. In fact, many of the raids are conducted to grab other hard-to-trace commodities, or to steal cash and valuable personal items from the crew. In October of 1999, a ship transporting $10 million worth of aluminum was attacked by pirates after setting out from Kuala Tanjung in Indonesia. Ten men boarded the vessel and captured the crew, taking their money, jewelry, watches, and other items. The crew members were then set adrift aboard a lifeboat and spent the next eleven days at the mercy of the ocean's currents before being rescued by Thai fishermen. The ship itself was located a month later off the coast of Goa in India, its cargo long since sold off on the black market.

In March of 2001, a merchant vessel carrying tin, zinc, and spices was boarded and seized by pirates while cruising off the coast of Sumatra. Once the crew was subdued, they were loaded onto a small boat and taken to a nearby uninhabited island. Once there, they were abandoned and left to fend for themselve while the freighter was taken to the Indonesian island of Bintan. After arriving at the port it was handed over to an international crime syndicate, but just nine days later it was found and recovered offshore near the Philippines.

In July of 2019, a group of brigands boarded a large South Korean ship called the *CK Bluebell* near the Anambas Islands in Indonesia. Using speedboats to catch the cargo vessel, the pirates assaulted the ship and quickly overcame what little resistance the crew had to offer, leaving the captain and another officer with minor injuries. The group then proceeded to raid the *Bluebell*, making off with over $13,000 in cash. They also took a number of the crew's personal effects, including mobile phones, clothing, and even shoes—all items that could be quickly and easily sold for cash once they visited a market back on shore.

In a sign of just how common these high-seas muggings have become, the *Bluebell* and its crew continued on with their usual route, carrying their cargo to the next port of call. While diligent and admirable, the problem with that was that in doing so they were hundreds of miles away from the spot where the pirate attack took place by the time they reported the incident. This made it impossible for the authorities to actually track down and find the perpetrators of the crime.

Because the standard operating procedure for pirates in Asia is to not take hostages or ransom passengers, there have been fewer deaths associated with piracy in that part of the world. This has meant that much of the activity that has taken place in the South China Sea has not been reported on as extensively as the attacks that occurred off the coast of Eastern Africa. Therefore, the general public has remained largely unaware of the frequency with which pirates have seized cargo vessels passing through the Strait of Malacca and the Singapore Strait. Most are not even aware that piracy is an issue in that part of the world.

But the shipping companies and international conglomerates that operate in the region are certainly aware of it, as are the nations that have a vested interest in keeping the trade routes flowing. That is why those countries have formed a coalition called the Regional Cooperation Agreement on Combating Piracy and Armed Robbery against Ships in Asia—or ReCAAP for short. Its members include the US, China, Japan, South Korea, and more than a dozen other nations, all of which have committed naval ships to help patrol the South China Sea. These efforts have paid dividends. In recent years, the number of pirate attacks has dropped off significantly. So much so, that by the start of 2020, the number of reported raids had fallen to their lowest number since the early 1990s.

While ReCAAP seems to be a major success in terms of international cooperation and in reducing piracy, some experts believe the numbers are a bit misleading. Although pirate activity does seem to be down in parts of the South China Sea—particularly in Malaysia and Indonesia—it is on the rise in other areas, perhaps signaling that the pirates have not been defeated, they have just relocated.

The Sulu Sea

Case in point, at the same time that the number of pirate attacks were dropping off in the Indian Ocean and the South China Sea, they also started to rapidly rise in the Sulu Sea near the Philippines. In 2016, the number of raids in that part of the world escalated sharply, even as ReCAAP forces were taking control of the Strait of Malacca. Early pirate raids were tentative and aimed at slow-moving targets that were easy to catch and board. But as they became more successful, the pirates became more brazen too.

Intelligence reports indicate that the pirates of the Sulu Sea tend to be Islamic militants using a familiar plan of attack. These oceangoing raiders have focused on raiding and capturing very large merchant vessels with the goal of holding them for exorbitant ransoms. But while pirates in other regions have usually gone after targets of opportunity, these new marauders are specifically preying upon the biggest ships they can find. The logic behind these attacks is that the biggest ships out on the ocean are owned by the largest and wealthiest companies, which have the deepest pockets when it comes to paying out ransoms.

Cargo ships are not the only thing these Islamic pirates are ransoming. Just as kidnapping crew members and innocent travelers was a successful tactic in Somalia, the same approach is proving to be true in the Philippines. An increasing number of people have been captured by these brigands, who are happy to ensure their safe return for a hefty price.

One of the higher profile abductions occurred in 2016 in the waters to the south of the Philippines, which is a region where the Islamic militant group Abu Sayyaf have been active for decades. The group mainly consists of members of the indigenous Moro who have been fighting for independence for centuries, first with Spain and later with the United States. Today, they continue that struggle with acts of terrorism and piracy against the Philippine government.

In November of 2016, a fifty-three-foot yacht named *Rockall,* owned by German couple Jürgen Kantner and Sabine Merz, was captured by pirates. During the raid, the outlaws kidnapped Kantner, but shot and killed Merz when she allegedly pulled a gun on them. A spokesperson for the Abu Sayyaf told members of the media at the time that the pirates were simply defending themselves when they fired back at the woman.

Kantner was later taken into the dense jungle that covers much of the Sulu province, a small island located inside the Autonomous Region in Muslim Mindanao, a self-governing part of the Philippines. The province is home to most of the country's Islamic population, making it a more Abu Sayyaf–friendly region. Its thick forests are the perfect home for the militant group, allowing them to maintain a number of hidden camps that are extremely difficult to root out and destroy. Thus, launching a rescue operation to free captives is an incredibly challenging proposition.

Once they were safely back in the jungle, the kidnappers sent word that they would set Kantner free provided they were paid a $600,000 ransom for his release. When those demands were not met after a three-month deadline came and went, the extremists beheaded the German sailor. The murder of Kantner was a clear message that the pirates were willing to brutally back up their threats when necessary.

What made this story particularly noteworthy was that this was not the first run-in that Kantner and Merz had with pirates while sailing around the world. Eight years earlier the couple had also been attacked by Somali brigands off the coast of Africa and spent fifty-two days in captivity in that county. Eventually they were released and sent home after a sizable ransom was paid on their behalf by friends and family.

Upon their return to Germany, Kantner became an outspoken critic against paying ransoms to pirates. He felt that it only encouraged them to continue their illegal activities and rewarded them for stealing ships and abducting innocent human beings. At the time, the *Rockall* was still in the hands of the Somalis who had kidnapped him and Merz, but Kantner later returned to Somalia, snuck back to the beach where they were held prisoner, and stole his boat back. This allowed the couple to resume their round-the-world sailing adventures, which unfortunately came to an end eight years later following their fateful encounter in the Philippines.

As has been seen elsewhere, the rise of piracy in the Philippines has resulted in a coalition of countries that have pledged to help defend merchant ships and hunt down the buccaneers. Taking a page out of the anti-piracy playbook, Malaysia, Indonesia, and the Philippines have agreed to set aside long-standing cultural and political differences to focus on a common foe. These three nations have begun working together not only to protect each other's people and ships, but to share information about when and where attacks are occurring. They have even agreed to allow naval vessels from each of their partners to pursue pirates into waters governed by one of the other countries in the coalition, an important step in helping to hunt down and eliminate the pirates.

The goal is to prevent piracy in the Philippines from getting out of hand as it did in Somalia and the South China Sea. By working to combat the problem while it is still in its early stages, the hope is that attacks against passing ships can be prevented, keeping the loss of lives and property to a minimum. Only time will tell if the coalition will be effective, but it is an important first step in keeping the modern day buccaneers from taking over.

The Gulf of Guinea

In West Africa, it is already too late to curb pirate activity. With the reduction of the number of attacks taking place in the South China Sea, the Gulf of Guinea is now home to the most troubled waters on the planet. Each year, there are dozens of successful raids carried out there, making it the latest focal point in terms of international maritime security.

Located off the coast of Western and Central Africa, the Gulf of Guinea features more than 3,700 miles of coastline spread out over more than a half dozen countries. The gulf, which features numerous islands, covers nine hundred thousand square miles before it merges with the Atlantic Ocean, making it a wide open body of water that is similar to the Indian Ocean off the coast of Somalia. And not unlike that part of the world, the Gulf of Guinea offers pirates ample opportunities to strike at cargo ships coming and going from the region.

Commercial shipping traffic is plentiful in the gulf, with cargo being sent to and from Europe and Southern Africa. But the most appealing targets for waterborne bandits are the oil ships that come out of Nigeria. The country is the largest oil-producing nation in Africa, and much of its production is shipped out to the rest of the world via the Niger Delta. The river empties into the Gulf of Guinea, so there is a lot of petroleum passing through the area at any given time. Much like in the South China Sea, the valuable cargo is an almost irresistible draw for pirates.

When it comes to ransoming ships and people, the pirates in the Gulf of Guinea are much more in step with their Somali counterparts than the East Asian and Filipino buccaneers. It is not uncommon for them to capture ships and kidnap crew members, only releasing them when large sums of money have been paid. This tactic has become so common that by 2019 abductions in the gulf accounted for 82 percent of all crew-related kidnappings in the entire world.

Much like in Somalia, piracy in Western Africa is driven by a lack of opportunities for young men in their home countries. Throughout most of the region poverty is a persistent challenge, along with high unemployment rates, violent crime, and a general lawlessness that pervades most of the nations along the Gulf of Guinea. With so many big issues to wrestle with on land, most of the regional governments do not have the time nor resources to crack down on piracy. This combination of variables has provided the pirates—which often have ties to international crime syndicates—a safe haven on land from which to launch their operations.

The pirates that ply their trade in the gulf are known to be extremely violent as well, often torturing and beating the individuals that they abduct. Their preferred method of attack on a ship typically involves using speedboats to chase down their target, then spraying the deck with automatic weapons before boarding. The level of ruthlessness that these brigands display is generally higher than what is found amongst pirate gangs from other parts of the world. Because of this, the number of injuries and deaths associated with these attacks is also much higher.

The vast majority of the pirate attacks that take place in the Gulf of Guinea fall inside the territorial waters of the nations that line its coast. This has made tracking down and punishing the pirates a significant challenge as—unlike in Asia or the Indian Ocean—creating a coalition there has been especially difficult. Countries like Nigeria, Cameroon, Gabon, Benin, and Togo have had a distrust of one another for decades. Breaking down those barriers has not been easy, nor have those nations requested much in the way of outside assistance when it comes to solving their piracy problem. As a result, the number of attacks only continues to grow and the attacks themselves become much more audacious and violent in the process.

2018 was an especially busy year in the Gulf of Guinea in regard to pirate activity. The number of incidences more than doubled from the year before and accounted for the vast majority of acts of piracy that were reported worldwide. That year, all six of the reported ship hijackings that took place around the globe occurred there, while 130 of the 141 hostages that were being held by pirates in various parts of the world were in that region too. On top of that, 2018 saw eighty-three sailors kidnapped in various locations across the planet; of those, seventy-eight took place off the coast of West Africa.

As the pattern of attacking and raiding cargo ships continued into 2019, the International Maritime Bureau (IMB) issued a call for action in the Gulf of Guinea. The nonprofit organization, which was established to combat all crime that takes place on the high seas, is hoping that improved communication and reporting between the shipping companies can help reverse the trend. The IMB is also seeking intervention by naval forces from outside the region to help quell the growing threat that is found there before it has the chance to have an impact on a wider scale.

An End to Piracy?

For now, there are no more dangerous waters on the planet than those found off the coast of Western Africa. Eventually, a coalition of forces will have to come together in order to change that, but there are significant hurdles that need to be overcome before that can happen. The general lawlessness that exists on a larger scale in that part of the world not only has contributed to the rise of piracy there, but serves as an obstacle to overcoming it as well.

The question is, will the waters of the Gulf of Guinea become the place where modern day pirates make their last stand or will another location eventually rise up to take its place? Since piracy returned to the high seas in the early 1990s, there has always been some place on the planet where ships and their crews were in constant danger of being attacked. Western Africa is the latest in that long line of dangerous places.

None of those locations holds a monopoly on disfranchised people with few economic prospects and a willingness to do just about anything for a chance to improve their lives. This is a common story across the globe, and as long as there are people who fall into those categories, and have access to important shipping lanes, there is a chance that piracy will crop up elsewhere.

What *has* changed over the past two decades is the way that the countries that directly deal with pirate attacks have learned to react to the threat that modern buccaneers bring. In the 1990s, pirate activity was largely ignored and seen as a trend spawned by Somalia's failure as a nation-state. But as the attacks increased, became more violent, and threatened international commerce, those countries learned to put aside their differences and work together to put a stop to the ongoing raids. So far, that has been the key to ending piracy in just about every corner of the globe, and it will likely remain the answer in the future too.

That being said, history has shown us that if there is a way for someone to profit on the high seas by attacking ships, plundering cargo, and kidnapping other human beings, piracy will continue. From the

French corsairs.

opening of the earliest trade routes in the Mediterranean Sea and the Persian Gulf, to our modern world filled with global shipping and inter-dependent economies, pirates have been there practically every step of the way. Over the centuries, the age of the pirate may have waxed and waned some along the way, but even when they have been counted out, the oceangoing outlaw has always been there, lurking in the shadows, waiting for an opportunity to return.

The Tale of Madame Cheng

Not all of the world's most notorious pirates sailed the Caribbean or flew an English or Spanish flag. Some of the most successful, brilliant, charismatic, and intriguing pirates were not even European at all—or men for that matter.

Take for example Madame Cheng, a Chinese pirate who broke the shackles of her impoverished upbringing, as well as a male-dominated culture and era, to become one of the most feared outlaws that Asia had ever seen. She rose from humble beginnings to become arguably the most successful pirate in history, and yet somehow few in the West have ever heard her name, let alone her amazing story.

As with many pirates, Madame Cheng's childhood and early life are almost completely unknown. It is believed that she was born sometime around 1775 in Guangzhou, China, in the coastal province of Guangdong. Her birth name was Shih Yan, although she used the name Ching Shih as well. At a young age, she was sold to a floating brothel in the city, where she began working as a prostitute, quickly becoming a favorite with the upscale clientele who frequented the location. Even as a young woman she understood how to manipulate men into doing her bidding, routinely using her wits and feminine wiles to get what she wanted.

While she worked in the brothel, Ching Shih met a well-known and highly successful pirate named Cheng I. He was already infamous for his deeds in the South China Sea and came from a family that had been dabbling in piracy for decades. Cheng proposed marriage to Ching Shih, although his exact motivations for doing so are unclear. There are some historians who say that he fell in love with the beautiful prostitute, while others say that it was just a mutually beneficial business arrangement

264 % Crimson Waters

with both bringing something to the table. Cheng I had a growing fleet and a large crew at his disposal, while Ching Shih was well connected and had influence with the elite in Guangzhou. Regardless, together they became rich and powerful themselves by building a criminal empire.

Ching Shih agreed to marry her suitor on one condition—that she be made a full partner. Cheng I accepted those terms, giving her 50 percent of his business and establishing her as his equal in all of the syndicate's dealings. The couple were married sometime around the turn of the nineteenth century, later adopting a son named Cheung Po who became the legitimate heir to the family business. Ching Shih, whose married name changed to Cheng I Sao—which meant "wife of Cheng"— also gave birth to two other sons in the years that followed.

As the husband and wife outlaws built their burgeoning crime syndicate, they began extending olive branches to former rivals. The plan was to stop competing against one another in an effort to slice off a small piece of the pie, but instead work together for the benefit of all. Over time, this pitch worked and Cheng I was able to convince his competitors to join his organization, building a large and formidable armada that became known as the Red Flag Fleet.

In its day, the Red Flag Fleet was one of the most dangerous pirate organizations in all of Asia. Consisting of hundreds of ships and thousands of men, Cheng I's armada was feared by merchants and the military of the Qing Dynasty alike. The fleet sailed with impunity across the South China Sea, frequently raiding ships and villages. In just a few short years, he and Madame Cheng were able to build a pirate organization unlike anything the world had ever seen. But that was only the beginning of the story.

In November of 1807, Cheng I died while sailing off the coast of Vietnam. The details of his death are unclear, with some reports saying the ship he was on at the time was caught in a typhoon, while others say it was a tsunami. Either way, a mysterious accident occurred, taking the life of the pirate leader at the age of thirty-nine.

Upon learning of her husband's death, Madame Cheng immediately made a move to consolidate her position within the Red Flag Fleet. She

Madame Cheng.

was already instrumental in running the pirate organization, but she feared one of Cheng I's rivals might attempt to steal control away from her. Worse yet, infighting could break out between the various captains, causing the entire operation to collapse in on itself. Always an ambitious and driven woman, she was not about to let that happen.

The first thing that Madame Cheng did was promote her adopted son, Cheung Po, to a leadership role. He had already been involved in the operation of running the fleet and was, without question, loyal to his mother. To solidify his importance to the organization, he was named captain of the fleet, which conveyed the idea that a man was in direct command of the ships. Despite his lofty title and position, the young man took his orders and direction directly from Madame Cheng herself.

Next, she connected with some of her husband's closest family members to remind them that she was part of the family too. More importantly, she let them know that she had no intention of relinquishing control to any of Cheng I's rivals. On the contrary, her intention was to maintain control herself, continuing to build upon the plans that her husband had already set in motion. With their support, Madame Cheng was able to maintain her sway over the ship captains, most of which soon came to accept the change at the top.

Even before she had married Cheng I, Madame Cheng was tough, smart, and well connected. After joining forces with her husband, she was even better suited to take the helm of what had become one of the most powerful criminal organizations in Asia, if not the world. That she maintained her prominence amongst outlaws and pirates after her husband's death is a testament to her strength and cunning as an individual.

With her leadership role secured, Madame Cheng went about instilling discipline and order amongst her underlings. In order to do that, she created what she called the "code of laws," which were designed to govern the behavior and actions of the pirates under her command. Anyone who disobeyed those rules would be punished harshly and without exception, no matter their rank or standing within the organization.

While no written record of the code of laws has ever been found, historians say that the rules covered a wide range of offenses. The harshest of those laws was perhaps failing to obey the direct orders of a superior officer—which would result in an immediate beheading. The pirates were also forbidden to steal from any villagers who assisted the organization, which helped to foster support amongst the general population along China's coast. Desertion or dereliction of duty was also punishable by death, as were sexual relations—consensual or not—with any female prisoners.

The code of laws helped to establish the Red Flag Fleet as a single, unified group. The rules called for the sharing of plunder and the creation of a communal treasury that benefited everyone. Ships or individuals were rewarded for bold actions with a slice of the booty that they directly obtained, but the majority of that plunder was put into a public fund used to improve the boats and other infrastructure. Those funds were also used to pay the outlaws who sailed under Madame Cheng's command.

If there was any thought that a female pirate lord would be weaker or more forgiving than a man, Madame Cheng quickly proved otherwise. Not only was she as ruthless as any male pirate, she was also as driven and organized. With the organization wholly under her command, she unleashed the Red Flag Fleet onto the South China Sea with orders to raid and plunder any ships or villages that they came across. The raids were as much about ensuring a steady supply of treasure to fill the communal coffers as they were about instilling fear in the local populace.

The fleet's attack on Sanshan village is a good example of just how brutal Madame Cheng could be as a leader. According to historical records, the pirates attacked and captured the town, then systematically beheaded all of the men who lived there. With that nasty bit of business out of the way, all of the women and children were rounded up with the intention of holding them for ransom. When no ransom was forthcoming, all of the surviving villagers were then sold into slavery.

Under Madame Cheng's rule, the pirates became bolder and more successful than ever before. Their raids spanned the coastline of China, with ships and towns stretching from Canton to Macau under constant attack. The Red Flag Fleet's influence became so great, that it actually came to control large sections of the coast, imposing taxes and tariffs on a number of the communities found there.

With the fleet's influence growing, the Qing Dynasty decided that it had to do something to try to curb the growing pirate activity. In January of 1808, they assembled a fleet to challenge the pirates and potentially break their hold on the seas. But before that offensive could be launched, Madame Cheng got wind of the impending campaign against her. She then ordered her men to make a preemptive strike, capturing or destroying the Qing ships while they were still in the harbor. This forced the Chinese navy to commandeer fishing boats in an effort to face off with the Red Flag Fleet. With so few, not to mention inferior, vessels at their disposal, the navy's efforts proved disastrous and futile.

The Qing efforts against the Red Flag Fleet were not singular, but were bolstered by the assistance of another pirate organization eager to vanquish the competition. The O-po-tae were once allied with Cheng I, but had splintered off following his death. Finding it difficult to operate in the South China Sea in the shadow of Madame Cheng's mighty outlaw armada, the rival group hoped that by helping the Chinese navy they might break her stranglehold on piracy in the region. The Red Flag Fleet proved to be a much bigger challenge over time than anything that the Qing or O-po-tae could defeat.

With the Qing threat diminished, Madame Cheng's fleet continued to grow in size and power. Under her control the organization prospered, eventually encompassing more than a thousand ships and eighty thousand men. This alone made it a nearly unstoppable force on the open ocean and along the coasts. But it was the vision and dedication of the pirate queen herself that helped push the Red Flag Fleet to ever higher levels of wealth and influence, even attracting the attention of the European powers that controlled the wealthy international trade routes.

In time, Madame Cheng was not content to just raid Chinese ships and coastal villages. Her ambitions eventually brought the fleet into contact with the Portuguese and British as well, leading to friction with those two nations. Things grew even more heated in 1809, when the pirates captured a representative of the East India Trading Company. Until that point, the Dutch and English had mostly been content to leave the pirate group alone, but once the Red Flag Fleet began to interfere with European trade, it became impossible to ignore the growing threat that it posed.

Early showdowns between the pirate fleet and European warships went in favor of Madame Cheng and her men. Their sheer numbers, and dedication to their leader, helped to galvanize them to outside threats, making them a difficult enemy to defeat. The harsh code of laws that she instituted brought discipline and a deep bond amongst the outlaws, many of which would fight to the death, even against overwhelming odds. That ferocity took the Europeans off guard during their initial confrontations, although they would soon learn not to underestimate the well-organized and driven brigands.

Thanks to its size and unprecedented success, the Red Flag Fleet drew the attention of numerous foes. Fighting off the Qing Dynasty on one front, pirate rivals on another, and European powers on a third eventually began to take its toll. Madame Cheng and her captains did their best to fend off all challengers, but defending their turf was becoming increasingly more difficult. The Red Flag Fleet was stretched thin, making it harder and harder to continue to pull in the loot that was needed to keep it well maintained and operating at full capacity.

By September of 1809 the fleet was beginning to suffer significant losses. The Portuguese in particular had stepped up their campaign against the pirates and won some important battles against them. The impact that the Chinese buccaneers had on trade throughout Asia had grown to a point where the European nations could no longer sit idly by and ignore the growing threat. Corporations like the East India Trading Company were putting enormous pressure on their governments to help them deal with the pirate problem, which continued to increase in size under Madame Cheng's leadership.

The traditional Chinese boats—known as junks—were quickly

becoming a liability for Madame Cheng and her men. For much of the sixteenth and seventeenth century, the ships were well suited to take on their European counterparts, but the Chinese were not very interested in continuing to develop a modern navy. Meanwhile, countries like England, Portugal, and the Netherlands regularly implemented new designs that were faster, more heavily armed, and more maneuverable. Because of this, it soon became evident that the Chinese junk was far outclassed on the water, making it more difficult for the Red Flag Fleet to stand toe-to-toe with the imperialist Europeans.

Chinese junk ships.

From September of 1809 through January of 1810, the Red Flag Fleet and the Portuguese navy based in Macau engaged with one another in a series of continually escalating battles. These showdowns quickly demonstrated just how powerful the muskets and cannons of the Europeans truly were. With rifled barrels on their main guns, the Portuguese were surprisingly accurate, even at long range. And when their cannon balls did hit, they packed an explosive punch that inflicted an immense amount of damage.

Even in the earliest of engagements it became increasingly clear that the pirates were vastly outgunned. In one naval battle that took place early on in the conflict, two Portuguese ships sunk or incapacitated sixteen junks without suffering much in the way of damage or taking significant losses of their own. Just a day later, the Europeans attacked an armada made up of two hundred Red Flag Fleet vessels, once again inflicting great damage using their superior range and maneuverability.

When word of the Portuguese success against the pirates reached the Chinese government, it sent emissaries to Macau to propose a joint campaign against the Red Flag Fleet. Madame Cheng's enemies were attempting to unite against her, combining their forces to take on their shared adversary. When she heard of this arrangement, Madame Cheng sent her ships out to sea in an effort to prevent the Chinese and European navies from connecting. A major nautical battle took place in late November, with the pirates largely successful in achieving that goal. The Qing fleet never united with the Portuguese as they had promised, although the pirates had suffered heavy losses to ensure that this merger did not occur.

By December, the Red Flag Fleet had moved the bulk of its ships closer to Macau in the hopes of forcing a final showdown with the Portuguese. The Europeans had more than demonstrated their superior firepower, but the pirates planned to overwhelm their enemies by using the vast numbers of men and junks that they had at their disposal. Once again, things did not go quite as planned, with Madame Cheng's forces coming out on the losing end. The fleet lost another fifteen ships, with dozens more damaged, forcing the pirates to retreat.

To make matters worse for the pirate queen, following this humiliating loss to the Portuguese, an allied pirate feet defected to the Chinese government. With the losses mounting and their enemies closing in, the Black Flag Fleet, a satellite pirate group that worked closely with Madame Cheng's organization, broke away and accepted an offer of amnesty from the Qing Dynasty. It was a difficult betrayal to accept, but her own men continued to stay loyal both to her and the code of laws that helped bind them together.

Finally, in January of 1810, the Red Flag Fleet and the Portuguese engaged in the decisive battle. The Red Flag Fleet assembled its largest force yet, consisting of more than three hundred ships and twenty thousand men. The armada closed in on the much smaller Portuguese fleet, but as with previous engagements, the Europeans came out victorious. Using their vastly superior maneuverability, speed, and firepower to overwhelm the pirates, they inflicted heavy losses, sinking numerous vessels in fairly short order.

After a long and protracted sea battle, the Portuguese captain ordered all guns to concentrate fire on a large Chinese junk that served as the flagship for the pirate fleet. Thanks to their improved range and accuracy, the cannons rained down explosive artillery on the enemy vessel, smashing its hull to shreds and quickly sending it to the bottom of the sea. With their main ship obliterated, the Red Flag Fleet quickly dispersed, seeking refuge in nearby shallow waters where their pursuers had a more difficult time following.

When the smoke had cleared and the battle was over, the Red Flag Fleet was—for all intents and purposes—no more. Madame Cheng still had thousands of loyal followers and dozens of ships under her command, but the European vessels were so superior to the Chinese junks that even a handful of Portuguese galleons were capable of inflicting massive damage. Morale amongst the pirates plummeted and their once mighty armada now looked to avoid engagements with their enemies rather than to confront them head on.

Reading the writing on the wall, Madame Cheng sent emissaries to the Qing emperor seeking a pardon for herself and those under her command. Her goal was to seek amnesty not only for herself, but all of the thousands of men who had remained loyal to her to the end. But the Chinese officials were not ready to let all of the pirates go free so easily, which created an impasse in the negotiations. Sensing things were at a crucial stage, Madame Cheng went to visit the emperor herself. After the two met face-to-face, the vast majority of the pirates that served under the infamous Madame Cheng were allowed to go free, with some even deciding to join the Qing navy in an official capacity.

The disbanding of the Red Flag Fleet marked the end of an era in the South China Sea. By that point, more and more European ships were traveling to Asia on trade and diplomatic missions, and it had become increasingly more important to ensure that those waters were safe to navigate. As with other parts of the world, piracy had been deemed unlawful and punishable by death not only by the Chinese, but by the English and Portuguese too. Even the opinion of the general public had turned against the once feared and respected buccaneers, who had now come to be seen as outlaws, murderers, and thieves rather than folk heroes.

After she officially received her pardon, Madame Cheng was allowed to live a normal, albeit luxurious, life. In her negotiations with the Qing emperor she managed to retain most of the wealth that she had accumulated while in command of the Red Flag Fleet. That assured her enough riches to last several lifetimes and made the transition into retirement far easier.

Not one to simply accept a quiet life in some remote village, Madame Cheng put some of her wealth to good use by opening a gambling den and brothel in Macau. She also used her extensive contacts in the Qing government and European traders to become a merchant herself. This only served to enhance her already considerable wealth and reputation.

Madame Cheng remained active in politics, business, and trade throughout the rest of her life. She even served as an advisor to the Qing Dynasty during the First Opium War against the British. That conflict took place in 1839 and had long and lasting implications for the future of China. By winning that war, the English took control of the trading routes to the country and further clamped down on piracy in the South China Sea.

As for the notorious Madame Cheng, she lived out the remainder of her years in Macau, where she was greatly revered for her business acumen. She had managed to rise from humble beginnings to a woman of wealth and power, something that was almost unheard of during the nineteenth century. In doing so, she also became quite possibly the most successful pirate in all of history, amassing a vast fortune while commanding a fleet that consisted of hundreds of ships and thousands of men.

Madame Cheng passed away in 1844 at the age of sixty-nine. With her death, the last of the truly great pirate leaders of Asia—if not the world—slipped into the history books. She left behind a legacy that is unparalleled by any other buccaneer, easily making her one of the most legendary pirates that ever took to the high seas.

Epilogue

H istorians date the first recorded evidence of piracy back to 1400 BCE, although in all likelihood there were probably outlaws roaming the Earth's waterways long before that. It is believed that boats were first developed as far back as 4000 BCE, which means someone, somewhere, was probably already using those early rafts for some type of illegal activity long before anyone bothered to write about it in a scroll or paint a depiction of it on a stone wall.

When you consider the fact that piracy still runs rampant in certain parts of the world today, it starts to dawn on you—the human race has been dealing with pirates for somewhere in the neighborhood of five thousand years, give or take a few centuries. Sure, there have been times when pirate activity has been greatly reduced or even eliminated altogether. But when the opportunity presents itself, it always seems to return in some form or another.

It does not really matter whether the first buccaneers appeared on the Mediterranean Sea, the Persian Gulf, or the South China Sea. The act of piracy has been shared almost universally across the human race, regardless of geographic location, culture, or religion. It did not even matter if a country was landlocked or not, as pirates have existed on rivers and lakes around the world too.

Human history has shown that for a pirate to be successful, they only need three things: water, a boat or ship, and the opportunity to prey upon others. Of those, that third ingredient is probably the most important, as most pirate activity across the centuries has been driven by

The Jolly Roger.

opportunity. Sometimes that opportunity came in the form of raiding random ships or villages that just happened to be in the path of the outlaws, whereas at other times it meant plundering the ships and outposts of enemy nations in the name of a king or queen. In the modern age, it means preying on large, faceless corporations with deep pockets and plenty of resources.

Over the centuries, pirates have also proven themselves to be highly adaptable and resilient. They learn from the tactics of their enemies and adapt to shifting political and economic conditions. The best buccaneers learn to read not only ocean tides, but the tides of change—shifting their methods, ideologies, and allegiances whenever it suits their needs.

Adopting new technologies and techniques has also been a trademark of successful pirates across the various ages. Early on, that meant improving their ships by adding sails, oars, and rudders to increase speed and maneuverability. Later, the seafaring brigands learned how to navigate the globe by the stars, build vessels that were fast and light, and use cannons to their tactical advantage. Today, technologies such as GPS tracking, two-way radios, and automatic weapons have changed the game for the modern day pirate.

All of these factors—and others—have allowed the pirate to endure in one form or another for millennia. Over the course of the past five thousand years, human civilization has reshaped itself countless times. Empires have risen, fallen, and been forgotten. The world expanded to immense proportions, and was then made small again thanks to modern technology. Fortunes have been won and lost, while new centers of power have come and gone.

However, through it all, the human condition has remained mostly the same. Across the ages, there have always been the haves and the have-nots. The wealthy and the poor. The privileged and the downtrodden. As long as that continues to be the status quo, there will always be a generation of new pirates waiting to be born. Waiting for their opportunity to follow in the footsteps of the buccaneers who have come before them.

That is just as true in the twenty-first century as it was when the first person took up arms against another out on the water. This does not seem likely to change anytime soon either. The lure of easy money and lucrative payoffs is just too enticing to pass up, even as the risks continue to rise. The history of piracy is still being written, with undoubtedly more to be said on the subject in the decades and centuries to come.